EATING INDIA

Anoop

Always my idol

love

April '09

BY THE SAME AUTHOR

Life and Food in Bengal
Bengali Cooking: Seasons and Festivals
Feeding the Gods: Memories of Food and Culture in Bengal
Land of Milk and Honey: Travels in the History of Indian Food

EATING INDIA

EXPLORING THE FOOD AND
CULTURE OF THE LAND OF SPICES

CHITRITA BANERJI

BLOOMSBURY
LONDON · BERLIN · NEW YORK

First published in Great Britain 2008
This paperback edition published 2009

Copyright © 2007 by Chitrita Banerji
Illustrations © 2007 by Polly Napper

Bloomsbury Publishing Plc, 36 Soho Square, London W1D 3QY

A CIP catalogue record for this book is available from the British Library

ISBN 9780747596387

10 9 8 7 6 5 4 3 2 1

Typeset by Westchester Book Group
Printed in Great Britain by Clays Ltd, St Ires pk

Bloomsbury Publishing, London, New York, Berlin

The paper this book is printed as is certified independently in accordance with the rules
of the FSC. It is ancient-forest friendly. The printer holds chain of custody.

FSC
Mixed Sources
Product group from well-managed
forests and other controlled sources
www.fsc.org
Cert no. SGS - COC - 2061
www.fsc.org
© 1996 Forest Stewardship Council

www.bloomsbury.com/chitritabanerji

For Jai

Cooking is at once the most and the least localized of the arts; it owes its development to commerce and to travel, and its preservation to stout regionalism; it must find its character in the resources at hand, yet may enrich these by some of the good things from outside. Every enlarging contribution was made by clever, articulate and traveled men, yet the burden is carried and handed on by obscure local women. The history of cooking, with its interchanges and migrations, is indeed hard to pin down.

—Sybille Bedford, *A Visit to Don Otavio*

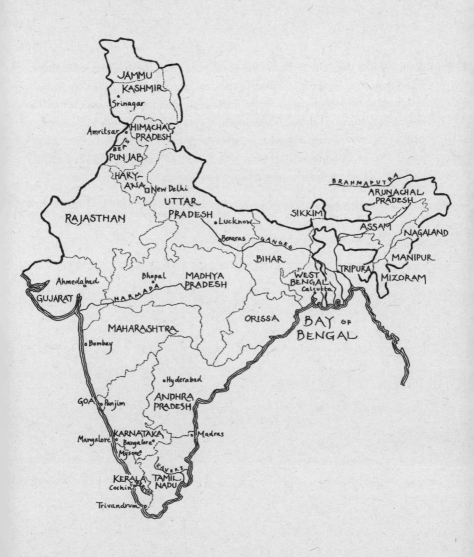

CONTENTS

NOTE TO THE READER

This book is based on several trips I made to India between 2003 and 2006. My journeys there did not follow a linear chronological or geographical sequence; nor did I set out to write a comprehensive chronicle of the cuisines of India. My selection of destinations (some of which I visited more than once) and cuisines was based on what seemed to promise the most interesting revelations. My objective was to see how much authenticity in food and cookery could possibly survive in the changing, young-old, immigrant nation that is India.

For the convenience of readers who have not been to India, I have used the older, more familiar names and spellings of cities, towns, and rivers.

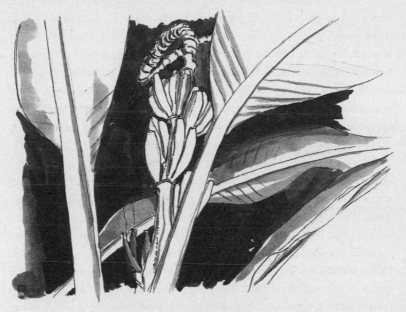

PROLOGUE

It was a frigid white morning in Boston. Sorting through a pile of mail, I had come upon a square beige envelope, one corner embossed with a colored illustration—a young banana plant, leaves drooping gracefully, standing next to an earthen pitcher with a green coconut on top. For Hindu families like mine, both banana and coconut are highly auspicious, and their presence is obligatory at most rituals and ceremonies. This envelope had to be an invitation of some kind. The card inside sported a large blue and gold butterfly, symbol of Brahma the Creator, patron saint of marriage and union. Opening the card, I read the invitation. The son of a longtime family friend in Calcutta was getting married. They wanted me to come.

I looked out of my window. Forlorn, leafless trees under a gray sky, piles of grungy snow on the street, people walking with the insular gait of a North American winter—head down, scarves pulled up to the nose, gloved hands in pockets for extra protection from the cutting chill. The mild, sunlit, gregarious cheer of winter in my native Bengal was utterly implausible in this landscape of solitude. I examined the card again. It felt like eons since I had taken part in a wedding in India. Not being closely connected to the Bengali/Indian community in Boston, I had also missed weddings at which the immigrant imagination tries to re-create ancient homegrown traditions. Should I make an exception by accepting this invitation, and how would I feel if I did?

As I kept staring at the card, a very different image rose before my eyes—a luscious, rippling swath of green falling away from both sides of a green ridge. It was a freshly washed banana leaf on which a long sequence of foods was being served to be savored with eyes, nose, fingers, and mouth. Not just any old banana leaf, but the one off which I had eaten at my aunt's wedding many decades ago. From half a world away, half a lifetime back, it sent me an imperious summons to remember and relive. Time and space melted away to make me a small child seated at a trestle table, fingers eagerly poised to dip into the nutmeg- and mace-scented rice pilaf (or polao, as we called it in Bengali) heaped on the leaf. Around the pilaf was arranged a number of other items, each endowed with its own promise. For the child that I then was, the feast was the culmination of a long day filled with unsettling emotions, exquisite music, loud and chaotic activity, and, above all, color and smell.

The vision of this fragrant, opulent, sapid banquet lingered in my mind throughout the day. It not only revived numerous distant memories, it roiled my thoughts and feelings as if an expert cook was stirring my brain with her spatula. Or was it the hand of a dairymaid—like the ones who frolicked and flirted with the young god Krishna as described in mythology—churning cream for butter? Whatever the culinary metaphor, I found that the distant past was suddenly overwriting the present.

My aunt got married at a time when ceremonies were conducted at home, not in rented halls. Nobody seemed to mind the chaotic upheaval of realigned spaces, the bumping into upended furniture, or the crowds of relatives milling around for days. The roof of my grandparents' large, rambling four-story house was converted into a kitchen and banquet hall. Under a red and white canopy, the guests sat in front of long trestle tables. Bengalis, like most Indians, have always eaten with their fingers. Instead of plates and cutlery, each person was given a banana leaf. Rows of tiny lightbulbs strung up on bamboo poles illuminated droplets of water that lingered on the glossy surface after the leaf had been washed. On one corner of the leaf sat the discreet embroidery of a pinch of salt, a wedge of lime, and two green chilies. As the feast progressed and different items were served in the traditionally approved sequence, a tapestry of colors and textures came to life on the palette of basic green. The consumer became an actor in a painterly enterprise.

Eating off a banana leaf was a vastly different experience from eating out of a ceramic, porcelain, or metal plate. Your fingers got wedded to the sensory connotations of flaky luchis, soft vegetables, grainy legumes, and fluffy pilaf, even as your fingertips interacted with the silkiness of the leaf. When the pieces of carp or bhetki or other fish swimming in a redolent sauce were ladled out, you had to quickly blend the pilaf with them, lest the sauce run away to the edge of the leaf and spill over on the table. As for the pièce de résistance, a malaikari of enormous freshwater prawns, the green banana leaf provided a perfect foil for a mélange of hues. Scarlet-orange shells covered the heads and tails of the prawns, contrasting with their pale flesh. The sauce that covered them was ruby red, gleaming with the richness of spices, coconut milk, ghee, and the coral oozing from the heads.

Even the palate cleansers that followed—sweet-and-sour chutneys made with tomatoes, plums, or pineapples—glowed with deep jewel tones on the leaf in a way not possible on inorganic surfaces of porcelain, ceramic, or metal. Mopping up these viscous delicacies required a manual and digital dexterity that eating with cutlery did not. But toward the end, most people broke off pieces of crisp pappadams that came with the chutneys and used them as impromptu spoons to scrape the leaf clean in preparation for the final course, dessert. On that evening, the guests began with the Bengali classics, an assortment in creamy white—sandesh, rosogolla, and mishti doi (sweet yogurt). These were balanced by the dark, juicy brown of pantua (a deep-fried sweet made with cottage cheese and evaporated milk) and the orange-flecked gold of darbesh exuding the scent of mace and nutmeg.

Replete at last, the diners received a final touch of green—a chaser of sharp-sweet paan (betel leaf), scented with camphor water, and wrapped in a cone around sweet spices, shredded coconut, and tiny crystals of sugar. A banquet that had taken two days to prepare had to be consumed in a leisurely manner to do justice to its taste and nuance. And the pensive chewing and savoring of paan afterward was, as the ancients knew well, the perfect segue from ingesting to digesting.

At home, for everyday meals, we ate off china and enamel plates instead of banana leaves. But the numerous offerings of this plant, as well as its symbolism, were very much a part of our consciousness. During my first year in college, my mother gave me a cotton sari whose color was called "young banana leaf green." It had a narrow border, woven with white silk thread that intensified the vividness of the green. Draping the sari over myself, I stood for many minutes in front of the mirror, entranced with the effect of the green on my body. Even the ruthless Mughal conqueror Babur was impressed with the plant, which he described in his memoir, *Baburnama*, as "a good-looking tree with its broad, flat, beautiful green leaves."

On the rare occasion when I felt I had done something that deserved a reward, I would ask my mother, the culinary genius in our extended family, to construct an entire meal out of the offerings of the banana plant. And she would oblige. There was banana blossom cooked with diced potatoes, coconut chips, and tiny chickpeas, seasoned with bay leaf, cumin, whole green chilies, and garam masala; banana blossom mixed with ground mustard and shredded coconut, gently steamed inside an envelope of banana leaves; the subtly glowing ivory pith of the banana trunk (used in ancient Sanskrit poetry as the perfect simile for a desirable woman's leg), cooked with tiny shrimp, or seasoned with whole mustard, turmeric, and green chilies; croquettes made with the spiced mashed flesh of a plantainlike green banana.

In snowbound Boston, however, such images were the stuff of fantasy and, over the years, had receded into the unlit corners of my mind, until the arrival of the invitation resurrected them. Instead of sending off a polite letter explaining why I couldn't come, I surprised myself by seriously considering a trip.

I had no illusions about recapturing the chaotic exuberance of my aunt's wedding. Urban weddings these days have become events organized in a professional manner, with far less chaos, intimacy, and personal involvement of family members. People rent halls, hire caterers, and reduce the disruption at home. Having seen the film *Monsoon Wedding*, I was even prepared for the once unthinkable presence of an event planner. The rituals of the Hindu wedding are complex, lengthy, and arduous but, even so, modernity has made room for some degree of comfort. When my aunt got married, the bride was fed a predawn meal that combined fruit, yogurt, and rice flakes, which had to sustain her through a daylong fast until the ceremony started in the evening. Brides today are permitted light snacks to keep up their energies and spirits for the ceremony itself. As for the wedding feast, I had heard and read too much about the waning of traditional Bengali cooks to expect even a near-duplication of that banana-leaf spread.

Still, I resolved to go. Preparing myself for all kinds of letdowns—wasn't the past always more attractive in remembrance than in actuality?—I made ready for this impulsive voyage. It was not till the second leg of the journey, when I was on the plane from London to Calcutta, that I saw what the leaf was trying to tell me. This didn't have to be an attempt to recapture a bygone golden era. Rather, it was an opportunity to examine current realities, an opportunity to be relished as much as a banquet from the hands of a master.

During all my years as a food writer, I had never stepped out of the well-defined territory of my native Bengal. Championing the cause of regional cuisine as the only authentic culinary identity, I had scoffed at the mere mention of "Indian" food or curry powder, which I came across often enough in the United States. Yet it was becoming more and more apparent, even from faraway America, that an inevitable fusion of influences from disparate areas was changing the nature of regional foods and eating habits in modern India. And, in fact, there was nothing new about this trend. The same Bengali cuisine that I wanted the world to know and appreciate, instead of focusing on the ersatz curries and tikka masalas available in Indian restaurants everywhere, has also evolved and changed over the centuries. Even a casual look at the pages of Bengali narratives going back to medieval times reveals significant differences from the way we cook and eat in Bengal today. With the passage of the centuries, Bengali cuisine has eagerly taken and absorbed exotic ingredients, and repeatedly been modified by external influences. The same is true of other regional cuisines in the subcontinent.

In this context, what *was* authenticity? I had to ask myself. In an unstable, mobile age, when large numbers of Indians are leaving home and migrating to other parts of their country in search of jobs and opportunities (as people do in America), when do the borders of regional uniqueness relax and let a pan-Indian identity emerge? Is it possible for specialties rooted in ingredient, terrain, altitude, soil, and cultural beliefs to survive in a time of rapid perpetual motion? The time seemed ripe for an expedition.

"What would you like, madam, the beef or the chicken?" asked the stewardess in her clipped British accent.

Dragged out of my speculations, I looked at the menu card. There it was again. "Chicken tikka masala with rice and vegetables." Even on a British Airways flight, there was no getting away from a dish that supposedly owed its origins to enterprising Punjabi restaurateurs trying to make a living in different cities after being uprooted from their home territories by the 1947 Partition of India. Despite a jab of reflexive annoyance at the ubiquity of this nontraditional, contextless dish, I couldn't help acknowledging a reluctant admiration for a community that had successfully created brand names out of chicken tikka masala or tandoori chicken. Like McDonald's with their Big Mac or Burger King with their Whopper, the Punjabis are making their creations a part of the urban eating vocabulary in the West.

The smile on the air-hostess's face was waning as she waited for me to choose. It was not too difficult to decide that between several items of plastic airline food, the best option for me had to be the one with a modicum of spice, fragrance, and color. Chicken tikka masala it was, on the flight to Calcutta. Giant freshwater prawns in a rich red sauce, or steamed banana blossom with ground mustard, would, like the ideal of authenticity, continue to elude me until touchdown in the land that had given birth to all of us—me, the banana tree, the prawns. Even there, it was possible that what I ate would fall short of what I thought it should be.

PART ONE

Chapter One

BENGAL: LAND OF A THOUSAND RIVERS

Bengalis love fish. Mention Bengali food to anyone in India, and the first image it evokes is that of fish and rice. The second image is that of sweets made from chhana (fresh cottage cheese). Geography is responsible for the first, an accident of history for the second. Although a wedding invitation started me on this Indian culinary odyssey, the history of Bengali sweets had been intriguing enough for me to have made an earlier exploratory trip to a destination hundreds of miles from my native region.

From a high aerial perspective you can see Bengal (and historically, this includes both the Indian state of West Bengal and the country of Bangladesh) as an enormous delta in the eastern part of India, crisscrossed by rivers and rills too numerous to count. The smaller ones join up with the major rivers like the Ganges, the Padma, and the Brahmaputra, but eventually, they all find their way into the salty waters of the Bay of Bengal. On the map, you will see the emptying out of this collective water pitcher identified as the Mouths of the Ganges.

Fly lower down, and you see the land that makes the delta—alluvial soil, renewed every year with the silt deposited by flooding rivers, precious as gold to the farmer. In poetry and literature, "golden Bengal" is a recurrent image. In physical terms, it is an extraordinarily fertile land, with the Tropic of Cancer running through it, just south of my city, Calcutta. Emerald acres of rice; dense groves of bamboo, banana, coconut, and palm; orchards of mango and other fruits; fields bursting with greens and vegetables; and rivers, lakes, ponds, and canals teeming with fish— Bengal seems to have been more than ordinarily favored by nature. In the sixteenth and seventeenth centuries, long before it had been split into two, this one region supplied much of the food for the imperial Mughal army. But behind the beauty there is the darkness, and the varied seasons that produce so much of Bengal's food can often take on a fearsome, destructive aspect. Ruinous monsoon floods, violent autumn cyclones bred in the Bay of Bengal, searing summer droughts—all are visited on Bengal by nature. Overall, however, this is a land that has fed her people well.

The presence of the rivers and the lakes and the rich coastal waters bordered by the mangrove forests of the Sunderbans, have automatically made freshwater fish a major part of the Bengali diet. Even the crustaceans that Bengalis adore—prawn, shrimp, and crab—are harvested from lakes, rivers, and estuaries, not the open sea. Moreover, fish here, as in many parts of China, is not merely food. As a symbol of prosperity and fertility, it touches many aspects of ceremonial and ritual life. A Bengali Hindu wedding, like the one I was about to attend, is replete with such symbolism.

Both my parents loved to shop for food. In our extended family, my mother's kitchen was famed as a renewable source of gastronomic delight. And the one thing she loved above all was fish, no matter what its size, texture, or density of flesh and bone. As a picky and temperamental child, I didn't share her enthusiasm. Until I was old enough to go to college, when an expansion of my world helped develop my palate, there were only a few kinds of fish that I tolerated. The rest, however much they were recommended by mother and grandmother as "brain food," were anathema, particularly the tiny, excessively bony creatures that were either crisply fried or made into fiery, red-hot concoctions with julienned potatoes.

As I grew into my teens, what particularly aggrieved me was being dragged to the fish market by my mother, despite vigorous protests. She was determined that I should grow up with some sense of where my food came from. I hated the noise, the crowds, and the slippery, wet surface of the aisles bordered with gutters where the fishmongers, sitting on high slabs of concrete, threw out fish offal and dirty water with careless abandon even as they loudly touted their goods. Sometimes, my mother bought a fish head to cook with roasted moong dal—a specialty that makes Bengali fish lovers salivate, while outsiders grow queasy. Choosing a majestic carp, she would command the fishmonger to cut off the head and then portion it. With fascination bordering on horror, I watched as the man picked up the huge fish in both hands and ran it with one swift, yet powerful movement against the blade of the bonti, a Bengali cutting instrument whose curving blade rises vertically out of a thick wooden wedge placed on the floor. As he triumphantly held up the head with its exposed dark red gills, it seemed more alive than the whole fish. Instinctively, I closed my eyes and held my breath lest some fishy spirit haunt me. Returning home from the market, I scrubbed my face, hands, and arms with soap and water, and rubbed down my dress with wet hands, hoping to delete the odor of fish but uneasily aware of its lingering potency.

It was not until many years later that I saw Louis Malle's film *Atlantic City,* with the unforgettable image of Susan Sarandon rubbing her hands and body with lemon juice after serving oysters in the bar. As a disgruntled teen, my only comfort came from recalling the story of the fisherman's daughter in India's great epic, the *Mahabharata.* The young woman helped her father in his work and ferried passengers across the river in their little dinghy to make extra money. Although she was beautiful, her odor was strong enough for the neighbors to call her Matsyagandha, "She

Who Smells of Fish." One day, a holy man came to the river and asked her to ferry him across. Sitting across from her, he was so overwhelmed by her beauty that he asked her to have a child with him. When she agreed, he rewarded her by permanently changing her body chemistry. From that time, no matter what she did, she emitted only a beautiful floral fragrance. Every time my mother took me to the fish market, I wished with all my heart that I would find a generous holy man at the entrance, who would make the offensive smell vanish.

Arriving in Cambridge as a graduate student, I discovered that nothing symbolized the contrariness of an outsider's life better than one's reaction to fish. In New England, a long maritime history has created an eating universe ruled by cod, halibut, tuna, salmon, bluefish, swordfish, and other inhabitants of the great Atlantic, so much so, that the word *fish* is almost synonymous with seafood. But in those early days after arrival, I was ignorant enough to repeatedly fall into the trap unwittingly set by generous American hosts.

"Do you like fish?" they would ask as they took me out to dinner.

"Oh, yes," I would respond with Bengali enthusiasm, having easily tired of the large pieces of chicken covered with fatty skin, the hamburgers, and the recalcitrant cuts of meat labeled "London broil" that were served in the dormitory cafeterias of that time.

And so they took me to well-known "fish" restaurants. Each time, I ordered an item with a new name, and each time, I encountered the strong, briny flavor guaranteed to put off a person used to eating freshwater fish. In Bengal, where the rivers rule the land, the ocean is rarely explored as a source of fish. In fact, marine fish are traditionally considered inferior to fish harvested from lakes and rivers, and are consequently much cheaper. All my favorite varieties were freshwater ones. Confronted by the disconcerting flavor of the fish served to me in America, I assumed at first that what I didn't like was the blandness of the preparation, the total lack of spices. If only the Puritan palate could embrace the tangy seasonings of my native land, what a difference it would make, I reflected as I picked at my portion. Since I didn't know how to cook, this was a natural mistake. Gradually, however, I figured out that this ˙ as a cultural, not a culinary divide: it was the seafood itself that tasted so foreign to me. And despite the many years spent here, I have not been able to cross it. The offerings of the sea, with a couple of exceptions, do not quicken desire in me. It is, however, a Bengali limitation, not an Indian one. The food of India's coastal states, like Goa, Kerala, and Maharashtra on the west, and Orissa on the east, includes many kinds of seafood transformed by intensely flavorful spices.

There were five days to go before the wedding, when I landed in Calcutta. I was glad to have that time to get over jet lag and revisit some familiar haunts. Calcutta, supposedly founded by the British trader Job Charnock who landed in the area in 1690, grew out of three villages and became a major port for the East India Company's early operations. It was also the first capital of British-ruled India. Throughout the nineteenth century and the early part of the twentieth, the city was an intellectual and political hub, and Bengalis were renowned for their scholarly, literary, and artistic accomplishments. Much earlier, however, in the ancient and medieval period, Bengalis were also famed for their success in maritime trading. The rivers of Bengal were the conduits of goods that made their way to seaports in distant locations. Aside from agricultural crops and dairy products, Bengal also produced high-quality cane sugar, indigo, and fine textiles. After the independence of India and the partition of Bengal in 1947, however, the region was caught in a cruel downward spiral, with the influx of refugees from East Pakistan/Bangladesh, economic downturn, loss of industries, and a pervasive disaffection among the middle class. Regretful longings for a glorious past dominated the conversation in many living rooms and coffeehouses.

These days, however, I'm often reminded of an old Bengali fairy tale about an adventurous prince who arrives at a deserted castle and discovers a beautiful girl lying in an enchanted sleep. Looking closer, he sees a small gold stick near her head, and a silver one near her feet. Being a clever fellow, he makes the right guess and wakes her with a touch of the golden stick. She tells him that she has been abducted by an evil demon who puts her in an enchanted sleep with the silver stick when he goes out hunting. During recent visits to Calcutta, I have had the sense of a search going on for the golden stick that will help the city wake to a new era of renaissance and possibility. And though the small towns and rural areas of Bengal are far removed from the aura of a metropolis, they, too, project a sense of looking for revival.

On the morning of the wedding, I drove up to the groom's family home in Calcutta's Salt Lake area—a onetime extensive marsh that has been gradually filled and developed to meet the needs of a growing population. Fish was much on my mind. The glorious fish and prawn dishes of feasts past paraded before my eyes: kalia, jhol, jhal, ambal, malaikari, murighanto, dal made with fish head, and that extraordinary adaptation from the British, the "fish fry" made with fillets of bhetki marinated in a paste of onion, ginger, and green chilies before being breaded and fried crisp. Two other misnomers resulting from the colonial experience—the chop and the cutlet—were also part of the festive meals in the old days; and, as children, my cousins and I loved them. A Bengali chop is a round or oval potato cake stuffed with minced fish or meat, which is dipped in eggs and bread crumbs and then fried. A cutlet, which can be chicken, meat, or prawn, usually means one of those elements seasoned and pounded lightly to form a long, flat oval that is then breaded and fried. Fries, chops, and cutlets are usually served with a tomato-cucumber-onion salad and a mouthwatering, brain-exploding sauce called kasundi that has nothing colonial about it. It is made with the tart green mangoes of summer, mixed with pungent mustard oil and ground mustard. To any Bengali, it is to die for.

Aside from the pleasures of eating, I also wondered whether fish as a ritual item in a wedding had survived. On the first day of the wedding (Hindu wedding ceremonies take three days to be completed and consummated), the groom's family usually sends an array of gifts, called tatto, to the bride's home, the most spectacular item being a whole fish—a rui (Bengali carp), the biggest the family can afford to buy. I still vividly remember the princely specimen that had appeared at my grandparents' house on the morning of my aunt's wedding, its silvery-pink scales gleaming in the sunlight. The enormous head was decorated with patterns drawn with an oil-and-vermilion paste, and garlands of jasmine encircled its portly girth. Was it possible, I mused, walking in through the gates embellished with banana-leaf banners, to obtain a fish of that size in this age of overfished rivers?

Before I could find out, however, I was stopped in my tracks by the activities going on in the family garage, transformed into a makeshift kitchen. Three portable stoves, enormous kadhais (Indian woks), wide-mouthed cooking pots, and two sets of grinding stones for spices, were fueling the orderly frenzy that precedes a traditional Bengali meal. An old man wielding a spatula directed operations, loudly berating his assistants, who halved, sliced, chopped, and diced vegetables as if their lives depended on it. With his long gray hair knotted into a tight bun, gray beard, betel juice–stained mouth, and checked lungi (a saronglike wrap from waist to ankle), the man was almost a twin of the master chef my grandfather had hired to cook for my aunt's wedding. Could it be that I was wrong in assuming that wedding feasts were no longer cooked at home?

Sadly, I wasn't. As my host informed me, the cooking in the garage was only for the benefit of relatives, friends, and visitors from foreign parts who show up for the occasion and stick around for the day, some being helpful, some adding to the chaos, but all expecting lunch, which has traditionally been the main meal of the day. A closer look at all the items on display indicated that I was in luck. This was to be the kind of traditional Bengali meal whose disappearance everyone bemoaned these days, the kind that began with an odd Bengali favorite, the one hardest to duplicate in an American kitchen—shukto.

A bitter vegetable dish eaten as a starter with rice during the midday meal, shukto remains a perennial puzzle for outsiders. More common among Hindus than Muslims, shukto's unique value is based on the gastronomic theory that it prepares the tongue and the stomach for the courses that follow. That theory, in turn, is derived from the ancient Indian science of Ayurveda, which ascribes specific attributes to each fruit, vegetable, and spice. The system decrees that certain foods are "hot," and therefore ideal for fueling the body in winter, while others are "cold" and therefore suitable for the torrid hot summers of India. Shukto, considered a cooling dish, includes such vegetables as eggplant, white radish, green banana, potato, green papaya, and, most important, bitter melon, called karola in Bengali. The bitter melon is sometimes supplemented with the equally bitter-tasting leaves of the neem (margosa) tree or those of patol, a climbing gourd. Only the surest of hands can create the perfect balance between the bitterness of these vegetables and the seasonings, which include ground ginger, poppy-seed paste, and the typical Bengali five-spice mix called panchphoron. The right touch of ghee, added before the dish is removed from the stove, intensifies its unique flavor.

You certainly won't find shukto coexisting with chicken tikka masala in Indian restaurants abroad. Even in Bengal, it is essentially a home-cooked item. But like fish head, it is a cultural marker, identifying a regional palate. It is also an acquired taste, like beer, and for those who have acquired it, there is no better starter to a leisurely, multicourse midday meal. Shukto probably got its honored status in Bengali Hindu gastronomy in medieval times, with the spreading of the Bhakti movement, preached by a charismatic figure named Chaitanya who emphasized non-violence, equality, and, in terms of food, vegetarianism. He also happened to be personally fond of dishes containing shukuta (dried neem leaves). Two biographies written by his contemporaries provide detailed descriptions of the vegetarian meals served to Chaitanya by his devotees, and quote at length from his discourses on the benefits of vegetables, especially the wide variety of greens that flourish in tropical Bengal.

The vegetarianism didn't last long in a land of fish lovers (except among a small group); but a distinctive and elaborate vegetarian cuisine, which developed during the peak of the Bhakti movement, still survives, delighting both vegetarians and aficionados of fish and meat. To compensate for the lack of protein and to add taste and body to vegetarian dishes, Bengalis often use dried pellets of ground dal, called boris (wadis in Hindi). In rural Bengal, making boris became both a ritual and an art. Women would bathe, wear fresh clothes, and grind large quantities of dal of different varieties with water on the grinding stones that were essential equipment in every kitchen. Once the dal had been made into a paste, and salt and seasonings added to it, the women would take two big handfuls and set them out on a clean cloth to dry in the sun. These were called the Old Man and the Old Woman, and were meant to be symbolic offerings to the gods—a common gesture of appeasement in many kinds of food preparation. The rest of the dal was whipped for greater smoothness of texture, and small pellets of it were set out on large mats or pieces of cloth to dry in the autumn and winter sun. Once dried, they could be stored for many months. The mark of a gifted bori-maker was in the airiness of the consistency she achieved through whipping the dal paste. Some boris, made with milled urad dal, were called phul-boris and were almost of meringuelike consistency. They were good enough to eat by themselves, after being deep-fried. Sadly, this art, along with many other delicate kitchen skills, has almost disappeared. Boris are usually mass-produced these days, and the drying process takes place inside an oven, not under the natural warmth of the Bengali sun.

The foundation of many Bengali vegetarian dishes, which strikingly differ in taste and flavor from those of other Indian regions, is to be found in the unique application of delicate yet unmistakable spices. Perhaps the most indispensable is the mixture called panchphoron (five flavorings), a combination of whole nigella, cumin, mustard, fennel, and fenugreek, in equal proportions. Thrown into heated oil, with one or two dried red chilies, the spices emit an inimitable aroma that indicates the presence of a Bengali kitchen, whether in London or New York, or Bengal itself. Ginger, black pepper, and ground mustard provided varying levels of piquancy until the sixteenth century, when the chili pepper was introduced by the Portuguese traders and adopted enthusiastically by Bengali cooks. Today, it is hard to imagine almost any vegetable preparation without the green fire of fresh chilies, slit in the middle, the seeds left intact.

One of my personal favorites, the seed of the opium poppy, also has a foreign connection. It is used in other cuisines, but its prolific, enthusiastic, even single-minded utilization is only to be seen in Bengal, especially in the westernmost areas of West Bengal, bordering on the state of Bihar. Indians discovered opium as a narcotic in the eleventh and twelfth centuries from Arab traders who had learned about it from the Greeks. The drug itself is extracted from the latex of the poppy's seedpods, and the tiny, kidney-shaped white seeds have no narcotic effect, since they form only after the seedpod has dried up. For centuries, these seeds were simply a byproduct of the opium generation process. Their chief culinary application was in Islamic recipes for meat and chicken in which poppy-seed paste was used to thicken sauces and lend texture, the way flour is in a roux.

Things changed after the British East India Company, having dislodged Bengal's last nawab in 1757, established a stronghold over the province, a vast, fertile area that included the modern Indian states of Bihar and Orissa. Having discovered that opium could generate huge profits not only in the Indian market but also in China (where it was a prohibited commodity), and that Bengali opium was of higher quality than that grown in western India, the British forced Bengali farmers to convert all their arable land to poppy cultivation; food crops were brought in from neighboring areas. With narcotic supplies thus ensured, the British carried on an illegal trade, smuggling opium into China and raking up huge profits. In the 1820s, the Chinese emperor Tao-Kuang tried to restrict the import of opium, but the British fought back. The First Opium War, which raged from 1839 to 1842, ended in China's defeat, resulting in the humiliating Treaty of Nanking. In 1856, the Second Opium War began. After being defeated again, the Chinese responded by legalizing opium cultivation in their country. As a result, the profits of smuggling Bengali opium were disastrously reduced, and, by the early twentieth century, the British trade in the drug was governed by internationally ratified treaties and regulations. One of Britain's best-known writers, interestingly, whose books denounced powerful, exploitative systems, was born in 1903 to a civil servant who supervised opium production in a town called Motihari, in the Champaran area of Bihar. He was christened Eric Arthur Blair, but the world knows him as George Orwell.

Meanwhile, on the sidelines of drug-running, war, and colonial manipulations, the Bengali culinary imagination had found extensive applications for the enormous quantities of poppy seeds, called posto in

Bengali, that had suddenly become available. Posto's delicate, almost herbal flavor complements vegetables like jhingey (a ridged, zucchini-like gourd), potatoes, or eggplant. Combined with ground mustard, it makes a delicious sauce for fish, while the addition of tamarind allows it to be made into a tangy ambal (sour chutney). Whipped together with ground coconut and chopped green chilies, it is the raw material for crisp fritters that go down well with afternoon tea or as a side dish at lunchtime. Best of all, however, is the uncooked posto-bata—large quantities of posto, soaked in water, ground to a fine paste on a stone, whipped up with mustard oil, salt, and chopped green chilies, and eaten as a first course with rice. In the perishing heat of the summer, posto cools the body like few other things. An added bonus is its slightly soporific effect, which deepens the postlunch siesta for an ease-loving Bengali.

Over the years, I've often been nonplussed by the eating habits of American friends I've invited to dinner. Having spent the better part of a day, or even two, preparing an elaborate Bengali meal, I assume that guests will eat the way I've always been used to, a bit of everything, but in sequence, with portions of rice. Instead, many of my friends tend to heap all the items on their plate, mix them up, and proceed with dinner in a haphazard fashion.

"How can you possibly taste the differences between items?" I protest.

They assure me they do.

"How can you go back to vegetables after eating a big portion of richly spiced meat?" I say.

"Why not," they say, "if we feel like it?"

That, in a nutshell, is the difference between the long-established eating culture of Bengal and the easygoing pattern of meals in America.

The Bengali meal, whether it is a wedding banquet or an ordinary day's repast, is structured in a sequence. Plain boiled rice is the staple, and is mixed with a bit of each dish as you progress through the meal; in a traditional wedding feast, you may additionally be served pilaf and/or luchis (puffed bread) to eat with meat and fish. A bitter dish, such as shukto or neem-begun (eggplant braised with neem leaves), is always eaten first. If none is served, you start with one or more fried vegetables with dal. This may be followed by a complex vegetable dish, perhaps banana blossom combined with diced potatoes, chickpeas, and ground coconut, which my mother made for me so often. Then comes the fish course, almost a daily dish. While there are numerous ways that Bengalis cook fish, the best known is the jhol, as unique to Bengal as bouillabaisse is to France. Pieces of fish, such as carp; vegetables like potatoes, eggplants, and the small gourdlike patol; and boris (which plump up and absorb the delectable flavor and juice of the jhol) are all combined in a thin, flavorful broth. Mustard oil, which reduces fishy odors, is the favored cooking medium, not only for fish but also vegetables. Like shukto, jhol is a paradox, its simplicity belying the trickiness of achieving a perfect balance between flavor and spiciness. When meat (Hindus eat chicken and goat; Muslims also eat beef) is part of a meal, it always comes after fish. As for dessert, Bengalis have an extensive array to choose from, including a slew of items unique to the region.

This basic Bengali meal can be considerably extended by the addition of small tidbits, variations in the dals served, a sequence of complex vegetable dishes, time-consuming digressions involving fish heads, rich pilafs to go with the meat, and tart concoctions of seasonal fruits that precede the dessert. Matching the bounty of nature, the region has developed an epicureanism that stems from leisure, imagination, the practice of creating meals around the offerings of the seasons, and the notion of food as both art and pleasure.

As in most other societies, religion plays a big part in Bengali food. The Muslim festivals are celebrated with pilafs, biryanis, kebabs, meats in rich sauces, and desserts—items similar to those served by Muslims all over India. In general, the cooking of Muslim Bengalis tends to focus less on vegetables than on meat, and the use of onion and garlic is pronounced. Among Hindus, ritual beliefs are strong and influence the selection of foods on different occasions. While elaborate meals mark sacred and secular festivals, specific foods acquire special significance on different occasions. During periods of mourning, complex rituals are accompanied by severely abstemious meals prepared with austerity. After my grandfather's death, I observed his children being served a one-course meal of rice and vegetables cooked in a clay pot, the only seasoning allowed being a few teaspoons of ghee and a bit of sea salt. In traditional homes, numerous rules—even more complex than those related to keeping kosher—govern the purity of foods, the proximity of certain items, and the permissibility of vegetarian and nonvegetarian foods on different occasions for different people. Much of this lore, along with the art of cooking elaborate and seasonal meals, is slowly vanishing. Families have traded the inheritance of culinary and cultural traditions for the freedom of being nuclear and mobile.

Perched on a stool in the garage turned kitchen of the house in Salt Lake, I watched the old man pour out shukto into a large container and marveled at his strength. With hardly a pause for rest, he lifted one of his enormous woks onto the stove and pulled forward a tray containing rows of cleaned parshey, one of Bengal's favorite fishes. Usually eight to ten inches long, these slender silvery beauties are cooked whole.

"What kind of sauce are you making for them?" I asked as he quickly dusted the fish with salt and turmeric powder.

He pulled out a plate containing dollops of freshly ground spices and pointed to mustard and posto. In the wok, the mustard oil heated up and released its characteristic aroma. The old man threw in a pinch of whole nigella seeds and several split green chilies before putting in the fish, sautéing them, and adding the spices. Leaving the contents of the wok to simmer gently, he began to organize ingredients for making several vegetable dishes. A little later, as he transferred the fish to a large enamel serving bowl, the heady smell of ground mustard and green chilies brought back the redolence of meals I had eaten during earlier visits from America. My father was still alive then, and my journeys were filled with anticipation, of the food he would buy from the market and the delightful dishes my mother would make for us to share. Parshey being a favorite of mine, my father always bought some for my first lunch—fat, oily specimens, their bellies bulging with roe, cooked in a pungent mustard sauce similar to the one that I had just watched being made by the old man.

There are more varieties of freshwater fish in Bengal than weeks in a year—or there were, according to narratives written as late as the mid-nineteenth century—and these were to be found all over the land. Poor peasants who had no money to spend in the market could simply wander out to the paddy fields during the monsoon and pick up handfuls of small fish from the standing water. The so-called climbing perch, moving across land in search of water when lakes or ponds dried up in the summer, also became food for the finder. But as in so many countries, the growth of population, habitation, pollution, and overfishing has left its mark on Bengal. In urban markets, fish is now an expensive commodity. Mythology, however, dies hard in the collective memory, and there are several species on which the Bengalis have lavished imagination, affection, symbolism, and desire in equal measure. The large rui—especially the head, which is part of the ceremonial meal made for the son-in-law every summer—and giant prawns both fall into that category. But perhaps no other fish arouses as much emotion across the board as ilish—the Bengali shad, which the British called hilsa.

The mystique of the hilsa can be understood only in the context of a larger Bengal that was split into two by the 1947 Partition of India—West Bengal (in India), and East Pakistan, which later became the country of Bangladesh. For the inhabitants of pre-Partition Bengal, the only line of demarcation between east and west was the geographical line of the River Padma. The people on the eastern side were called Bangals and those on the western side were Ghotis—both jocular terms used to convey rivalry, derision, superiority, and plain difference. Over time, the division was further reinforced by demographics, Muslims forming the majority in East Bengal, and Hindus in the west. Cooking techniques and food preferences reflected both religious and subregional differences. However, a common bond of culture and language persisted through the centuries, creating a unique Bengali identity recognizable all over the subcontinent. Rice and fish remained the ideal Bengali meal on both sides of the border.

Nothing exemplifies this Bengali identity better than the region's love affair with hilsa. The two major rivers in the east and the west, the Padma and the Ganges respectively, have always been the prime sources for this fish, which begins life in estuarine waters and then moves up-river to spawn. During my school and college years in Calcutta, I often heard heated discussions between members of my family (rooted in West Bengal for countless generations) and their friends and colleagues who had migrated from East Bengal, about which was superior in flavor and taste—the hilsa from the Ganges (that we swore by) or the one from the Padma. But this was a minor difference. There was absolute, indissoluble agreement over the fact that no fish can rival the hilsa's exquisite flavor or delectably tender flesh, not the large rui with its ceremonial and ritual status, nor the giant prawn with its rich, coral-filled head, nor the myriad other specimens that fill the waters of Bengal. In appearance, too, it had the edge, a full-grown specimen being nearly two feet in length, its small silver scales shimmering vividly, its eyes like pale blue gemstones even in death.

To me, hilsa is both a memory of joyful family meals and a symbol of loss. It is a fish that is strongly linked to the Bengalis' seasonal appreciation of food. The first drenching downpours of the monsoon, when all creatures stir back to life after the searing, draining torpor of summer, are celebrated with that classic Bengali meal—khichuri (rice and dal cooked together, flavored with ghee, ginger, and whole garam masala) and freshly caught hilsa. On other days during the monsoon, when the plump, kidney-shaped roe (much like shad roe in appearance) is available, it is gently dusted with salt and turmeric and sautéed in mustard oil to be eaten with plain rice. As for the fish itself, recipes for hilsa are too numerous to document, with families each adding their individual quirky touches.

Like banana blossoms, hilsa was also an item with which my mother sometimes constructed an entire meal. We started with a few pieces of fried fish and hilsa roe. But the plain rice was enlivened by pouring over it the oil in which these had been fried—the bare teaspoon of mustard oil in the pan usually increasing to half a cup with the rendered fat from

the fish. The head came next, fried, broken up into pieces, and combined with the leaves and stems of a green called pũi. The bulk of the
fish was divided into two portions, one cooked with a ground mustard
paste, its pungency merging into that of the mustard oil, the other
(bonier portions of the back) made either into a jhal with hot red chili
paste, or an ambal with tamarind pulp.

The likelihood of such meals has dwindled almost to the point of
nonexistence, not only for me in the absence of my parental home, but
also for the region. The severely polluted Ganges is producing fewer and
fewer fish, and very few of these are allowed to reach full-bodied matu-
rity. In recent years, every time I have visited the fish markets of Calcutta and asked about hilsa, the vendors point to specimens that have
been imported from Bangladesh—the hilsa from the Padma that is bigger in size, and yet, to the West Bengali, deficient in taste and flavor. And
even those may soon disappear as Bangladesh keeps exporting large
quantities of frozen hilsa to Europe and America for eager Bengali
expatriates. Bengali tradition, based on the ecological awareness that
comes with an agricultural way of life, imposed a ban on eating hilsa
during the crucial months of late spring and summer, thus allowing the
fish to grow, mate, and spawn. But the urge to consume, in an age when
technology can fly things from one corner of the earth to another, is too
powerful to be stemmed by such considerations. This graceful "darling
of the waters" may well be doomed to an existence only in memory and
legend.

A rising crescendo of voices, rapid footsteps, and the loud blowing of
conch shells—the auspicious sound that drives away all evil influences—
shook me out of my remembrances of things past. The tatto (gifts from
the bridegroom's family to the bride) was being brought out. As the
procession of relatives emerged, I left the garage and went up to admire
the large trays holding cosmetics, jewelry, decorative objects, saris, kur-
tas, packaged nuts and dried fruits, and covered terra-cotta pots filled
with sweets and sweet yogurt. Artfully decorated with colored paper, red
cloth, and gold ribbons, the assembly of gifts gladdened not only my eye

but also my heart. Even if the hilsa's demise was imminent, at least this beautiful custom from the vanished world of my childhood had survived. I looked for the tray containing the whole rui fish and, sure enough, it was there, though its dimensions fell far short of the one I remembered from my aunt's wedding.

Once the gifts had been loaded into several waiting cars and the party had driven off, I went inside the house to see the groom. In the Bengali marriage market, he had been an eligible bachelor, with a well-paid job as the marketing director for a multinational corporation. He was waiting upstairs for lunch to be brought up. While the rest of us would eat the meal cooked by the hired chef in the garage, the groom was allowed only a ritually pure meal that his female relatives, after bathing and wearing fresh clothes, were preparing in the family kitchen. Dressed in a set of new clothes, his forehead decorated with patterns in sandalwood paste, a thick garland of marigolds round his neck, he sat waiting patiently on a square piece of carpet. Following tradition, the meal would be set before him on the floor, which had already been washed thoroughly. This very early lunch was to be his last meal until the wedding rituals were completed late in the evening. When he saw me, he smiled shyly. I imagined he looked very different in his office, wearing a suit and tie instead of the traditional Bengali dhuti-panjabi, projecting authority and decision. Here, on this important day, he had to be a passive recipient of the gestures of ceremony, faith, ritual, and affection.

I sat down beside him and we chatted inconsequentially, until the United States was mentioned.

"I'd like to go there, someday," he said. "But I wouldn't want to live there. Don't you ever regret living in a foreign country?"

"It doesn't feel foreign anymore," I said.

He nodded, but I was not sure he believed me.

"Did you always think you'd have an arranged marriage?" I asked, emboldened by his question.

"I wasn't sure, at least not while I was a student, when I did go out with a couple of girls. Later, after I started working, my family began to talk about marriage. At first, I was reluctant, but then I saw some of my friends getting married. Those were arranged marriages, and they seemed very happy. I'm the last one in our group to marry. I think it's a good decision. My parents know what's best for me because they know me better than anyone else. And it's not as if I'm marrying a total stranger. We've been introduced; we've met a few times."

I thought of my own rebellious generation, the way some of us had fought our families' decisions, thrust aside family involvement or advice. I remembered the peculiar sense of envy with which I had sometimes envisioned the youth of the future—much less hobbled by convention, bolder and more independent in making decisions. But things don't change the way you expect them to. Despite their addiction to MTV, blogs, iPods, cell phones, tight jeans, burgers from McDonald's, and mushroom pizzas from Domino's, the instinct for caution and conformity apparently remains strong in today's young people when it comes to the important decisions of life.

The sound of conch shells again: three women, the groom's aunts, were coming up the stairs, carrying the food. It was a strictly vegetarian meal, untouched even by a whiff of fish. Nor could cooked rice be a part of it. That daily staple, without which life is unimaginable in Bengal, is omitted from most ritual meals except during the ceremony of Annaprasan, "first rice," when a six-month-old infant is fed his or her first grains of cooked rice. When any other ceremony does require rice, it is usually in the form of popped rice or dried rice flakes. The women placed before the groom a gleaming silver plate and several silver bowls filled with different items. On the plate was a stack of pale golden luchis, fried disks of fine white flour, puffed up like balloons and emitting the aroma of pure ghee. Once again, I was swept away from the present to a distant childhood when my mother's luchis, light as air, were one of my favorite foods. During my early years in America, one of the beckoning pleasures of going home was the prospect of sitting in my mother's kitchen to watch her knead the dough, roll it out into small disks, and fry them one by one. After the first five or six were done, she would pick one up and hand it to me. Few gastronomic experiences equal the unalloyed pleasure of piercing the top skin of the luchi with your finger, letting out the hot, fragrant air, tearing off a bit, and putting it in your mouth for a slow, heavenly dissolution.

The young groom wrapped half a luchi around a portion of slow-cooked potatoes in a tamarind-chili-asafetida sauce, and put it in his mouth. As he chewed, a smile of relish lit up his face—probably the way my face did when I tasted my mother's luchis—making it seem even younger. The women looked at each other and laughed, as if they were relieved that the surrogate god for the day had approved of what they had prepared and offered to him. Eagerly, they helped him to other items—a thick dal flecked with coconut and ginger chips and exuding the aroma of garam masala, several other vegetable dishes, and the obligatory finale of yogurt and sweets.

Halfway through the meal, a further commotion of people and cars downstairs announced the arrival of the reciprocal tatto sent from the bride's family. This, too, included a large rui fish, and the women around me excitedly chattered about the fish head that the chef downstairs would cook with roasted moong dal.

The hired chef was a master of efficiency and skill, but we started lunch much later than I had expected. The excellence of the cooking, however, provided more than ample compensation. It had been many years since I had eaten such an elaborate traditional meal. The shukto was followed by fried eggplant slices, pumpkin-flower fritters, fried julienned potatoes, and a highly seasoned dish of shredded cabbage, cubed potatoes, and green peas. After that came dal with the fish head, which was a major enterprise to eat, but entirely worth it. Then we sampled the delicate parshey in mustard–poppy-seed sauce, followed by a more highly seasoned dish of shrimp combined with shredded coconut and ground mustard. The final item was a rich, garam masala–infused kalia, made with pieces of the carp. No meat was served—a wise decision, I felt, since the evening's catered feast was bound to include chicken and goat meat. Instead, we ended with two favorite Bengali desserts, mishti doi and sandesh.

Doi, as yogurt is called in Bengali, is universal food. It is used throughout India—in the north for raita and lassi, in the south for making curd-rice—and eaten plain everywhere, either as a digestive or as a cooling food in summer, mixed with fruit and rice flakes. It is used for marinating and cooking meat and has auspicious connotations in Hindu religious rituals. But probably no other culture has made it into a dessert that is not only sweet, but soothing, emollient, and deeply satisfying. Even the lactose-intolerant may find it worth the risk of eating the Bengali mishti doi (literally, sweet yogurt). It bears little resemblance to the breakfast yogurt of America or Europe, which is sweetened with the addition of fruit preserves or flavored with coffee or vanilla. Made in terra-cotta pots with rich evaporated milk and yogurt cultures, Bengali mishti doi has a custardlike consistency, often with a thick, extra-creamy layer on top called māthā. Only a whisper of the natural tartness of yogurt can be tasted, yet it is not in the least cloying. Mishti doi is rarely made at home, the domestic cook having long realized that the professional product is far superior. Each of Calcutta's legendary sweetshops has a particular style of making mishti doi; each is delicious. One of the best known, fancifully named Payodhi (literally, the ocean of milk) by the poet Rabindranath Tagore, is made by a confectionary called Jalajoga.

Sandesh is another unique Bengali creation, made with fresh cottage cheese (chhana), which is kneaded until it reaches the appropriate consistency—again, a skill better achieved by the professional confectioner. The kneaded chhana is cooked with sugar into different types of consistencies to make different types of sandesh. The soft sandesh or kanchagolla sold near the Kalighat temple in Calcutta is extraordinarily delicious. Some confectioners may flavor their product with lemon, mango, or saffron. Sandesh in which the chhana has been cooked to a harder and drier consistency, called karapaker sandesh, tends to keep better and travels well. Bengalis have a custom of carrying a box of these sweets when going to visit someone either after a long interval or with the purpose of delivering some pleasant news, such as an impending wedding or the birth of a child. There is a linguistic serendipity in the fact that the word *sandesh* not only denotes a sweet, it also means "news" in both Bengali and its mother language, Sanskrit.

After lunch, as the younger people gathered in one of the rooms and the others simply lolled in their chairs, overcome with a pleasant lethargy, I decided to make a temporary escape from Salt Lake. I would go back to the apartment my husband and I had inherited from his parents, at the other end of town in Ballygunge. After the excitements of the day, the sumptuousness of the lunch, and the many memories that had buffeted me throughout, I almost wished the wedding ceremony could be postponed, so that I could have a relaxed and solitary evening. The thought of eating again, and that also to be a catered feast heavy on spices, lipids, and proteins, was intimidating.

Had it been possible for me to choose, I would have ended the long day with a late-night meal consisting of tiny portions of what Bengalis consider comfort food, which my mother always made impeccably— rice, dal, and mashed potatoes. It is a simple, delectable, nutritious meal, but only those who have the gift can elevate it to art. The rice in this case is not the well-known basmati, but a Bengali variety called gobind-abhog (literally, food for Gobinda, another name for the god Krishna). Its tiny grains emit a distinctive aroma that is further enhanced if you add a little bit of ghee to your portion just before eating. The dal I longed for was the red lentils that are commonly eaten in Bengal, though not so much in other parts of India. Lentils can be cooked in a hundred different ways but when I needed comfort, my mother always made her exquisitely delicate version, flavored solely with salt, ghee, and slit green chilies that had been blended into the dal to impart their heat and fragrance. As for the mashed potatoes—aloo bhatey or aloo bharta, depending on which side of the Bengali divide you came from—the Bengalis have come up with a sharp, zestful version that owes nothing to milk, butter, or broth, and everything to pungent mustard oil, chopped green chilies, and, optionally, chopped onions. The potato came to India with the Portuguese, but was slow in being accepted in the Indian

kitchen where several native varieties of taro and sweet potatoes provided starch, texture, and volume to daily meals. But the South American tuber was popularized during British colonial rule in India, and it is
now fair to say that no other region in India glories in using potatoes
(by themselves or in combination with other vegetables, fish, and meat)
as much as Bengal. Of all the potato concoctions that the regional imagination has come up with, nothing satisfies more than this spirited mash.

Of course, there was no prospect of the fantasies about my mother's
cooking turning into reality: she had stayed back home in Cambridge.
Instead, I made a pot of tea to revive myself and, after drinking it, went
for a long, rambling walk in the direction of Gariahat, a well-known
shopping and residential area in south Calcutta. I had several hours for
solo entertainment, since the wedding ceremony would not take place
until much later in the evening. Under a winter sun, aslant and gentle, I
watched chattering children and giggling teenagers coming home from
school and remembered similar afternoon meanderings with my friends.

On the way home from school we often made a detour to a little
park where our two favorite street-food purveyors did business. One
served the quintessentially Bengali snack, mashla-muri. Puffed rice (muri)
was expertly tossed up with finely chopped onion and green chilies,
roasted brown chickpeas (also called Bengal gram), tiny pieces of coconut, mustard oil, salt, and a swirl of thin tamarind paste. The man had
an uncanny sense of proportion and knew exactly how much to make for
four or five or six customers. Once the mixing was done to his satisfaction, he poured out the mashla-muri into paper cones—filling each right
to the brim—and handed them to us. We resumed our walk, munching
happily, eyes watering from the chilies, noses quivering with the sharpness
of the mustard oil, tongues shivering from the intensity of tamarind.

Mashla-muri, in some form or other, has been part of Bengali eating
forever. But for our other mouthwatering treat, we were indebted to the
immigrants from northern India who had made Calcutta their home. The
basic element of this concoction was a tiny sphere of fried dough, tautly
crisp outside and hollow inside. It goes by several names—golegappa, pa-
nipuri, phuchka—all of them Hindi, and is commonly eaten stuffed with

spiced potatoes and dipped in tamarind water, once per mouthful. But the snack we loved, called churmur, went one step further. The spicy potatoes (often mixed with crushed chickpeas) were tossed with tamarind water and a touch of mustard oil, mixed thoroughly with several handfuls of crumbled phuchkas, and heaped on a dried shaal leaf—a commonly used disposable plate. More phuchkas were crumbled and sprinkled on top. A smaller portion of leaf was stuck into the pile, to serve as a malleable spoon, and off we went, happily gorging ourselves.

This afternoon, I slowed down to watch a group of schoolgirls and felt irrationally gratified when they stopped in front of a vendor for mashla-muri. Another group, a little farther off, opted for aloo-kabli, or potatoes and chickpeas cooked and tossed with roasted cumin—red chili powder and lemon juice. During recent visits, I had not seen any of the street vendors selling the churmur we so loved, but phuchkas were still as popular as they used to be. It occurred to me that even in street food, the Bengali propensity for adopting and adapting was evident long before the advent of the Punjabi restaurants and Western fast-food chains. The American motto I had fallen in love with and internalized during my years as an immigrant—Change is good—could equally be a Bengali or even an Indian one when it came to food. The façade of unyielding traditionalism is just that—a façade. So is the idea of unmitigated regionalism. In reality, curiosity, experimentation, and metamorphosis all are at work. The only thing to fear is that the more artful elements of cuisine—whether on the street or in the kitchen—might vanish from lack of time, patience, and, most of all, enthusiasm, which is crucial to the preparation of good food.

"Look at these, Didi, see how beautiful they are? Why don't you buy some?"

Didi. Elder sister. I live in dread of the day when shopkeepers, stall owners, or sidewalk salesmen will make the inevitable transition and call me Mashima, or Aunt, carelessly pushing me up the generation ladder. But not yet; at least, not this time.

I had inadvertently stopped in front of a sidewalk flower seller, many of whom buy small consignments from wholesalers in the big

market and try to get the custom of the passersby. The man was point-
ing to a huge bucket filled with water in which stood bunches of
tuberoses. The fragrance was intense and beautiful, although the real
season for tuberoses was the monsoon. I let myself be tempted and
bought a dozen tall stems to take back to the apartment.

By the time I got back to Salt Lake and found the rented hall where the
wedding was taking place, it was past eight o'clock and the ceremony was
in progress. The chief actors—the groom, the bride, and her father—were
sitting on a carpet underneath a red and white canopy, along with two
priests. The bride, a glittering figure in red silk, gold jewelry, and flower
garlands, was being given away by her father, a priest guiding them
through Sanskrit mantras and ritual gestures. While the faces of the young
couple were vibrant with happy expectation, the father of the bride
looked tired. Very likely, he had followed tradition and fasted all day and
prayed to the gods for the future happiness of the couple. Hinduism, like
Catholicism, has room for plenty of fasting and, in Bengal, the traditional
calendar is dotted with occasions for rigorous self-denial, though there are
no prolonged periods of fasting like the Islamic month of Ramadan.

The wedding went on. The father got up and left, having given
away his daughter with the endowment of the proper dowry and renounced all claims on her. From now on, her husband would be responsible for her livelihood or, as the Bengalis put it, "rice and clothes." After
many rituals and offerings of flowers, prayers, and incense to gods and
ancestors, it was time for the most spectacular part of the ceremony,
where food plays a pivotal part. A priest built a fire with jute sticks in a
large copper vessel, for the bridal couple to make a series of offerings.
The first item was khoi (popped rice). As two pairs of hands held the
clay bowl filled with khoi and tipped it forward, a shower of white
poured out and the flames leapt high with a whooshing sound as if Agni,
the god of fire, was signifying his pleasure at the offering. Next in line
was a bunch of small sweet-and-sour bananas that have sacred connotations in Bengal. After that came a plateful of cut fruit and another one
of sweets. Agni was being generously nourished.

At the end of the ceremony, the pair made their way to another part of the room where a plate of sweets was set before them. Each broke off a piece to feed the other. As they did so, amid much laughter and jubilation, I watched the tenderness with which the groom brushed the crumbs from the bride's lips and hoped they would share their lives without any unbearable conflict or misunderstanding. My earlier conversation with the groom about having an arranged marriage came back to me. Comfort and security were not the only benefits of going along with your family's wishes. Participating in age-old rituals, in which the first step toward intimacy was through food, opened up a rich sense of possibility—of desire aroused, desire gratified, perhaps even a kind of love that nonconformists cannot imagine.

It was time to visit the banquet room where the wedding feast was still going on. As I had anticipated, this banquet bore no resemblance to the kind of food we had eaten for lunch that very day, or to my aunt's wedding feast on a banana leaf. With time, a kind of internal globalization had shaped the modern banquet. Instead of hewing solely to Bengali traditions, it had come to include many northern Indian dishes that were so popular in restaurants. The naan and navratan korma, the pakoras and raita, the rice pilaf and chicken tikka masala were all items that would be familiar not only to Indians, but to Westerners who have eaten in Indian restaurants. These were further supplemented by Chinese chow mein and South Indian dosa and sambhar. I confess I was somewhat disheartened. After the extraordinary lunch, this catered feast, however generously presented, did not arouse hunger. I decided to quietly slip away and go back to my apartment.

But as I went to say good bye to the married couple, one of the groom's aunts came hurrying after me.

"Surely," she panted, "you're not going to leave without eating something?"

"I'm not hungry," I said.

"Oh, but you have to eat something. You must. Otherwise, it will bring them bad luck. You know that."

Of course. How could I have forgotten? The unfed, and, by

implication, slighted guest is a dire image that haunts all families who are celebrating an important occasion. In the Hindu code of hospitality, the guest is considered the equivalent of a god, and no deity can be allowed to leave without having accepted something. Even in this unbelieving modern age, a host will generally insist that even a casual visitor not leave without having a bit of food—sweets, cookies, samosas, anything available. I was about to retrace my steps back to the banquet room, when she gestured to me to wait. In a few minutes, she came back from the room where the newlyweds were sitting with their friends, waiting to eat dinner at the end of their long day. In her hands she carried a box with the logo of a famous sweetshop.

"Here," she said with a smile, "this is for you to take home. But break off just a little bit of sandesh and put it in your mouth before you leave. I know it can be difficult to eat a big meal when you're tired. And it's been a long day, hasn't it?"

I smiled back at her and ate half a sandesh. It was the perfect solution. Thanking her for the gift of sweets, I then said good-bye to the bridal pair and the rest of the family. Halfway down the stairs, I looked back. Dinner had finally been brought to the young people. The groom was serving some rice pilaf onto the bride's plate; she was looking down with a shy smile.

Back in the apartment, I put the box of sandesh in the refrigerator and collapsed onto the couch. CNN International was airing a news magazine, but instead of following the pictures on the screen, my mind kept getting crowded by the images of the day, particularly the flamboyant meeting of food and fire, sanctioning the union between a man and a woman standing together. No matter how much I tried to imagine it, I would never know what it was like to have a relationship cemented with such time-tested rites. But even as I wondered if I had any regrets, I knew the answer. Tradition and ritual had always aesthetically appealed to me, and the cultural context even provided me with comfort, but I had never been able to define myself through their observance. If anything, it was my native Bengali food that gave me the strongest sense of identity.

Chapter Two

IN PURSUIT OF THE PORTUGUESE:
FROM BENGAL TO GOA

Early next morning, I made a pot of tea and took out a saffron-flavored sandesh from the box given to me by the bridegroom's aunt. Sandesh is not really one of my favorite sweets but, along with rosogolla, it holds top billing in the gallery of Bengali desserts. It is impossible to visit any city in Bengal without being offered one or both of these. Both are made with chhana (cottage cheese), but sandesh is dry, whereas rosogolla (literally, ball of syrup), as its name implies, is a sphere of chhana that is cooked in mildly sweet syrup. It is supposed to have been invented (perhaps through a happy accident) by a nineteenth-century confectioner named Nobin Chandra Das, whose son, K. C. Das, opened the epony-mous Calcutta shop in the 1930s, a shop that still survives.

Like most Bengalis, I had always assumed that these and a host of other chhana-based sweets had evolved out of the regional imagination, until I came across the theory that the Bengalis had learned to make them from the Portuguese who settled around the Bay of Bengal in the seventeenth century. It was a startling, almost incredible idea. In India, the Portuguese presence is linked so vividly to the west coast—Vasco da Gama landed in Calicut in May 1498, Goa became a Portuguese terri-tory in 1510 and remained so until 1961—that their arrival and acti-vities on the east coast are easily obscured, the more so because of the larger role played there by the British, the French, even the Dutch. To think of the Portuguese having a hand, however indirectly, in the evolu-tion of these quintessential Bengali sweets was like being told that the French had taught us to make shukto. And how often had I, the Bengali food writer, described these items as being the true, authentic product of Bengal?

Sweets are a major part of eating in India. North to south, east to west—the subcontinent is one gigantic sweet tooth, constantly demand-ing gratification. Not only are sweets eaten as dessert to conclude a meal, as they are in the West, they can appear right in the middle of a meal in areas like Gujarat and Rajasthan, be served at breakfast and at teatime, and be eagerly consumed as snacks at any time of day, as candy is in the West. The extensive availability of street food in Indian cities and towns plays into this. Morning and afternoon, confectioners can be seen frying jilebis (descended from the Arabic *zalabiya*) and imratis, crisp yellow and orange sweets made by squeezing lentil-based batter into hot oil in convoluted patterns and soaking the resulting fried pieces briefly in syrup. As for sweetshops, while Calcutta appears to have the highest ratio of number per square mile, every city has more than enough to destroy the willpower of the moderately abstemious passerby. Home cooks contribute their portion to the family, rice pudding being the universal favorite, followed by a variety of laddoos, crêpes, and steamed confections. Even the gods love sweets, which are the commonest food items offered during the rituals of daily worship. Traditional Bengalis of my grandmother's generation firmly believed that it was unhealthy to drink water on an empty stomach. The remedy was to pop a sweet into your mouth before lifting the glass of water. If no proper sweets were available, there was always the ubiquitous batasha, a spun sugar bonbon of meringuelike texture.

The culinary difference between Bengal and other regions in India is seen in the ingredients used for making sweets. Non–Bengalis use whole milk and evaporated milk of varying consistencies, as well as legumes, flour, semolina, rice, and coconut, but never chhana. What I had overlooked, in spite of having grown up in India, was the long-standing belief among Hindus outside Bengal that deliberately "cutting" or spoiling the milk of the sacred cow by the addition of acid is a sin. The salty panir that we commonly see in northern Indian cooking came in with the Muslim conquerors from western and central Asia (the word is derived from the Farsi *peynir*), and it remained confined to Muslim homes for many centuries. It was certainly never offered to Hindu gods. Enjoying cheese, as in the West, is also not part of eating in India.

What then happened to break the taboo in Bengal? There is no documented evidence prior to the eighteenth century of chhana being used for sweets. In households with access to a large supply of milk, evaporation was the method of choice to preserve excess amounts in prerefrigeration times. Kheer (evaporated milk) sweetened with white or brown sugar, is well loved by itself. If milk did get "spoiled" naturally, because of hot weather or some other precipitating factor, the Bengalis probably fed the liquid and solid portions to their farm animals and domestic fowl such as ducks and geese. But once the Portuguese had settled around the Bay of Bengal and the Bengalis discovered that they were very fond of fresh cottage cheese—*queijos frescos*—some enterprising person must have welcomed the economic opportunity of making cheese and supplying it to these foreigners.

It was probably two other factors that served to persuade the Bengalis themselves to make use of chhana as food. The Portuguese happened to be extremely skillful confectioners, as testified by European travelers. François Bernier, a French doctor who spent seven years in India, from 1659 to 1666, noted that "Bengal likewise is celebrated for its sweetmeats, especially in places inhabited by the Portuguese, who are skilful in the art of preparing them and with whom they are an article of considerable trade." Second, as single men not interested in going back home to find wives, the Portuguese settlers actively pursued marriages with local women. Very likely, the early marriages were with Muslim women and Hindu women of the lower castes. Given the familiarity thus generated between the Europeans and the Bengalis, and, given their common predilection for sweets, it doesn't take too much imagination to see how some creative Bengali confectioners might have started experimenting with chhana and transforming it into sweets of a new kind—especially if they were Muslims. Many Bengali Muslims happened to be hereditary cooks and confectioners—some descended from royal chefs in the courts of Muslim rulers—and they were not hampered by any sense of a religious taboo. But the Hindus must have followed soon after.

Eating my morning sandesh, I was reminded of a journey I had made to Goa the previous year. I was so intrigued by this reconstructed history of Bengali sweets and the Portuguese origins of chhana that I simply had to discover if there was anything resembling chhana sweets in the cuisine of Goa, which is much better known for its Portuguese culinary influence.

I flew to Bombay, where I stayed for several days with Sandip and Mou Maiti, two friends who had migrated from Calcutta. Sandip is a software entrepreneur and Mou a schoolteacher. The timing of the visit was serendipitous, allowing us to jointly celebrate Saraswati Puja—a spring festival in honor of the Hindu goddess of learning and music, who is worshipped with great fanfare each year in Bengal. When I told Sandip and Mou about wanting to make a trip to Goa to follow the trail of Bengali sweets, they were filled with excitement. Sandip had friends and colleagues in Goa he had been thinking of seeing for some time. Impulsively, he decided to come with me. We could both stay with his friend Gourav Jaswal, he told me, and promptly called Gourav to let him know of our impending arrival. Even at the last minute, getting train tickets was no problem. We credited the goddess Saraswati for this bit of good fortune. Perhaps she, too, was curious about the possible heathen origin of chhana sweets that had been bought from a Bengali store in Bombay and offered to her in the Maiti home.

We were taking the Jan Shatabdi Express operated by India's Konkan Railway, named after the Konkan region on India's western coast. The train left Bombay from Dadar station at the ungodly hour of five thirty in the morning and was scheduled to reach Goa around one thirty. For the first part of the journey, while the train snaked southward down the Konkan coastline, I dozed, unresponsive to offers of tea and food provided by the railway company. Beside me, I could hear Sandip rustling through the newspapers and magazines he had brought, and smell the strong spices of the meal that was served to him. When at last I woke, the concrete landscape of Bombay and its burbs had vanished and the verdant hills of the Western Ghats mountain range were flashing past my window. For the next few hours, the vista of trees, hills, and rivers glowing under a blue sky alternated with the impenetrable darkness of long tunnels running through the mountains. Despite the closed windows of our air-conditioned compartment and the lingering odors of the railway lunch, I imagined I could smell the perfume of clove and cardamom and see the climbing vines of the pepper tree—all the spices that had drawn foreigners to India's western coast, in ancient and medieval times. The magic of that past transported me from the rocking and rattling of a train in motion to the rise and fall of a large Arab dhow riding the waves with a cargo of spice that would end up being sold in the markets of Genoa or the Rialto of Venice, and flavor the banquets of imperial Rome.

Goa is a tiny territory and most destinations there are easily reached. Disembarking at Thivim station, Sandip and I drove to the Dona Paula suburb of Goa's capital Panjim, where Gourav Jaswal and his wife, Gulnar Joshi, lived in a spacious two-storied house perched on a small hillock. Although I was aware of the 450 years of Portuguese presence in Goa, I was still astonished by the sheer number of churches I saw along the way. At any point, it seemed, you could throw a stone and hit a church. And this was not even the area of Old Goa, where the Jesuits built the extraordinary Basilica of Bom Jesus, along with many other elegant houses of worship.

At first sight, Goa does live up to many of the claims made by tourist brochures. The beaches are beautiful, the people friendly. History is woven into every part of the landscape. When I climbed the wide red stone ramparts of Fort Aguada, built in 1612 by the Portuguese as a reference point for vessels coming in from Europe, I was rewarded with a breathtaking view. The intense blue waters of Aguada Bay, which is a confluence of the Mandovi River and the Arabian Sea, glittered under the late-setting western sun. The blue of the water, the creamy gold of the sand, and the intense green of the bushes that grow close to the shoreline and stretch backward were juxtaposed in a magical congruity. What kind of sand gives birth to such lush foliage? I stood and imagined the medieval past, the Portuguese ships docking, and the adventurers, conquerors, and missionaries disembarking, each consumed by a particular vision of what India meant—wealth, dominion, conversion of heathens.

As for the Indians, they must have been struck by the first Europeans to suddenly arrive on their shores. In a warm tropical region, where dark skins and bare bodies were the norm, these men with white skin and exotic clothes must have looked like the inhabitants of another planet. A later description of the locals' reaction to the Portuguese who first came to Sri Lanka could well have come out of Goa. The Sri Lankan king was told that they were "a race of very white and beautiful people, who wear boots and hats of iron and never stop in any place. They eat a sort of white stone and drink blood." The last two items could well be the *queijos frescos* they loved, and the red wine that they drank instead of water.

Panjim is probably the cleanest capital city in India, and it is astonishingly green. The air is clear and breathable and an amazing number of people speak fluent English. In and around the markets, I saw women dressed in brightly colored cotton saris, their movements imbued with a swift gracefulness. I remembered having heard that the Konkan region is famous for its beautiful women.

The unique Indo-Portuguese style of architecture—stuccoed walls, tiled roofs, long verandahs encircling the building—that has been preserved in some neighborhoods creates the delightful sense of a time warp. In an area called Fontainhas, where the yellow stuccoed walls of houses, shops, and restaurants glowed in the strong western sun, I found an art gallery filled with the white and blue porcelain tiles so typical of Portugal, yet completely incorporated into the local artistic corpus. Cohabitation inevitably meant osmosis. Why should I be surprised that our Bengali sweets came with an Iberian touch?

In the context of India's long history, the 450 years of Portuguese presence in Goa doesn't seem all that remarkable. But their ruthless sense of mission—monopolizing the spice trade, colonizing the area, and proselytizing the natives—had the effect of almost obscuring the older Hindu and Muslim civilizations of this region. It is easy to perceive Goa as a Christian enclave in India, rather than a territory inhabited by people of different faiths. The Basilica of Bom Jesus, consecrated in May 1605, remains the most outstanding symbol of this first attempt at domination by a European power. An enormous paved courtyard surrounds the basilica. Even in midmorning, the sun was merciless and the heat from the stone courtyard was palpable through my shoes. Inside, it was blessedly cool and since it was not a Sunday, there were only a few visitors. The basilica's main altar is dominated by a huge statue of Saint Ignatius in priestly vestments. On a small pedestal in front of the statue is the tiny figure of the infant Jesus after whom the church is named. The basilica also houses a magnificent mausoleum with a glittering silver casket, inside which lie the remains of Saint Francis Xavier. Although the saint's body was not embalmed or treated after death, it has escaped decay, and this miraculous "incorruptibility" continues to draw thousands of visitors to the basilica. I sat on a church bench watching worshippers come in and stand in contemplation of the altar and the casket of Saint Francis. Culture dies hard; before leaving, they expressed devotion to the Christian God and Christian saints with the age-old Hindu gesture of namaskar—heads bowed, palms folded together and raised to touch the forehead.

My evening's experience was wildly different from the quietness of a devotional enclosure. Along with our hosts Gourav and his wife, Gulnar, and several of their friends, Sandip and I went to Calangute Beach, one of the favored locations for foreign tourists. Ever since the hippies discovered it in the sixties, Goa has always been a haven for Westerners longing to escape their dreary northern winters. But as I saw in Calangute, the crowd has changed somewhat from the laid-back, pot-smoking, bag-toting flower children of an earlier generation. Many of the young and not so young foreigners crowding the area looked tougher, meaner, and captivated by harder drugs. The unfamiliar languages ranged from Dutch, German, and Norwegian to Hebrew—the last indicating the large numbers of Israeli youth who come to Goa to relax after finishing their compulsory stint in the Israeli Army.

Quite a few foreigners in Goa have become impromptu settlers, as we discovered talking to a man with a shaved head. He had arrived from Germany six years earlier and never gone back. Dressed in an Indian dhoti and kurta, he was busily rolling out dough in a food stall to make parathas, which were then stuffed with meat and vegetables by several assistants. The long lines waiting to buy these "rolls" implied that this was a tasty concoction, but there was nothing of Goa about it. A stuffed paratha is very much a northern Indian item, though it has colonized almost every city in India.

It was in an incense shop that I came face-to-face with the sadder, if not darker side of tourism in Goa. Lured by the exquisite scent coming out of the shop's tentlike enclosure, I went inside, hoping to buy some incense to take back to America. On a ragged carpet sat a little girl of eight or nine, her appearance clearly a mixture of India and the West. I asked for the owner of the shop, and she replied in an unnaturally poised tone that she could sell me whatever I wanted; her mother had left her in charge. I asked if they lived in Goa, and she nodded. As I was making my selection from the packets of incense sticks, the mother, a pretty young European woman, came back. She, too, had come to Goa several years earlier—a drifting, accidental tourist, unhappy at home, looking for something better in a sunlit ancient land. Within a few months, she had become involved with an Indian man. But he disappeared after she told him about her pregnancy. With no money to buy an air ticket, and with no strong family ties back home, she had simply drifted into a mode of day-to-day survival in Goa. I looked again at her daughter before I left the shop, and wondered what kind of thoughts jostled each other behind those somber, almost adult-looking dark brown eyes.

The next day, our host suggested that Sandip and I have lunch with him. He would also show us around town. Gourav runs a consulting company called Synapse that helps clients resolve business problems through innovative techniques. Sandip and I went over to meet him there. The bright young people who work at Synapse were delightfully friendly but, as we talked, I could see how perplexed they were by a person who was willing to travel hundreds of miles merely to flesh out obscure information about Bengali sweets. I lost no time in explaining that I was equally interested in sampling the broad range of Goanese food.

We drove around town, stopping wherever I saw anything interesting—the type of aimless exploration that makes for the best kind of traveling. One gratifying experience came from a bakery whose bread, I discovered, including the French-style baguettes, could easily compete with those of classy bakeries in the West. It should not have been a surprise. This, after all, is the land of *pão*, the Portuguese word for Western baked bread, which is so different from more traditional Indian breads, leavened or not.

Some Goans even prefer to eat their most famous dish, vindaloo (derived from a Portuguese meat stew made with garlic and wine) with *pão* instead of rice. On one of my other trips to India, I had visited a retired Bengali banker, Samit Ghosh, and his Goanese wife, Elaine Marie, who live in a Bangalore suburb called Whitefield. The couple's home is an enormous estate named Pairi Daeza. Behind high walls was the most lavish private garden I had ever seen. For the passionate cook, it was a paradise, in which you could simply stretch out your arm and pluck the bay leaves you needed for a dish, or pick a couple of star fruit to slice up for a tart salad. Both Samit and Elaine are food enthusiasts, and I had the pleasure of watching Elaine cook mackerel vindaloo for our dinner. Until then, I had assumed that vindaloo was always made with pork. It took a Goanese woman to disabuse me of this notion. When we sat down to dinner, which included, among other items, the famed Goanese dish of sorpotel, Elaine surprised me by refusing to eat rice with her vindaloo. For her, nothing equaled the satisfaction of mopping up the tongue-blistering hot gravy with large pieces of soft white *pão*.

By one thirty, we were all consumed with hunger, and Gourav stopped the car in front of his favorite restaurant. I had asked him earlier to find a place that served good fish. A love of fish, to the point of eating it nearly every day, is something the people of Goa share with Bengalis. The difference lies in the Goan preference for marine species like salmon, mullet, mackerel, sardine, skate, and prawn. In a poem, one of Goa's best-known poets begs the god of death for one day's reprieve, just so he can enjoy the fish that has been cooked for him.

"Well, here we are. You'll have the best fish curry of your life," declared Gourav. "It's made with kingfish, which is also called surmai, and the taste is absolutely divine."

Again, that word—curry. A slippery eel of a word, bent and stretched to cover almost anything with a spicy sauce, a king of misnomers, and yet, to those who use it, the perfect definition for whatever they are trying to describe at that given moment. I've had a beef with curry for many years, long enough now to have quit protesting its application or urging the user to find a more accurate word. If Goanese fish curry was delicious, I was ready to sample it.

On the restaurant menu, in any case, there were more than enough exotic Portuguese names to cheer me. There was assado, bafad, caldeirada, barrada, feijoada, temperado, sorpotel, cafreal, xacuti, and of course vindaloo (derived from the Portuguese words, *vinho* [wine] and *alhos* [garlic])—a whole vocabulary of eating that is linguistically Iberian, yet firmly rooted in the use of indigenous ingredients like tamarind, kokum (a sour fruit), and tefla (a berry), as well as common Indian spices. Even bacalhau (Portuguese salt cod), which has now become a luxury because of lack of availability, is cooked in a style that is an intriguing blend of East and West, with chickpeas, potatoes, macaroni, onion, garlic, olive oil, cloves, and cinnamon. As for curry, when it appears as *caril*, a historic glamour temporarily washes over the inadequacy of the English term.

Gourav was right. The kingfish was superb. So was the pomfret that Sandip ordered. I was less impressed, however, by the chicken xacuti. Despite its Portuguese name, it is not a dish limited only to Christians; Hindu Goans also cook and serve it frequently. The sauce is composed of a long list of spices, including dill and poppy seeds, roasted and ground together. Coconut milk, green chilies, and cilantro are added to give the finished product a greenish tinge. Perhaps it was the plethora of spices that drowned out each other; perhaps the chef in this particular restaurant simply had a better hand with fish than chicken.

I heard someone at the next table ordering sorpotel and tried to see what it looked like when the waiter brought it in. Sorpotel (also spelled sarapatel), as I had learned earlier from Elaine Marie, should be eaten several days after it has been made, to allow the flavors to blend. The main ingredients are pork meat, liver, and heart, as well as fresh pig's blood blended with a bit of vinegar. This, like several other Goanese dishes, has a fiery taste; some recipes include as many as sixty dried chilies for three pounds of meat and offal. Other spices used in sorpotel are those common to many meat dishes—cloves, peppercorns, cinnamon, turmeric, cumin, onion, garlic, ginger, and green chilies. Tamarind, another mainstay of coastal Indian cooking, provides the requisite tartness. All of these make sorpotel an easy dish to preserve, almost like a pickle, even in a hot climate. But the use of pork makes it anathema for Muslims, while the inclusion of pig's blood may put off the Hindus.

Goa's best-known dish, vindaloo, is usually made with pork as well.

It keeps so well that in prerefrigeration days, one could even use it as travel food. The meat is marinated for five or six hours, or even overnight, in a mixture of spices (garlic figuring plentifully) and vinegar. Onions are then fried in oil, and the meat and spices added for slow cooking. One reason for the development of pork as a major element in the diet of Christian Goans is that there is very little pastureland in the area for cows or goats to graze. Pigs, on the other hand, like chickens and ducks, are resourceful animals that can feed themselves through foraging and rooting in any kind of land and also by consuming kitchen scraps. Once Christianity had been introduced, the Islamic ban on eating pork and the Hindu reservations about a dirty, foraging animal became irrelevant.

As Gourav, Sandip, and I made our way through lunch, I kept observing as many tables as I could. Nowhere on the customers' plates nor on the menu was there any sign of one of the basic building blocks of a Bengali/Indian meal. Dal doesn't seem to figure as a separate course in Goa. The Portuguese influence cannot explain this omission; after all, Goa did have a rich history and cuisine of many centuries before their arrival. Instead, the indigenous diet has been shaped by Goa's coastal geography. The common elements of that cuisine were rice, fish, and coconut, along with local spices. To a certain extent, that still remains the foundation of Goanese cooking. The different kinds of dal that are so integral to meals in other parts of India, from Bengal to Gujarat, from Punjab to Tamil Nadu, could be overlooked by the coastal palate of Goa because of the easy availability of seafood and meat. The Hindus have also made much of locally grown vegetables—the astonishingly tender okra, combined with onion, ginger, garlic, tomato, and a teaspoonful of vinegar; young jackfruit (as tasty as the tender meat of kid goat); eggplant; bitter melon seasoned with many spices and, to the Bengali, the heretical addition of tamarind pulp; and cabbage cooked with grated coconut and seasoned with onion, ginger, and garlic.

As a Bengali and a prawn lover, I was eager to sample as many Goanese prawn dishes as I could. But time was not on my side. In one restaurant, we ate skewered prawns for dinner, and for the first time I was willing to concede that a marine prawn can be as delicious as the offerings of Bengal's lakes and rivers. In Goa's fertile coastal domain, there is an astonishing array of marine fish, ranging from tiny specimens to larger ones like salmon, mullet, mackerel, sardines, and others. According to some sources, 117 varieties of fish have been identified in the markets of Goa. The fish curry that I ate with Gourav and Sandip has probably been made in Goanese kitchens for a thousand years, except that neither chilies nor vinegar were available before the arrival of the Portuguese. Other recipes for curried fish and prawn have also evolved out of local ingredients and stood the test of time. But Goanese cooks have borrowed European techniques and created dishes like fish cakes, prawn pies, breaded fish fillets, whole baked fish with stuffing, and smoked and salted fish.

The one item that dominates and unites all the contrary elements in a Goanese kitchen, Christian, Hindu, or Muslim, has to be the coconut. So pervasive is its influence that even in recipes that call for cow's milk, the Goanese cook will use coconut milk. The primacy of the coconut tree, especially in contrast to the banana tree that Hindus in Bengal so revere, is enshrined in a legend popular among Goanese Christians, and it is a charming instance of rewriting a Middle Eastern story with an Indian alphabet. It describes how Joseph and Mary fled with the baby Jesus through a countryside that is clearly in India. At one point, tired and worn out, they stopped near a banana tree and asked for shelter, but the tree refused to help. Then the family neared a coconut tree and made the same request. The tree dropped its large fronds to cover them, allowing them to rest undisturbed and recover from exhaustion. In acknowledgment of this act of generosity, Mary blessed the tree, saying it would be fruitful throughout the year and that every part of it would benefit humankind. The people of Goa, along with many other Indians, have joyfully utilized the leaves for thatching homes, the spines to make brooms, the trunk as timber, and of course the fruit as a protean source of nourishment. By contrast, the fate of the accursed banana tree has been to die after bearing fruit only once.

Not only is the coconut used in a hundred different ways to cook fish and meat in Goa, it also plays an important role in desserts. A very simple rural sweet, pathoyeo, made to celebrate the beginning of the harvest season, consists of rice, palm sugar, and ground coconut spread on a turmeric leaf, which is then folded, sealed, and steamed gently. Other indigenous sweets made with coconut, palm sugar, legumes like moong beans and chickpeas, rice, and semolina, have taken on names from the language of the Portuguese rulers—cocada, doce de grão, mongonne, doce-baji.

The merger of East and West has produced a whole corpus of cakes, custards, puddings, and creams for the Goan to enjoy, especially during Christmas and wedding festivities. Undoubtedly, the king of all Goanese desserts is bebinca, a legendary, multilayered cake, an absolute must at formal banquets and meals. It is the perfect example of two widely disparate culinary imaginations at their creative best. Baking breads and cakes is definitely a technique imported from the West and associated with Christian eating traditions. Combining flour and eggs to make something sweet is another. Among Hindu Indians, sweets were considered appropriate offerings for the gods, and could therefore never include eggs, which are considered nonvegetarian. Eggs, in fact, are an oddity, since the Hindus, even while they ate fish and meat, imposed a taboo on eggs for a long time. Foreign travelers noted this, among them the itinerant Portuguese priest, Father Sebastian Manrique, who traveled through India, from Bengal to Punjab, in the seventeenth century. Rice pudding in India, for instance, never includes eggs as it does in the Western kitchen, since it is one of the commonest foods offered to the gods. The creamy consistency is achieved by evaporating the milk before the rice is cooked in it.

Bebinca calls for coconut milk, sugar, flour, egg yolks, ghee, grated nutmeg, and slivered almonds for garnishing. The final product consists of eight or ten separate layers, each baked separately in a pan coated with ghee. The process takes hours and, even so, is fraught with disaster for the unwary. The taste, however, is ambrosial, as I discovered the few times I have been fortunate enough to taste it, in Goa and elsewhere. Goans who have settled in other parts of India, often buy bebinca from shops when they visit their home territory and bring it back for nostalgic mouthfuls. It can be frozen and kept for quite some time. The use of ghee instead of butter, of coconut milk instead of regular milk, turns a Western cake into a richly modified Eastern entity.

Delighted though I was to find and sample bebinca and other Goanese sweets, there was no trace of any dessert made with the chhana that supposedly the Portuguese had taught Bengalis to make. I spent hours poring over documents in the Xavier Centre of Historical Research and in the State Central Library, where the senior librarian, Maria de Lourdes, is herself the author of a Goanese cookbook. Nowhere did I find any indication that anything resembling the sandesh or rosogolla or the host of other Bengali chhana sweets had ever been part of the Goan repertoire. Yet the possibility, if not a confirmation, of the Bengalis learning the sweet secrets of chhana from the Portuguese settlers in their land unexpectedly affirmed itself in an article I found that had been written around 1921 in a journal called the *Indo-Portuguese Review*. In writing about the descendants of the Portuguese in Bengal, the author, D. M. Terreiro, commented that the Indians were tied to the Portuguese with "tender ties of love." What better than love to break down taboos and inhibitions and arouse the urge to experiment, taste, and enlarge the boundaries of the senses?

On the train back to Bombay, I was suddenly reminded of one of my favorite paintings of Krishna as a young god—the work of a great Bengali artist, Jamini Roy. It shows a chubby blue-skinned infant (blue was the metaphorical representation for a dark skin) wearing a yellow dhoti, holding out two palms expectantly, while his mother rotates the butter churner in an earthen pot of cream. Although the son of a king, Krishna was sent off to be brought up by a dairy farmer and his wife, to keep him safe from the murderous intentions of a Herod-like uncle. Few other gods have aroused as much popular affection and tenderness as Krishna the dispossessed royal child, loving and being loved by the people of a rural community. The numerous stories (mostly from the medieval period) about his childhood depict a mischievous imp who often got into trouble and loved to steal cream and butter from his mother's larder.

Visualizing the beautiful details of the Roy painting, it struck me that, in that world, there had been no chhana to steal, no sandesh or rosogolla to relish. Whatever one may think of the Portuguese arrival in India and their dominion in Goa, modern Bengalis can be thankful to them for having expanded their culinary world beyond what was once available to the gods.

Chapter Three

ROAD FOOD ON THE HIGHWAY

Revisiting Goa in my mind, a year after that memorable trip, was the perfect prelude for the long food exploration I was planning. I knew it would never be possible for me to know any other city as intimately as Calcutta, the place of my birth, just as I would not appreciate any other regional cuisine in India as intimately, instinctively, and with as much sense of history, as I did that of Bengal. But Goa had been an experience that made me eager to see the India I did not know. I felt a bit like those medieval knights who were always setting off on quests, seeking outlandish beasts, damsels in distress, magical tasks, the Holy Grail. What I hoped to find, in the destinations I had selected across India, were cuisines and stories, rich with native imagination and currents of external influence.

During the few days I still had in Calcutta before starting out, I found myself compulsively wandering the streets, instead of visiting friends, or shopping, or going to see Bengali films. Under a smoggy sky, my city had become a mélange of old colonial buildings, crumbling bare-brick walls, a few quaint neighborhoods untouched by time, and brash new glass and concrete office towers, multiplex shopping malls, and intrusive overpasses arched over existing roads. In the outlying areas mushroomed new housing estates with modern amenities like gyms, swimming pools, playrooms, grocery stores, and clubs. Life here and in most of India was being churned with an unprecedented fervor.

Despite the frenetic clip of modernization in some areas, India's roads remain a stubbornly old-fashioned part of her geography. The British, who ruled for two hundred years, focused their energies on creating an extensive rail network for the transportation of people and commodities. But these were not sufficient to meet the needs of an enormous land and its ever-growing population. Today, growing numbers of trucks, buses, and cars, as well as the age-old bullock carts, traverse India on potholed, rudimentary highways, making them a cacophonic, chaotic, perilous way to travel. Meanwhile, the ease of air travel and virtual travel steadily erode the magic of the road. But for my food odyssey to be well rounded, I needed a taste of highway travel. The best place for such an experience was the ancient, historic road that began right ouside my city and ran all the way across the heart of India.

Ever since I had arrived to attend the wedding, I had been hearing and reading about an ambitious new highway project undertaken by the Indian government. It was called—rather grandiosely, I thought—the Golden Quadrilateral. I downloaded a map from the Internet and studied it. The plan consisted of a system of superhighways and lesser roads connecting the four major metropolitan centers—Delhi, Calcutta, Bombay, and Madras (the last three now called Kolkata, Mumbai, and Chennai)—to each other and to other major cities throughout the country. It was a much-needed makeover for the twenty-first century, with a budget of several billion dollars, and a timeframe of fifteen years for completion. However, given the way things work in India, I knew that progress would be snarled and uneven. While spiffy-smooth multilane highways might quickly grow out of a city like Bombay, lesser-known areas could easily languish for decades with incomplete roads. For me, though, it was the continuing expansion of an existence along these roads that mattered. Could roads be built without people? Could laborers work without food? Could travelers journey without eating?

I remembered the very first journey of my life—a vacation trip by train from Calcutta to Puri in the neighboring state of Orissa, famed for its Hindu temples and exquisite beaches. My cousin Rani and I were going with my mother and her parents. The adults were excited about visiting the great Jagannath Temple in Puri, where they would make offerings and prayers, and eat the sacred "bhog" cooked in the temple for devotees. Bhog is strictly vegetarian, consisting of rice and dal and a concoction of many vegetables cooked together in a pot. It is amazingly tasty.

On the train, however, Rani and I, both eight years old, had no thought for the religious observance or ritual foods to come. Instead, as I still remember after all these years, we watched with lip-smacking anticipation while our mothers took out the tiffin carrier (a series of nesting aluminum containers held together by metal rods on the sides, possibly the best innovation to come out of the British colonial era) containing our home-cooked dinner. As the lids came off, irresistible odors filled the train compartment. We leaned forward eagerly to see and smell before touching and consuming the traveling Bengali's traditional nourishment—soft, airy luchis; slow-cooked potatoes flavored with cinnamon, cardamom and asafetida; kasha mangsho (tender goat meat coated in a rich and fragrant sauce); and an assortment of sweets. What bliss to plunge your fingers into this food and munch your mouthfuls to the synchronized rhythm of a swaying, noisy train running through a night-dark country.

In the morning we were woken by loud cries of "Chai garam," as the train pulled into a station. Young men and boys were loudly announcing hot tea for sale. As soon as the train stopped, the passengers opened the compartment doors and the vendors jumped in carrying large aluminum kettles full of milky, sweet tea in one hand and a basket full of conical earthen mugs in the other. They poured the tea into the mugs, called khuris, and offered packaged cookies to those who wanted them. The khuris were the perfect disposable cups; after finishing your tea, you simply threw them out of the window, where they smashed to bits, to be swept away by the station cleaners later, or, simply degrade into the landscape if you threw them out of a running train. Behind the tea sellers came other vendors, carrying other breakfast fare ranging from oranges and bananas to boiled eggs still in their shells, puffed rice, and roasted chickpeas. Rani and I were considered too young to be permitted to drink tea, but on the occasion of this first long journey, our parents relaxed the rules enough to let us sip from their khuris. Oranges and cookies made the perfect breakfast, downed with water from the thermos we had brought with us.

The pleasurable excitement of that kind of family vacation was no longer on the horizon. But I was filled with a different kind of excitement. Not only was the starting point of the Golden Quadrilateral project right outside Calcutta, it was the continuation of a historic road that went back several centuries. India old and new, fused into a renewable highway, was waiting for me.

As I contemplated the prospect of being on the road, I was reminded of the near-mythic connotations that the road and its travelers have in America, my adopted home. They have been celebrated by countless writers (not only Kerouac but many others as well), poets, and singers; the minstrelsy of the road has become a large part of the American consciousness. And road food—from a kaleidoscopic panoply of eateries offering signature regional cooking—is an institution that sustains the mobile culture of this country. In India, the colonial past and the post-independence years have created a similar magic around train travel. While dining-car fare, when it does exist (on the newer, more sophisticated long-distance trains) is depressingly banal, it is countered by the joyful tradition of carrying your own food and sharing it with your family and friends, as I had learned from my first train journey. My more recent trip to Goa had been both reaffirmation and letdown from the point of view of food. The tea sold on the platform came in horrible little plastic cups, designed like the khuris to be discarded, but these were more likely to poison the land. The food served by the railway company (included in the price of tickets and therefore hard to ignore) was grimly overspiced. And the only snacks sold by itinerant vendors were the chikis, brittle candy made with peanuts or sesame seeds. It made me even more curious to find what was available for travelers and workers on the highway. It also evoked for me images of India's ancient and medieval past, when the road was the only way to travel.

From ancient times, India, like China, has fascinated travelers of every persuasion. But of all the great countries with an ancient civilization, probably none has been more open to the outsider. A succession of emperors and conquerors established their strongholds over huge swaths of the subcontinent's territory, but none felt the need or the desire to build a Great Wall. In this land, with an innate diversity of inhabitants and bountiful natural resources, the magic of roads, rivers, and bordering seas never failed to take hold of the imagination of natives and foreigners. Successive waves of people came to India, lured by the promise of fortune, power, opportunity, adventure, and enlightenment. Those who stayed added their imprint to a perennially evolving civilization. The land became a crucible for the shaping of an unpremeditated immigrant nation.

In the sixteenth century, a dynamic and visionary Afghan ruler, Sher Shah Suri, built a highway called Sarak-i-Azam that spanned the width of the subcontinent, from Bengal in the east to Punjab in the west. In a way, it was as ambitious a concept as the Great Wall of China, though its purpose was not defense. Sher Shah's goal was to foster good governance and efficient administration, as well as to promote trade and commerce throughout the empire. But it is safe to say that he could not have imagined how durable this highway would be in linking disparate parts of an enormous country, how its aura would continue to captivate travelers and pilgrims down the centuries. In colonial times, the British extended the road all the way to Peshawar and Kabul and renamed it the

Grand Trunk Road. Kipling, that quintessential voice of the Raj, made it the playing field of his unforgettable hero, Kim. He called it "such a river of life as exists nowhere else in the world." In the traumatic aftermath of the 1947 Partition of India, when droves of refugees fled across the newly drawn borders, the road became an involuntary escape route, as well as the site of massacres.

In the new millennium, the Grand Trunk Road still retains its luster and romance. Every time I reread *Kim* and let myself be caught up in a past that seemed almost more vivid than the present, I relished the knowledge that the starting point of this legendary route—India's equivalent of the Silk Road—happened to be my hometown, Calcutta. Compared to the nation's capital, Delhi, Calcutta is a young city. But this historic route, running from medieval to modern times and now becoming part of the Golden Quadrilateral as National Highway Number 1, has always lent it a special burnish in my mind. Contemplating the Grand Trunk Road is a way to be connected to both past and future.

When Sher Shah built his highway, he also arranged for inns and hostelries to be constructed every few miles for the convenience of travelers. I often imagined the medieval movable feast that unfolded on travelers' platters as they moved east to west. At the starting point in Bengal, it had to be rice, vegetables, and fish. In the northern reaches, they would find wheat-flour chapattis (bread baked on a griddle), dal, panir (salted cottage cheese), and maybe some kebabs. In Punjab, the hot naan bread cooked in a tandoor would be served with mustard greens and rich halvahs. But the fellowship of the road did not meld rich and poor. Compared to the merchants, traders, noblemen, and courtiers traveling with all the comforts of wealth, the peasants, laborers, and itinerant holy men—Hindu sadhus, Buddhist monks, or Sufi mystics—could only have commanded minimal resources. Road food, for them, was probably little more than rice and dal cooked in a pot over an open fire. If they were lucky enough to get hold of vegetables and seasonings other than salt, those too would go into the pot. This roadside pottage is the likely ancestor of one of India's commonest staples—khichuri in

Bengal, khichdi in Hindi-speaking areas, kedgeree in colonialspeak. It has as many incarnations as Hindu gods. When Buddhist monks traveled across India in medieval times, the khichuri cooked in the evening on a roadside fire was their sole meal. And when a Bengali wanted to celebrate the arrival of the life-giving monsoon rains, he also made khichuri, but with ghee and spices that the monks could not afford. One version of this rice-and-dal dish, topped with spicy sauces, is called kushuri and is found on the streets of Cairo, as an Egyptian fellow student once told me. It was probably introduced there along with the British armed forces, many of whom were Indian recruits.

Fascinated as I was by the history and legend of Sher Shah's opus, I knew it wasn't possible for me to travel the whole length of the Grand Trunk Road. I had already read a lot about different stretches of the road, especially the part that ran through the state of Punjab and ended at the Pakistani border. Punjabi truck drivers, aggressively rushing down the road, refusing to yield to other cars and trucks, have become the stuff of legend in modern India. They are the ones who have popularized the Punjabi eateries called dhabas that serve quick, hot, nourishing meals of naan bread cooked in the tandoor, thick bowls of dal, tomato-and-onion-laced vegetables, and sometimes meat or chicken. They are the ones who transport vital supplies across the country. And late at night, they are the ones who stop to pick up roadside sex workers, for short-term pleasures and the possibility of long-term devastation.

Far from Punjab, I simply wanted to travel along the eastern end (or beginning) of the road for as long as needed to form some idea of what sustained the laborers and travelers. Putting aside the vision of medieval foot traffic, horse-drawn carriages, and palanquins carried by bearers, I set out in a mundane motorcar. Passing the airport, I noticed an impromptu shrine. A painted clay statue of Hanuman, the monkey god, had been placed under a large peepul tree. A steady stream of men and women stopped to make offerings of flowers and sweets that were being sold nearby. Devoutly, they folded their hands, prayed for a few minutes, and went their way. The sight reminded me of a report I had read about construction coming to a halt on another part of the Golden Quadrilateral project because an old temple sat in the middle of the area through which the existing highway would be widened to four lanes. Residents of the villages on both sides of the temple were protesting the move, claiming that destroying the temple would bring disaster on them. Old India was as vigorous and had as much of a decibel level as the slick, Americanized new India that the government is forever trying to project to the world.

From the car I watched the stream of trucks, vans, and cars, their drivers honking impatiently, hogging the right of way, cursing wildly when the odd bullock cart or two obstructed them. It was nothing more than what I expected. But what struck me was the complexity of the construction that became visible soon after I got out of the city.

The Golden Quadrilateral project was really underway with an extensive network of ramps, overpasses, and arteries, in various stages of completion, branching out of the original highway. Until now, I had not been sure how much of what I read was government propaganda. I looked at the groups of men and women toiling away, some doing work manually that is mostly mechanized in developed countries. Through the open car window, I heard shouted instructions in Bengali, Hindi, and dialects I could not understand. Many of these laborers were transient migrants from Bengal's neighboring states. Some of them would give up and move on to other projects when the strain on their bodies became too much to bear. But the loudmouthed supervisors and well-dressed contractors would remain a fixture on the landscape until the project was completed.

Driving along, I observed the women carrying stones and bricks in shallow, woklike containers on their heads. Others were visible, breaking large bricks and stones into pieces with hammers. It was hard to imagine how they found the strength to do the work. Scantily clad men, their bare legs white with road dust, stood mixing concrete. Others manned the vehicles that poured tar over finished sections of the road.

How did this motley crew of itinerant laborers and overseers sustain themselves, especially on the long stretches that were far from towns and villages, where the usual sweetshops or tea shops were not to be found? Did they eat chapattis and vegetables, or rice and dal, or dry food like puffed rice and roasted chickpeas, or snacks like samosas (savory turnovers) and pakoras? I pressed on, looking for roadside stalls or makeshift restaurants.

Out of nowhere rose the vision of a long-forgotten roadside meal eaten by a migrant community that had been an intrinsic part of my early life—the rickshaw pullers of Calcutta. Most of them had come from Bengal's neighboring state of Bihar. Walking home from the bus stop in the afternoon, I sometimes saw them sitting on a shady pavement, eating their simple lunch. The food was always the same—roasted chickpea flour, called chhatu in Bengali, sattu in Hindi. They kneaded it vigorously with water and seasoned it with salt and some pungent mustard oil, before rolling it into small round balls in the palm of their hands. Onto battered metal plates with raised edges, they put some hot green chilies and maybe an onion or two. Each mouthful of balled-up dough was enlivened with frequent bites of chilies and onions, and washed down with large gulps of water. At times, I slowed my pace to a shuffle, simply to watch the completion of the meal. A loud belch followed the final drink of water. Then the plates and glasses were washed at a roadside tap and put away in the boxlike spaces under the rickshaw seats. Afterward, the men spread out their red and white checked gamchhas (thin woven towels they always wore round their necks as sweat rags) on the pavement, and lay down for a nap. Instant oblivion transformed their gaunt features into a peculiar smoothness. Afterward, it was difficult to be my usual picky self when my mother or grandmother set out the next meal for me.

On Sher Shah's road, it took me an hour to find what I was looking for—the typical makeshift unit of a tarpaulin roof on bamboo poles, a table and a bench, a couple of portable kerosene stoves, lidded aluminum pots, and large kettles. This was an eating stop for the road crew (though not those who did the hardest, most back-breaking labor and seemed the poorest) and some of the truck drivers. The customers, sweat-streaked and grubby-clothed, eagerly leaned forward to see what was being ladled out of the pots. As the chipped ceramic plates were set down on the table, I saw the fast-food option for that day—a mound of noodles, gleaming with oil and streaked with a reddish brown sauce. Bits of chopped vegetables and even rarer shreds of omelets dotted the pile of starch. Ersatz Chinese food has become the khichuri of the new millennium. I asked the driver of my car to slow down and pretend to fix something so that I could have a few minutes to take in the scene before me. The men ate with quick, ravenous, shoveling motions, drawing in the dangling strands with slurping noises. After a few moments, I noticed that they did not eat with their hands as is usual in India. Nor did they use chopsticks or forks. The utensil of choice was the teaspoon, a peculiarly postcolonial Indian adaptation to a foreign food.

Unable to suppress the thought that the medieval khichuri would have been a far healthier option, I looked ahead at the road and its ramps and offshoots that sprawled in dizzying loops, just like the platefuls of fried noodles. After hundreds of miles, India's Grand Trunk Road would end near the Pakistani border, outside the Indian city of Amritsar. I expected it would be smoother and straighter there, running through the gold-flowered mustard fields of Punjab. But I would have to look for it at some future date. For now, I had to turn back to Calcutta and look southward. A hotter sun, rockier lands, and thicker coconut groves in a southern state beckoned to me. I was booked on a plane to Bangalore, capital of Karnataka, better known to the world as India's "cool" software capital. I was reasonably sure that road food there would be something other than a plate full of greasy Chinese noodles.

Chapter Four

A SOUTHERN THALI IN KARNATAKA

The Indian South carries an aura of distinctive identity, culture, and mythology, comparable in its specificity to that of the American South. If you draw a line west to east, halfway down the Indian landmass, you'll be left with a triangular wedge to the south, like a slice of pie. Think pumpkin, rather than apple, for that is a vegetable which grows in this area. The territorial pie includes the states of Andhra Pradesh, Tamil Nadu, Karnataka, and Kerala, and, through the centuries, its borders have merged, extended, and contracted under different ruling powers. Fabled labels identify the cuisines that have developed here under a blazing sun, washed by the waters of two oceans, nursed by rushing rivers, and contoured by hills and rocky plateaus—Coondapuri, Malabar, Chettinad.

The harshness and lushness of nature have created the original culinary molds, which then evolved through centuries of impact by other races and religions, imported ingredients, and cultural and colonial fusions. But they are bonded with an imperceptible yet definite thread of "southern-ness" that is further reinforced by an ethos that seems more ancient than what you encounter in other parts of the subcontinent.

For me, the southern state of Karnataka had always seemed one of the most fascinating locations for a culinary treasure hunt. An enormous area, it has a wide variety of topographies and climates, which have given birth to several distinctive styles of cooking and eating. A thousand years of food history is well documented in a series of texts, ancient and medieval. Bangalore, therefore, was one of the earliest destinations on my projected itinerary, one that I anticipated with avidity. And it did not disappoint. The city proved to be a surprising gateway to a varied, nuanced, yet bold cuisine that was unlike any I had encountered before.

Food, like race and ethnicity, can be all too easily stereotyped. The dismissive clichés about southern cuisines that I had grown up with—always vegetarian, swimming in coconut oil, having little to offer beyond bland idlis, dosas, uthhappams, and curd-rice—have thankfully crumbled away. Dosas (large crêpes made with a fermented dough of rice flour and ground dal) have in fact conquered India and become a favorite item among urban fast foods, especially for working people. But in a popular eatery or "tiffin room" in Bangalore, this utterly familiar item startled my taste buds with a lacing of chili-garlic-peanut paste in between its delicate folds. The proprietor and cooks, I learned later, were all Coondapuri Brahmins, a community whose cooking is marked by a liberal use of ghee and spices. Another restaurant served me a dal spiced with a mouthwatering Coondapuri blend of roasted desiccated coconut, whole red chilies, coriander, and fenugreek seeds, all crushed into an aromatic mix. As in the cuisines of neighboring Kerala and Goa, coconut is used in every conceivable form; it is a sign of prosperity and is an integral part of the cuisine. Meat, fish, and rice acquire sharp tones from the use of tamarind, fresh kari leaves, asafetida, peppercorns, jaggery (unrefined palm sugar), and cumin. One day, as I wandered around by myself, I was arrested by the sight of a roadside stall that displayed slices of fresh-cut star fruit sprinkled with an enigmatic spice mixture calculated to enhance the fruit's delicate acidity. Throwing caution to the winds, I sampled some. It was quite unlike anything I had tasted elsewhere. Over the next few days, I became conscious of such a powerful seduction that I wished I could indefinitely stay on, uncovering more of Karnataka's secrets.

As in any unfamiliar territory, I longed to find an interlocutor who would guide me with knowledge and enthusiasm. Some Bengali friends introduced me to Ajith Saldana, an author and food critic for a leading newspaper. He agreed to have lunch with me in a restaurant serving a wide variety of Karnataka's food. I let him do the ordering and waited with the eagerness of the person who knows little and expects much.

The waiter arrived with two large thalis. As I looked at mine, the first thing that struck me was the round-cut portion of banana leaf that covered the silver plate. Admiring the seductive play of colors and textures of food on a lustrous green surface, I was glad that the custom of eating off these leaves was still prevalent in the South. It was, however, a surprise to encounter it in one of the better-known restaurants in Bangalore, instead of in a traditional home or a temple.

The first thing I noticed was that this was not going to be a vegetarian spread. Fish and meat are eaten by the majority of the people of Karnataka, and the spice-coated fillets of fish on my plate, aflame with the redness of the local bedige, or bydagai, chilies, promised a gratification that was very different from what we find in fish-loving Bengal. Portions of different vegetable dishes were ranged neatly along the rim of the plate, and in the center was a small mound of rice. On one corner of the plate sat two fried yogurt-cured chilies, their stems curved into question marks. Fresh green chilies, which are an almost obligatory presence on a Bengali plate, don't seem to be popular in the South.

"Start," said my companion. "Eat, and tell me what you think."

Earlier, I had expressed a particular interest in sampling the coastal cuisine of his native city of Mangalore, a port on the Arabian Sea where Karnataka meets Kerala. Although it was named after a local Hindu goddess, Mangaladevi, Mangalore, located about 220 miles from the state capital of Bangalore (the two names are confusingly similar), has a sizeable Christian population—Catholic, born-again, and Protestant. In the days of the Roman Empire, it was a frequent port of call for Arab merchants as they carried on the spice trade between Asia and Europe, and, even after all these years, it continues to be one of India's busiest ports. In the past decade, Mangalore has grown almost beyond recognition, because of the fast-growing software industry, the multiplying educational institutions, and the prosperity engendered by remittance money sent by expatriate workers from abroad. As everywhere in India, the rapidity of this transformation made me wonder about the survival of the area's traditional cuisine.

Ajith Saldana pointed to some of the items on his plate and mine (he had taken care to order two combination platters to ensure the maximum variety of dishes) and said they were traditional Mangalore dishes. But, as I reminded myself, what tradition really meant was less than clear, in a country that has seen numerous waves of external influences and internal melding. The chilies on our plates were a reminder that almost every cuisine in India had undergone a radical shift with the arrival of the Portuguese, who brought the capsicums from the New World. Now the variety and ubiquity of chilies in India rivals that of countries like Mexico.

The waiter returned and set down small glasses of peppery, tamarind-flavored rasam and a basket of pale yellow pappadams. Again I saw deep-fried yogurt-chilies, which had been casually scattered over them. As I bent forward to inhale the subtle flavors, Saldana began to tell me about the different cooking styles that had evolved in Karnataka.

"Economics and caste were often the defining factors," he said, using his fingers to mix a bit of rice with some vegetables. I thought of the traditional demand for Brahmin chefs in my region of Bengal. In a caste-based society, the Brahmin was the lord, and his touch the purest. Food cooked by a Brahmin chef was therefore acceptable to all members of the caste hierarchy, a factor that could even override a particular chef's lack of skill.

"The Hebara Iyengars, for instance," my companion went on, "are renowned as wedding cooks. Their sense of andaaz [estimate] is legendary."

"What about religion?" I asked, following his example and ignoring the cutlery, although most of the guests in the restaurant were using them. I pointed to the fish and the meat on our plates, anathema to observant Hindus, Brahmins as well as non-Brahmins, in so many parts of northern and western India.

"It's not that clear-cut," Saldana said. "Take the Coorgs. They are descended from a martial race that subscribed to animist beliefs and ancestor worship before they became part of the Hindu mainstream. Then there are the Bunts. They are a Hindu landowner community and, to some extent, pioneers of the restaurant business in India, especially in the South. They are known for their hospitality and lavish cooking. On special occasions like weddings and festivals, they cook up elaborate banquets. Some among these groups not only eat fish and chicken, as Hindus do in your region of Bengal, they also eat pork. In fact, they serve pork at their wedding banquets."

I shuddered to think of the reaction of Hindu Bengali guests in Calcutta if they were confronted with a pork dish at a wedding feast. Although a Westernized minority happily samples ham sandwiches and other porcine delights, most Bengali Hindus consider pork as bad as beef, even though there are no quasi-scriptural injunctions about sacred pigs. Ancient Hindu royalty hunted the wild boar and shared the meat with guests. *Apicius*, a recipe collection from the days of the Roman Empire, mentions a dish of wild boar seasoned with cumin and black pepper, and I have always wondered whether the Roman chef got the idea for the recipe as well as the vital ingredient, pepper, from India via the spice trade. The domesticated pig of today, though, carries unhygienic associations. For many Hindus, it is a "dirty" animal, raised for food by the lowest members of the caste hierarchy. To Muslims everywhere, it is forbidden meat. It was easy to imagine that coastal Karnataka, however, had seen the trickle-down effects of a long association with the people of neighboring Goa where the Portuguese had once held sway and Christianity was dominant. Pork vindaloo is not only a general favorite in Goa, it is also proudly served at weddings and other festive banquets.

Mangalore's Christian community dates back to the sixteenth century, but their history is punctured by many episodes of cruelty and harassment at the hands of different ruling powers—the Portuguese who colonized Goa, the Maharashtrian invaders under the great Hindu warrior-king Shivaji, and the Muslim rulers of Mysore (now a part of modern Karnataka), Hyder Ali and his son Tipu. The latter was a great warrior who foresaw the threat posed to India by the British East India Company and repeatedly fought against them. Unfortunately, he saw little difference between a foreign power with colonial/imperial designs and the local Christians (proselytized by an earlier foreign presence, the Portuguese), who tended to look on the British as allies rather than enemies. After one of his decisive victories against the British, Tipu took revenge on the Mangalore Christians. They were stripped of their wealth, forced to convert to Islam, relegated to the lowest and most menial of jobs, and sold into slavery. Those who refused conversion were killed. Many were tortured. One particular Christian clan was spared, however, because of its members' expertise in cultivating betel leaves and areca nuts, to which Tipu's soldiers, like so many other Indians, were addicted.

Tipu met his death fighting bravely at the 1799 siege of Srirangapatnam (which the British referred to as Seringapatam, most notably in Wilkie Collins's novel *The Moonstone*). Most of the state then came under British dominion. The day before I had lunch with Saldana, I had visited a small summer palace that Tipu had built in Bangalore. Relishing the cool shade inside, after being out in the sun for many hours, I pondered Tipu's tragic fate. He seemed to me like a character in a Greek tragedy, a man of courage and heroism who is nevertheless fatally flawed and meets his end partly because of those flaws. At least, he had left behind an exquisite architectural memento. The entire first floor of Tipu's summer palace is a hall supported by carved teak pillars. Colonnaded spaces are a trademark of southern religious and royal architecture. Stairs lead upstairs to two sets of rooms and balconies where Tipu used to sit and listen to petitions, deliver judgments, and conduct state business. The surrounding gardens shelter the palace from the worst of the summer heat. In that cool and airy space, it was hard to credit the story about his cruel treatment of the Christians of Mangalore. In the end, of course, despite Tipu's orders for enforced conversion to Islam, those who survived cruelty, imprisonment, and hunger went back to practicing Christianity after the British finally took control of the region. And it is thus that pork continues to feature on the Mangalore menu.

Ajith Saldana happens to be a Christian from Mangalore and, as we continued with our meal, his food stories complemented the intriguing tastes on my Southern thali. With a gourmet's enthusiasm he described one of his favorite pork dishes, in which the meat is boiled with ground mustard, coriander, ginger, garlic, and shallots. Garam masala, fried in pork fat, is then added to the gravy. Another favorite in Mangalore is chicken cooked with coconut milk, roasted and crushed garlic, powdered cumin, and the caraway-like seeds called ajwain or ajowan. Some people, he said, laughing gently, call this dish "soul food." There was no time for me to eat this during my visit, but the mere description made me think of trying to make it at some future date in my American kitchen. I would not have the authentic local taste in my memory, but who was to say that my enthusiasm would not be a substitute for authenticity?

The Karnataka story I liked best, however, was about the alcoholic who spent his evenings drinking with his buddies until he had no money left. But however besotted he was, he always remembered to bring home a small bottle of toddy (a liquor made from the fermented sap of the palm tree) to ferment the dough for his morning idlis, the steamed cakes made with a rice-and-dal dough, which are served at breakfast throughout the South. These idlis, light and fluffy and imbued with the sugary fragrance of the toddy, are called sanas.

According to Saldana, sanas can be eaten for breakfast since they have a slightly sweet taste, but they are equally good when you dip them in the gravy of another Mangalorean favorite, sorpotel, a spicy pork preparation in which black sausage, made with pig's blood is added for extra flavor. Remembering my earlier visit to Goa, I said that the Goanese claimed sorpotel and vindaloo as *their* signature dishes, but Saldana emphatically dismissed the notion. But indeed there are remarkable similarities between the meat dishes made by the Christian communities of Goa, Mangalore, and Bombay.

For the final item of this Karnataka lunch, we ate not dessert but that odd Southern concoction called curd-rice—small-grained rice cooked with plain yogurt, seasoned (or tempered, as Indian chefs like to say) with fried mustard seeds, a handful of urad dal, salt, and fresh kari leaves. I looked at my portion in its little steel bowl and wondered whether it would taste bland after all the spicy dishes we had eaten. I need not have worried. Although the curd-rice is a chaser of sorts, the discerning gourmet jazzes it up with a few yogurt-cured chilies. Following my companion's example, I plunged my fingers into the bowl and crumbled a chili into it. The effect was potent. My first mouthful brought stinging tears to my eyes.

I fumbled for my napkin and dabbed my eyes even as I relished all the secondary undertones on my tongue—the delicate tartness of yogurt, the sharpness of mustard seeds, the strong herbal essence of the kari leaves, and the soft, clinging chewiness of the rice. And then came something else. Not a taste, but a scent, a maddeningly beautiful fragrance, familiar yet unidentifiable. I was fairly sure there was nothing new on the table that could have smelled like that.

"Your food is making me hallucinate," I told my companion, laughing. "First it makes me cry, then it transforms the smell of food into the scent of flowers. I'm not sure I'll survive this."

"Flowers?" he asked puzzled. "Oh, I know what you mean. One of the hostesses walked past you. Look, she's standing over there. You can see the jasmine garland in her hair."

A jasmine garland. How many years had it been since I had worn a jasmine garland? As college students, my friends and I used to buy jasmine garlands to wear in our hair on special occasions, like weddings or the Bengali New Year, or religious festivals during the monsoon, when the jasmine is most prolific.

"I wish I could find one for myself," I replied. "I've been wandering all over the city for the last few days and in the evenings I've seen so many women wearing these garlands, but I've never seen any flower sellers."

"It's a matter of knowing where to go. But you can have one right now."

He beckoned to the hostess and, when she came up to our table, asked her to get me a garland. To my astonishment, she quickly brought a small tray with a fresh garland and a couple of hairpins. Delighted beyond words, I wove the garland into my hair, making use of the pins she had provided. This was an ending to a meal that went beyond dessert.

Afterward, I went to have a look at Nilgiris. Opened in 1905, it is possibly India's oldest supermarket. A magically unfamiliar world unfolded for me inside. Shelves carried packages with names I had never come across. Even the pictures on the packages did not tell me what exactly some of the items were. I picked them up and turned them over in my hands but, without a translator, could not make out the Kannada text. Not everything was abstruse; there was the packet containing precooked bisibelebhath, rice coated with spices that tinted the grains a dull brick color. I read the English instructions for cooking. It seemed pretty simple. There were other rice and vegetable concoctions, too.

They confirmed what I had been hearing, about the mini cultural revolution in food coming out of the great information technology migration from southern India. Most of the techies who go to the West on temporary work assignments have no idea how to cook. Trying to save money, they huddle together in small apartments or houses, and they work long hours. But when it comes to food, many of them, especially the vegetarians, can't stomach the cheap foods available in Western cities. Eating out everyday in Indian restaurants is an expensive proposition, even assuming that such restaurants are accessible. Food processing companies in India have taken advantage of this situation and begun producing a wide range of precooked, nonrefrigerated packaged foods that these young workers can easily prepare for themselves. It is said that the suitcases of migrant software workers flying out of India are filled more with these packages than clothes. However, it is not simply the homesick techie who is benefiting from the availability of such foods. They are a welcome addition to the kitchen of busy working women in India, too, who may be inspired to experiment: with people from one region newly free to buy the packaged food of another, culinary horizons can expand with very little trouble. While the epicure might sneer at the mere idea of easy-to-prepare meals, there is no denying their ambassadorial role.

Nilgiris, being a supermarket, also sells fresh vegetables, soft drinks, milk and dairy products, pickles, cereals, and other household goods, including its own brand-name tea. After a delightful hour of browsing, I picked up several packages of yogurt-cured chilies. From the refrigerator near the counter, I also bought a can labeled Cocajal, containing the water of the young green coconut, indubitably the most refreshing drink on earth.

The Aryans who migrated into India from western and central Asia identified the lower half of India as Dakshinatya, the southern realm, or more familiarly in English, the Deccan. To my mind, it is the land without winter, a kingdom of the sun which is both a nurturer and a killer. Survival here requires a peculiar kind of fierceness, even in a state like Karnataka, a significant portion of which is green and fertile. A regional folktale about hunger and food is a perfect illustration of this spirit.

A young woman lived with her husband and mother-in-law in a small village. Life was hard for her: not only were they dirt poor, the mother-in-law was also a virago who relentlessly abused her and treated her like a slave. Every day, the young woman did all the chores and cooked the family meals—which were mostly rice and vegetables. Mother and son gorged themselves and gave her the scant leftovers. One day the mother-in-law gave the young woman a huge pile of fresh snake gourds (a long, slim vegetable, striped green and white, with a delicate taste that blends with many seasonings) and asked her to cook them for the midday meal. Tortured by hunger pangs and overcome by the delicious aroma of the ingredients she was using, the daughter-in-law decided that for once she was going to eat her fill. She made up a story about a sick neighbor wanting to see her mother-in-law, and got the woman out of the kitchen. After the vegetables were cooked, she poured the entire portion into the pitcher she used for fetching water from the river. Quietly slipping out of the back door, she made her way to the village temple where the goddess Kali was worshipped. It was generally empty at that time of day. Behind locked doors, she sat down and gorged herself on the contents of the pitcher.

But although no human eyes saw her feasting, the goddess did. Watching the young woman gobbling up such a huge quantity of food at incredible speed, the goddess's mouth fell open, and she raised her hand to cover it. Blissfully unaware of this, the daughter-in-law let out a large burp of satisfaction, went out, washed her pitcher, filled it with water, and returned home. By then, the mother-in-law was back and had discovered the trick played on her. Furious, she scolded the daughter-in-law for being a greedy liar and viciously beat her with a broom, but the pleasure of a full stomach made the young woman immune to pain. The next day, the whole village was in an uproar, for the priest had discovered that the image of Kali was covering her mouth with her hand. Terrified of catastrophic reprisals by the goddess for some unknown human misdeed, the villagers went into a frenzy of prayer and ritual offerings. But the goddess did not change her posture.

The daughter-in-law then declared that she knew how to make the goddess resume her original stance. She marched into the temple carrying a broom, locked the door, and proceeded to berate Kali for creating such a fuss simply because a famished woman had sat and eaten vegetables in the temple. "What is it to you, why should you care, you malicious woman? Take your hand down and restore people's peace of mind." The goddess stood unmoving. Livid with fury, the young woman then used her mother-in-law's trick; she went up to the image and thwacked the face several times with her broom. With a whimper, the goddess dropped her hand and stood as she had always done, arms by her side. The village was awed by this miracle and even the wicked mother-in-law began to fear her son's wife.

Modern Karnataka was called Mysore (the Anglicized version of the ancient Sanskrit name Mahishura) as late as 1973, when the Indian government changed the name. Its recorded history goes back to ancient times, when the region was conquered and ruled by kings from northern India. In the middle of the fourth century, two Karnataka dynasties wrested power from these northern rulers, an indication of the long-standing North-South tension in India. The founder of one dynasty, Mayurasharman, was not only a man of defiance and resolve; in a strictly hierarchical, caste-bound society, he displayed a capacity for radical re-thinking that the modern generation of software innovators could be proud of. By birth a Brahmin, he pursued his hereditary vocation as a priest until one day when he was subjected to undeserved humiliation in the royal court. Incensed, he abandoned his Brahminical life, became a warrior (normally the preserve of the Kshatriyas, the second tier of the caste ladder), and roused people to rebel. After toppling the ruling king, he crowned himself the ruler of northern Karnataka.

For me, however, an even more fascinating figure belongs to the twelfth century, a king named Someshvardeva II. He belonged to a later dynasty, the Chalukyas, who came to power in the sixth and seventh centuries and expanded their kingdom to include, not only modern Karnataka, but also Andhra Pradesh, Madhya Pradesh, Maharashtra, parts of Orissa and Tamil Nadu, and the greater part of Gujarat. Their domain, lying between the two great rivers, Narmada to the west and the Cauveri to the east, was the first great southern empire in India, a realm renowned for its art and architecture as well as its wealth.

Someshvardeva II, however, was not content to be a mere ruler and warrior. He was the author of an extensive Sanskrit encyclopedia, *Manasollasa* (a literal translation could be "The Spirit's Delight"), which is enough to convince any reader how important food was in ancient and medieval Karnataka. Any notions of a meek, vegetarian Southerner die a speedy death as the text outlines different methods of cooking pork, venison, rabbit, birds, and tortoises. As for those who love fish, the Chalukya text can give Izaak Walton's seventeenth-century treatise *The Compleat Angler* a run for its money. The king elaborates on the joys of fishing as a recreational sport, mentions thirty-five kinds of marine and freshwater fish, and gives meticulous instructions about fishing technique. Not merely a sportsman, he also appears to be an enthusiastic cook. One of his recipes—admittedly on the bizarre side—describes taking the reproductive organs of large fish and roasting them on a fire. When they have hardened, they should be cut into pieces, fried in oil, and seasoned with ground cardamom, black pepper, rock salt, and asafetida. Another suggests cooking fish in tamarind juice, sprinkling wheat flour over it, frying it crisply, and serving with a garnish of ground cardamom and black pepper. Tamarind, cardamom, and black pepper may seem a wildly unorthodox combination to my fellow fish-lovers in Bengal, but its essential Southern character is evident in many items on the Karnataka thali (dinner plate) even today. The region's most famous dish, bisibelebhath, is seasoned with tamarind, chilies, cinnamon, and cardamom.

Bangalore, the capital of modern Karnataka, has a food story embedded in its name. Originally, it was called Benda Kaal Ooru, or the town of boiled beans. According to legend, a king named Vira Ballala had gotten lost while hunting in the neighboring area. Tired and hungry, he came upon an old woman who had only a pot of boiled beans to offer him. The king gratefully consumed them, giving the town its name. Later, the British simplified the name to Bangalore. Recently, in a show of anti-imperialist fervor that has also changed the names of other Indian cities, Bangalore has been officially renamed Bengaluru, to more accurately reflect the original Kannada version.

It is a relatively young city, established in the sixteenth century by a local ruler, Kempe Gowda. Subsequently, the British moved the city to a higher altitude, and it became a favorite zone for retired officers of the British, and later, the Indian, armed forces. Although the residents tend to complain about the growing pressure of cars, people, and buildings, the city appears surprisingly green in contrast to many other Indian metropolises. Relics of colonial times still abound, the most eye catching being a glass pavilion in Lal Bagh, the city's public gardens. Built along the lines of the Brighton Pavilion in England, the structure houses the Bangalore flower show, yet another colonial tradition.

It was in Lal Bagh that I came across a familiar produce being marketed with a foreign label. Beneath a large, leafy mango tree sat a young couple, the husband dressed in a blue sarong and white-and-blue checked shirt, the wife in a red printed sari. Before her sat a leaf-lined basket, with a piece of paper sticking out that said, "American corn." At least twenty ears of corn, the husks peeled away, displayed their bright yellow kernels. But what made them American rather than Indian corn, I could not fathom. I had seen a similar sign in another city—in a glitzy, American-style food court, where a fast-food restaurant's menu included "American sweet corn" along with Western fast food like burgers and pizzas. But I had dismissed that as a mere bit of marketing; after all, anything labeled American sells to the Indian middle class. In Lal Bagh's leaf-laden arbor, presented by two people who seemed more rural than urban, the label was incongruous.

Besides, American or not, corn was the last cereal grain I was expecting in Karnataka. The state's contrasting geography has allowed several staple crops to flourish here—rice, wheat, sorghum, and ragi, a kind of millet that originated in western Africa and is supposed to have come to India either by way of Arab traders, or directly borne on the monsoon winds. A surprising variety of ingredients and styles go into the preparation of these grains. Coming from predominantly rice-eating Bengal, I had been intrigued by the reddish grains of ragi—especially when I learned that one of its original Sanskrit names means "the dancing grain." A friend served me a salted porridge made from gently roasted and ground ragi, which can also be made with brown sugar as a breakfast food. I must confess that I did not like the strange slippery texture of the porridge. Some grains, you have to grow up with.

The woman in Lal Bagh noticed my interest and held out a couple of ears of corn from her basket. The plump, shiny golden kernels looked fresh enough, though corn is not a food I am partial to. Despite my near two decades in America, I've never acquired a taste for the mild, sweet butter-brushed kernels that friends offer on occasions like the Fourth of July. If I have to eat corn, I prefer it the Bengali way—roasted over a charcoal fire, brushed with mustard oil, and seasoned with lime juice, hot chili powder, and black pepper. Only after many years in America had I learned that corn was prepared in a similar way in Mexico and other South American countries.

Regretfully, I shook my head. As she put the corn back in her basket, I took out my camera to take a picture of her. The bright red sari, dotted with white, yellow, and green, draping her dark skin and glossy hair made a pleasing counterpoint to the yellow corn in her basket. Suddenly, the husband was galvanized into action. He sat up and let loose a torrent of objections whose meaning was clear to me from his angry hand movements. He wanted me to put away my camera. I looked at the woman to see if she, too, considered it offensive or unacceptable to be photographed. For a few seconds, her face was unreadable, a beautiful mask chiseled out of the same native basalt you see in the statues and temples of Karnataka. Then, turning to her husband, she gave him a look of withering scorn that stopped him midtirade. Quietly she said something before facing me again, signaling regally with her hand that I could take her picture.

The steel beneath the surface of this apparently demure woman reminded me of the folktale about the young woman who taught the goddess Kali a lesson. It also deepened my regret at not being able to have a real conversation with her. Did she herself eat the American corn she was so eager to sell? Was it really significantly different from varieties that were considered Indian? Did she know that corn really did originate in the Americas, though its dissemination in India and other parts of Asia is mysterious enough to have generated several expert theories? Even if she didn't, I had a feeling that she would have appreciated the North American myth about a native people—those Indians who were not from India—coming to the succor of hungry, distraught newcomers from across the ocean, giving them corn, laying the basis for the feast of

Thanksgiving. Ascribing symbolism to food and its sources, as well as mythmaking about the offering and sharing of food, comes naturally to the Indian imagination, as demonstrated by a bit of Karnataka history. In a city near the border with the state of Andhra Pradesh lies the grave of Muhammad Gawan, merchant, scholar, and minister in the courts of three successive Deccan sultans in the fifteenth century. Despite his success and accomplishments, his end was violent. At the age of seventy-eight, he was murdered. A mango and a neem tree, the latter, whose bitter leaves go into the Bengali shukto, provide shade to his tomb, signifying the sweetness of his life and the bitterness of his death.

But I could not speak Kannada, I could not tell the beautiful corn seller any stories—mine, hers, or those of other people. We shared an ethnicity, but it was not enough. I could only walk away in silence.

That evening, when I went back to the hotel, I got a call from Samit Ghosh, whose Goanese wife, Elaine Marie, had once served me an exquisitely tasteful meal at their mansion outside Bangalore. Samit had mentioned a Bengali culinary outpost in Bangalore, a branch of the famous Calcutta sweetshop, K. C. Das. Over time, it has apparently become a landmark among Bangalore's eateries. The proprietor of the Bangalore enterprise is Biren Das, the great-grandson of Bengal's legendary confectioner Nobin Chandra Das, the inventor of rosogolla.

To me, it was an astonishing idea—that in a region so far from sweet-addicted Bengal, a traditional Bengali confectionary selling sandesh and rosogolla and other chhana sweets should be so successful. It was the first real example I came across of the colonizing of tastes within India in modern times. Samit, realizing how much I wanted to meet Biren Das and have a look at the confectionary where the sweets were made, had arranged a meeting for me. The next day, before going to Das's office, I went to take a look at his downtown restaurant, which also doubles as a shop. The clients, instead of being nostalgia-ridden Bengali migrants, were overwhelmingly local; the conversation all around was mostly in Kannada, laced with a bit of English, with only occasional snatches of Bengali and Hindi. The food was entirely vegetarian, but in the Bengali style. I saw plates heaped with the classic Bengali combination of luchi, slow-cooked potatoes, and a dal made with yellow split peas. Small bowls of confections contained rosogolla, chamcham, rosomalai, sandesh, and many other items—a sweet, juicy, spongy, milky, grainy, custardy, chewy assemblage. Any lingering disbelief I had was dissipated—armed solely with desserts, a Bengali had successfully colonized this distant Southern city. In a few decades, the children and grandchildren of the people eating in his shop would probably consider these sweets a part of their inalienable heritage, debating the exclusive sense of ownership that Bengalis in Calcutta still have. A new chapter was being added to the story of India's evolving feast right in front of my eyes.

Biren Das was waiting for me in the large building that houses his office and sweets-making operations. Dressed in the traditional Bengali dhuti-panjabi, he did not remotely resemble the success-driven MBAs being churned out these days by Indian universities. But wandering through the spotless plant where enormous quantities of milk are processed and made into fifty varieties of sweets provided plenty of evidence of his business acumen. Perhaps he saw some unvoiced doubt in my eyes that led him to say, "Did you know that merchants and businessmen in ancient India were called sreshthis, a word meaning 'those who are the very best'? They were expected not only to make money but also to discharge their debts to society, do things for the less fortunate."

Wondering if Bill Gates would like to be called a sreshthi, I trotted along behind Das as he led me upstairs and downstairs through the sweet labyrinth. Strange facts emerged. The milk is from Holstein cows; the yogurt culture for making mishti doi has been imported from Denmark since 1980; high-quality sugar is imported from the northern state of Uttar Pradesh. And most surprisingly, the Bangalore operation is not new; it was started in 1972 in response to the Bengal state government's decision to temporarily ban the commercial production of milk-based sweets, because of an acute milk shortage that no longer exists. After the tour, Biren Das, like a good host, took me into his comfortable office where an enormous tray of sweets waited for me. Knowing my limitations, I made sure to taste the Das family's greatest contribution first, the rosogolla. It was delightfully spongy and sweet. But it couldn't quite eradicate the longing for the remembered ones of the past—when I was a child, the rosogolla a special treat, the cows native to Bengal, and the production less scientific, less streamlined.

The success of K. C. Das's Bengali sweets in Bangalore is actually not as surprising as I had first thought. Bengali chhana sweets are famed and appreciated throughout India. They easily fill the lacuna in southern cuisines in which the favored desserts are different variants of rice pudding or vermicelli cooked in sweetened milk, while a second tier of sweets combines coconut, brown sugar, and legumes. Ripe mangoes in summer are another alternative. One item I found very attractive was the chiroti, a flaky pastry, soaked in almond-flavored milk and dusted with sugar before serving. The southern passion for coconut and palm sugar is reflected in another sweet, the holige, a thin wheat crêpe with a filling of dried or fresh coconut and palm sugar, gently fried in a skillet. One Karnataka confection, surprisingly, reminded me of the rich desserts of northern India. It is called Mysore pak, an artery-clogging, slow-cooked halvahlike sweet. The ingredients are simple—split pea flour, syrup, and ghee. But the proportions are deadly—double the amount of ghee as flour.

The town of Mysore, about ninety miles south of Bangalore, is more famed for silk and sandalwood than sweets. In the last few years, however, it has also become a secondary center of software enterprise. On my last night in Bangalore, I lay in bed and watched a television program about the employee training center operated in Mysore by Infosys, India's largest software company. The trainees were an international group, including many from China. During lunch, they congregated in the enormous company cafeteria, where there were many southern dishes to choose from—a luscious spread of dosas, idlis, rice, vegetables, and sambhar. The camera focused for a few minutes on a group of Chinese trainees sitting together. They were obviously enjoying every mouthful of this alien food, but instead of using fingers or cutlery, they ate with chopsticks. It was an amusing variation on the Grand Trunk Road vignette, where I had observed Indian laborers shoveling Chinese noodles into their mouths with teaspoons. I tried to imagine which would be more difficult to master—eating a dosa with chopsticks or noodles with a teaspoon—and failed. Sleep overtook me, followed by visions of Biren Das's Holstein cows frolicking like goats on the green grass of the Infosys campus.

Chapter Five

THE ANGLO-INDIAN TABLE

After returning to Calcutta from Bangalore, I was unexpectedly laid low by a long bout of sickness. Lying in bed for days, I found myself caught in an acute tension between physical inertia and a champagnelike bubbling of speculation about my unfinished project. The pull of unseen destinations, images of their past and present fusing together, the pleasurable fantasies about their food—all made the restricted quietness of life within four walls even harder to bear. India waited, trembled on the edge of vision, vanished, and appeared again to tantalize me with a thousand questions.

As my health improved, I began to see my all too familiar surroundings with a new kind of vision. My late parents-in-law had lived in this apartment for nearly two decades. Rifling through the pages of old books, journals, photo albums, and annotated music sheets, I glimpsed their earlier lives. The glass-fronted cabinets filled with silver medals, trophies, and awards spoke about my father-in-law's long and illustrious career in the military, before and after India's independence from the British.

I remembered the very first time I had come to meet them, and my surprise as I saw the dining table set with plates, forks, knives, and spoons. Even at home, it seemed, the retired colonel and his wife did not eat with their fingers as Bengalis generally did. Coming from a family that was firmly grounded in tradition, I found this unexpected colonial fetish mildly repelling and intriguing at the same time. As our intimacy increased, I realized that, having joined the British Indian Army at the age of twenty-two, my father-in-law, Prabir Chakrabarti, had adopted the culture of the British with all the enthusiasm of youth. Now, as I looked through the relics of his past, I mulled over what little had been disclosed to me and my husband by his parents before their death, and it seemed that the lives of three generations of the family, from my husband's great-grandfather down to his late father, represented yet another facet of the story of changing cultures in India's food.

Prasanna Chakrabarti, the great-grandfather, was a Sanskrit scholar, fiercely dedicated to the pursuit of knowledge and academic perfection. Having heard of a renowned pundit in Kathiawar (in the state of Gujarat), he left Calcutta, journeyed all the way across India to this remote western location, and enrolled as a student in the pundit's select academy. After several years of intensive education, Prasanna returned to Calcutta and became a professor of Sanskrit himself. The late nineteenth century saw urban Bengali society caught between opposites. The so-called Bengal Renaissance had already exposed the elite to modern Western ideas and concepts, especially to a scientific worldview. Yet, long-standing traditions and hierarchical systems continued to have a powerful hold on the general psyche. At that time, an orthodox Brahmin scholar like Prasanna would strictly observe many complex dietary rules and eating customs. He would make sure that the food had been prepared observing all the rules of purity and pollution set out in ancient Sanskrit scriptures. Sitting down to eat, he would first distribute tiny portions of food and a drop of water beside his plate, and dedicate them to the gods. What kind of struggles had a man like him experienced, caught between belief in observance and the unpredictable necessities of a long journey? Did any involuntary encounters—whether with the Jains, who carry nonviolence and vegetarianism to an exquisite extreme, or the Parsis, whose faith allows them to enjoy practically every food under the sun, or, worse, Muslims, who happily consume the Hindu's revered sacred cow—generate a greater degree of tolerance in him? Did it enlarge Prasanna's view of the contemporary world, even though he continued to teach a dead language?

His son Prafulla's early career was different enough from his father's to support such a possibility. A brilliant student, Prafulla did not study Sanskrit. Instead, he focused on a Western-oriented education, eventually becoming a scholar at Christ's College, Cambridge University. With a "double first" in mental and moral science (philosophy) under his belt, he went on to study law in London and became a barrister. On his return to Calcutta, he had to undergo the pain of penance in order to be accepted by Bengali society and to "recover caste"—penance that consisted not only of feeding gods and Brahmins, but also having to consume cow dung (a minuscule quantity, much diluted in water). But after that painful ritual, he fit right in with the city's Westernized elite and built up a successful law practice. He married and had three children, two daughters and a son.

Most unexpectedly, however, India intervened. Prafulla, the quintessential sahib, was bitten by the "Swadeshi" (freedom) bug. Instead of continuing with a lucrative law practice, he joined the Swaraj Party, which, with its radical demands for independence from colonial rule, was becoming a thorn in the side of the more moderate Congress Party led by Gandhi and Nehru, which was willing to settle for dominion status first before gaining full independence. The family mythology focused on the primary achievement of Prafulla's career as an activist—becoming the editor of a party-funded newspaper called *Forward*, which debated the hot political issues of the day and exposed the shortcomings of many politicians and government officials.

Neither my father-in-law nor his younger sister—Prafulla's two surviving children at the time when I met the family—had an adequate explanation for their father's radical change of direction. They were too young to grasp what was happening in their father's life, and the early death of their mother left them mostly in the care of an elderly, widowed grandmother. During my enforced period of inaction in my in-laws' apartment, I imagined the defection in terms of food. Like his father, Prafulla, as a young man, had traveled a long distance from home. But whereas Prasanna's journey was contained within the greater Indian cultural sphere, Prafulla had had to cross the ocean (often referred to as "black water" in Bengal), leaving behind a world where food and touch are inextricably linked from the earliest days of life. A traditional Bengali mother feeding her child is a prime example of this tactile connection. She picks up a bit of rice and fish and vegetable, rolls it into a ball in the hollow of her palm, and propels it deftly with her thumb into the waiting mouth. From her, the child learns to manipulate his food until his awkward fingers become the most exquisitely precise tools for food of all textures and consistencies. Could there be a greater contrast between this way of nourishing yourself and sitting down, say, at the college dining hall in Cambridge, wielding sharp steel utensils to cut into large portions of meat and fish?

Fanciful though it was, I couldn't resist theorizing that when Prafulla the British-trained lawyer became disenchanted with the regime of the colonial masters, he was also consumed with the need to resuscitate intimacy with his own culture—the kind of intimacy that allowed him to savor the sensuous richness of his native cuisine through the coming together of hand and mouth. I imagined him taking pleasure in a small gesture—discarding the knife, fork, and spoon for good, and eating Bengali food with his fingers.

On the social and political level, Prafulla's change of orientation from sahib to native was probably related to a growing awareness of the iniquities and discrimination perpetrated by the British Raj in India. His law practice would have exposed him to many such incidents, and confronted him with the conflicts of loyalty, identity, and culture that result from the encounter of races and the dominion of one over the other.

A prime example of such conflicts was a community prominent in Prafulla's city of Calcutta—the Anglo-Indians, forever yearning to belong to the ruling British community without ever quite succeeding. This term was used in a broad and somewhat imprecise way; children born of the union of Indians with other European races, such as the Portuguese, Dutch, or French, were all loosely referred to as Anglo-Indians, but mostly the term applied to those descended from intermarried Indian and British parents. Originally, the British men who came to India without wives and married (or formed liaisons with) local women were eager to provide the best opportunities for their children and sent them to Britain for schooling. However, developments in Haiti—the Slave Rebellion of 1791 and the mulatto uprising of 1806—made Britons more cautious about the children of mixed marriages. As a result, Anglo-Indians were barred from education in Britain.

Despite that, the Anglo-Indians in India, always Christians, ordered their lives, observances, customs, food, and festivals the same way as the British, thus perpetuating the incongruity of a Western life in an Indian context. Under colonial rule, they were given special professional opportunities. India's railways, for instance, were one of the preferred domains of Anglo-Indian enterprise. The 1956 Hollywood classic *Bhowani Junction*, based on a John Masters novel, has Ava Gardner in the role of Victoria Jones, daughter of an Anglo-Indian engine driver.

Among the local Indians, however, the Anglo-Indians, like mixed races in so many places, often aroused distrust, bordering on contempt. They were seen as pretentious, denying their Indian heritage to suck up to the British masters. After the British left India, many Anglo-Indians, fearful of their future, migrated to Britain, Australia, and Europe. Those who stayed had to struggle for acceptance, but they and their descendants are now integrated into India as one of its diverse communities, genuinely appreciated for their achievements. The Anglo-Indian community in modern India may be small, but its members are noted for their gregariousness, for the exuberance of their social life, their excellence in sports, the success of their men in the armed forces and of their women in nursing or administrative careers, and, most of all, their hospitality, liberally laced with alcohol. In spite of adopting the British way of cooking and eating (though they have never been averse to sampling popular festive items like biryani and pilaf), they have also made innovative use of ingredients drawn from the land that has been physically, if not always spiritually, their home. As a result, they have contributed a small but significant chapter in the evolution of India's food.

One accessory of the Anglo-Indian table (or, for that matter, the British, or even the Japanese table) is a bottle of a condiment—Worcestershire sauce. Indians like to claim that it is a native Indian product, created by a quick-witted cook employed by a British or Anglo-Indian master, in order to mask the taste of meat that had gone off. According to the legend publicized by Lea & Perrins, the British manufacturer, the sauce was born in Britain, an accidental byproduct dating to the 1840s. A container of spiced vinegar (made by the chemist according to an Indian client's specifications) had been left forgotten in the cellar and began to ferment. Before throwing it out, the chemist happened to sample it and thus discovered its unique taste. In India, racial prejudice sometimes manifests itself in derisive comments about Anglo-Indian food being nothing more than meat and potatoes smothered with this all-purpose sauce. Nothing could be further from the truth.

One of the greatest ironies of India's food story is of course the term *curry*, whose blanket application is so much at odds with the actual authenticity, regionalism, and idiosyncrasy of India's cuisines. This term has its roots among another group sometimes described as Anglo Indians: Britons who had served their time in India and returned home to retire. After a long absence, many of them had difficulty in adjusting to the life of their native land. Exotic, exasperating India, they found, had seeped into their bones, become the home away from home. The bland, unseasoned foods that their compatriots were happy to consume left these "returned" Anglo-Indians longing for the spiced food of their colonial domain. It was this desire that led to the birth of first-generation Indian restaurants in England, the so-called curry houses. Soon enough, curry became synonymous with Indian food, thus papering over all the subtleties of regional cookery and the variety of names—often precisely descriptive—that identified different preparations. The Anglo-Indians of India followed suit and used the term *curry* to indicate meat or poultry cooked with native spices, as distinct from the roasts, chops, stews, and puddings cooked in the Western way.

Another interesting food mutation courtesy of the British and the Anglo-Indian presence in India, is mulligatawny soup (a corruption of Tamil *milagu-tannir*, pepper water), more familiar today in Tamil and South Indian cuisines as rasam. The transformation of pepper water into mulligatawny soup rests on the colonial need to replicate the Western meal that consisted of separate courses. There was nothing in the Indian cuisines that could be served as a soup course, with the possible exception of the Muslim shorba. The British and their Anglo-Indian followers therefore took the Tamil pepper water and made it into soup with the addition of pieces of meat or chicken, stock, fried onions, and a variety of spices. The invention is credited to the British settlers of Madras in Tamil Nadu, who were sometimes referred to as "mulls" by their fellow Britons in other regions. Within a very short time, however, mulligatawny became a mainstay of British and Anglo-Indian kitchens throughout the country.

Although I did not know it then, one term that was very much a part of my daily life from childhood onward was also born of the Anglo-Indian presence—tiffin, a snacklike meal usually taken at midday. In the days before I went to school, I would watch from the third-floor balcony, the carpenters in my father's furniture workshop take breaks from work and sit around eating puffed rice, roasted chickpeas, samosas, or, on very hot days, rice flakes soaked in cold water and combined with shredded coconut and palm sugar. Sometimes, I ran downstairs and asked, "What are you doing?" perhaps hoping to be offered an exotic morsel. "We're doing tiffin," they would say and carry on, ignoring my hopeful glances. Later, when days were spent in school, my classmates and I were fed the traditional Bengali lunch of rice, dal, vegetables, and fish at an ungodly hour of the morning before the bus came to pick us up, since there was no such thing as the school lunch. To sustain us for the rest of the day, our mothers gave us small sandwiches, fruits, and sweets in modest-size lunch boxes. During midday break we ate this food, which we called tiffin. Even office workers took tiffin breaks. Among the Anglo-Indians, tiffin often consisted of leftover meats from roast dinners, reshaped as pies or meatballs, spiked with a variety of chutneys or relishes. One of the best known eateries in nineteenth-century colonial Calcutta, the Great Eastern Hotel, offered its Anglo-Indian and British clients tiffin consisting of "steak or chop, bread and vegetables," for the reasonable price of one rupee. But one has to wonder what the main meals were after snacks of this dimension.

While the age of gourmandizing may be significantly diminished, the Anglo-Indian community (most of it now in Calcutta) still celebrates festivals with uncommon brio. Christmas, being the high point of the year, is the time for magnificent culinary displays that combine the riches of East and West. The holiday table in a prosperous Anglo-Indian home can simultaneously accommodate roast duck or roast suckling pig, vegetables, salads, rolls, and enormous platters of mutton or chicken biryani. On other festive occasions, soup might be followed by baked fish stuffed with Indian spices.

One well-known Anglo-Indian concoction, honored with the title of chicken country captain, consists of pieces of chicken combined with onions, fresh-ground ginger, green chilies, and a bit of black pepper, fried in ghee and simmered gently with water until it is done. The origins of the dish are shrouded in mystery. Some believe it was the brainchild of a native captain of the sepoys (Indian troops working for the British). Another hypothesis is that it was created by a ship's captain. Whatever the authentic story, there is no controversy about its delectable taste.

Since the British tried to follow as much of their own traditions—culinary, sartorial, cultural—as possible even during long stints in India, it is only natural that their national favorite, fish and chips, would also be reproduced in their Indian kitchens. The fish that lent itself best to filleting,

breading, and frying was the bekti (bhetki in Bengali), a species frequent-
ing coastal and estuarine waters. The traditional favorites of Bengal, the
rui, the katla, the hilsa, rarely made their way to the British or Anglo-
Indian table. As a result of the years when Indian cooks worked in the
kitchens of British and Anglo-Indian families in Calcutta, the term *fillet*
became part of Bengali usage, with the final *t* being pronounced. In a further instance of adaptation, the fillets of bekti were spiced up with a
marinade of ground ginger, onion, and crushed green chilies before being fried. The accompanying tomato ketchup also entered the Bengali
kitchen through the mediation of Anglo-Indian cookery. When vegetables like eggplant, pumpkin blossom, or cauliflower, coated with chickpea
batter and deep-fried, were served as snacks with tea, a bit of tomato
ketchup was often poured on the plate to add tartness to the fritter.

Breakfast in Indian cities, especially in Calcutta, which was the capital of
British India for a long time and where the majority of the Anglo-Indians are
still to be found, was one meal that was significantly affected by the colonial
experience. Although the Portuguese are credited with introducing Western
bread to India, it was the dominant presence of the ruling British and their
Anglo-Indian cohorts that led to the popularity of toasted sliced bread and
eggs (boiled, poached, fried, scrambled, made into omelets). Westernized Indians, especially those who had the opportunity to go to England for higher
education, came back with many Anglicized habits, and it was in their dining
rooms that this Western idea of breakfast first acquired an Indian presence.
Since then, bread has become as common an item in Indian grocery stores as
it is in the West, and eating it is no longer limited to the urban elite.

As children, my friends and I looked forward to Christmas with much
enthusiasm primarily because of the plethora of special cookies, cakes,
buns, and pastries that flooded Calcutta's New Market at this time of
year. The suppliers were usually Anglo-Indian women of modest circumstances for whom this was a way to supplement one's income during the holiday season. While the market's fruitcake or plum pudding or
shortbread was purely Western, there were other delightful items that
testified to the Anglo-Indian penchant for using Indian ingredients in

inventive ways. One of these, called kulkul or kalkal, was a deep-fried sweet made with cake flour, semolina, eggs, butter, sugar, a bit of vanilla and, amazingly, coconut milk.

Cooped up in my in-laws' apartment, I watched the ghosts of Christmas long gone in my childhood fade away into a far more distant past, when my husband's grandfather Prafulla lived in a city where Christmas brought out the celebratory face of the country's rulers. Had he, I wondered, had any personal British or Anglo-Indian friends who invited him to their homes during the holiday season? If so, had he cut the knot of friendship when he took up the life of an activist? It was too late to find out. What is known only too well is that Prafulla's life ended with mystery and violence. He started receiving death threats, warning him to stop the political crusade in his newspaper. One afternoon, thugs stormed the offices of the newspaper he edited and destroyed everything. A few days later, Prafulla left home, saying he would be back in the evening, as usual, and never returned. His body was never found. His children were left almost penniless. His son, Prabir, my father-in-law, made a terse note in the family journal in which Prafulla had previously recorded the births of his children and the death of his wife: "Father disappeared on the 4th of April, 1938, from 3 Valmeek Street, Ballygunge."

Prabir was halfway through college at that time. The tragedy forced him to quit. He used his father's connections to find a clerical job in order to support his sister and grandmother. In a few years, however, he left the job and joined the army. He served in World War II—in Palestine, Egypt, and Burma—and, after India became independent, in India's wars with Pakistan and China. In the course of a long and successful military career, Prafulla's son reverted to the model of his father's youth. He staunchly espoused Western culture, enrolled his only son in a school run by Jesuit missionaries, arranged for him to take piano lessons at the Calcutta School of Music, tried to inculcate in him the rational, secular, post-Enlightenment worldview that he particularly admired, and always encouraged him to look beyond India for opportunities and professional fulfillment.

For senior army officers like my father-in-law, military life continued to be a throwback to the Raj, even as the country flexed its newfound

Indian muscles. The daily routine in peacetime included drinks in the evening, get-togethers at the club, dances organized on special occasions, and Christmas and New Year's Eve parties with plenty of alcohol. The officers' wives also had to model themselves on the pattern of bygone memsahibs—managing the servants, throwing parties, playing card games, having midmorning coffee and gossip sessions, and learning to cook Western/Anglo-Indian dishes at their ladies' clubs.

One afternoon, going through a bookcase, I came upon two clothbound, worm-eaten volumes—*Mrs. Beeton's Cookery Book* and *Mrs. Routleff's Economical Cookery Book for India*. The latter proudly proclaimed on the cover, "Ninth edition, revised and enlarged." As I gingerly turned the pages, the past—of the country, of the outsiders who had come and ruled it for so long without letting their Britishness be submerged, and of my parents-in-law, whom I never had the opportunity to know well—rained out with the crumbling dust that had accumulated for unknown years. Illustrations of archaic kitchen gadgets and cooking techniques stared at me from the fragile pages.

Clearly, the books dated back to the days when my mother-in-law was a young army wife, living in the central state of Madhya Pradesh. My father-in-law was stationed in a small town called Mhow, whose name is actually an acronym for Military Headquarters of War. It was founded in 1818 by Sir John Malcolm, after he concluded a treaty with the local rulers who had been resisting the British. After independence, Mhow grew in importance as a training center for the Indian Army. In the short time that I knew her, my mother-in-law had never mentioned getting lessons in Western cookery during the years she spent in Mhow. The food she had served me had always been the Bengali classics—fish, vegetables, dal, rice. So, I wondered, what had she learned from these books? Roast beef? Chocolate cake? Oxtail soup? As I kept turning the pages, the books provided some kind of an answer. Old typed sheets and small scraps of paper with scribbled notes fell out. Among the latter was a recipe for guava jelly. Another nameless confection required two cups of flour, one cup of sugar, a teaspoon of baking powder, two tablespoons of burnt sugar, one teaspoon of mixed spice (what?), sixteen teaspoons of butter, four eggs, and a small cup of milk. It sounded quite enticing, but there were no directions to follow with the ingredients.

The typed pages were more definitive. Both were headed "Ladies Club Meeting," one dated December 17, 1965, and the other March 9, 1966. The first had a recipe for a walnut cake with walnut frosting, and another for marzipan. The other page was titled "Pastitsieo [sic]—delicious dish from Greece by Mrs. Despina Sharma." I presumed the latter was the cooking instructor. The odd combination of macaroni, minced meat, onion, tomatoes, garlic, garam masala, ghee, flour, milk, eggs, and nutmeg did not seem Greek exactly, nor did it arouse much confidence as a viable recipe. But perhaps it worked if you were bold enough to try it. Here again was one of the countless examples of creating a new dish through fusion, in the not-too-distant past, and attributing to the product a fake authenticity—in this case, of the dish being genuinely European—that made it desirable beyond taste or texture.

It brought back to me the memory of my first visit to this apartment. That dinner table, laid with knife, fork, and spoon, did not seem so incongruous anymore, even though my father-in-law had, by then, long retired from military life. It was only one more facet of the multiple eating cultures that India has adopted and made her own.

By the time I was ready to renew my travels, I felt I had to start with some kind of a pilgrimage. Perhaps it was an element of deep-seated superstition that generated the thought. The illness had left me vulnerable in a way I had never been before. In a country that is overwhelmingly full of believers of every faith, it was not unusual to have moments of doubt about my own lack of belief. A current of thought ran through my mind: perhaps even the gesture of a pilgrimage, mingling with the faithful who forget themselves in the presence of a deity, and, more significantly, partaking of the offerings that were made in a temple, might give me some insurance (however illusory) against further misfortunes. It was exactly the way I had seen some of the elders in my family express themselves in times of trouble, to my youthful outrage. Now,

I found a grudging kind of humor in recognizing the ancestral strain in me.

After much pondering and poring over the map, I decided that the destination had to belong to another faith. I would go to Amritsar, in Punjab, which houses the holiest shrine of the Sikhs. Perhaps staying all this time in my late in-laws' apartment had something to do with the choice. My father-in-law was a great admirer of the Sikhs, many of whom were his fellow officers. He had spoken to me several times about their bravery and generosity.

There was another inducement—the Grand Trunk Road, which ran beyond Amritsar to the Wagah checkpoint on the border between India and Pakistan. Having seen its beginning near my hometown, I wanted to see the end on the edge of enemy territory. Two faiths, Hinduism and Islam, after coexisting in one country for a thousand years, had finally become hostile to the point of Partition, an outcome shaped in the crucible of colonialism. The border, unyielding now for more than half a century, would be an appropriate place to consider all the food and hospitality that had once transcended faith and bigotry, and served as the coin of common exchange and human fellowship.

PART TWO

Chapter Six

PILGRIMAGE AND PAGEANTRY IN AMRITSAR

The plane was late and the short winter day was long over by the time I reached Amritsar. For India's dynamic and prosperous community of Sikhs, Amritsar is what Mecca is to the Muslims. It is the site of their most important gurdwara, the fabled Golden Temple, which stands in the middle of an artificial lake evoking an ancient sacred "pool of nectar," from which the city takes its name.

Coming out of the airport, I was struck by the conjunction of a crescent moon and a rising Venus in the velvety night sky overhead. Together, they symbolized Islam, so vividly present across the border (which is only twenty-two miles from Amritsar) in theocratic Pakistan. Standing on the tarmac outside the airport, it was impossible not to feel moved by the sorrow and terror of the 1947 Partition of India, which drew a thin red line through the heart of Punjab. But as I drove into the city, the call to evening prayer rose from many mosques, while bells chimed to the accompaniment of aarti rituals in Hindu temples. It was a comforting reminder that for the most part, the two opposing faiths do manage a tolerant coexistence in modern India.

As an adult, I've never felt much enthusiasm for paying homage to the gods in shrines belonging to my own Hindu heritage. This is partly because of the discriminatory policies in some temples, partly because of the undisciplined crush of worshippers that often fills the temples, and partly because of the predatory behavior of priests and attendants, who not only demand payment for services (as guides, as interceders between men and gods) but also insist on the visitors' having to purchase flowers and food offerings from the temple premises. The few times I took my mother to visit the historic Kali temple in Calcutta, we were buffeted and jostled so mercilessly that the only way to make progress was to hold on to the grimy hand of the temple attendant as he pushed ruthlessly forward. I found it utterly antithetical to any devotional or spiritual impulse. The stone and marble floor on which we trod barefoot was slimed over by the crushed remnants of flowers and leaves, and as we neared the dark, enclosed shrine in the heart of the temple where the image of the goddess was housed, the smell of fresh flowers, incense, sweets, and human sweat combined with an age-old imprisoned odor that repulsed me. If Kali's temple was inclusive to the point of swallowing its visitors, it was a different experience altogether for me at another temple in north-central Calcutta, dedicated to the god Vishnu. I happened to be with a couple of Australian friends, who were utterly mesmerized by the intricate carved beauty of the temple spire—rising with otherworldly splendor in the shabby heart of the city. But when the three of us tried to go inside, several guards came rushing out to forbid entry. I pointed out that all of us were barefoot. But that was not the problem. In this temple, where Vishnu, the preserver of all creation is worshipped, my blatantly non-Hindu foreign friends were inadmissible. The same is true of the great Hindu temples of the South.

Given such experiences, the Golden Temple, which has weathered many violent episodes and remains serenely unaffected by the clamorous chaos of its surroundings, held a special promise. Aside from its physical grandeur, it is renowned for the spotless langar (communal eatery) that feeds all visitors, needy or not, Sikh or not, with unquestioning largesse. Food, in the form of cooked offerings, is also served in many Hindu places of worship, but the sheer numbers of devotees can make the eating experience somewhat fraught. The Golden Temple, from what I had heard, would be different.

Compared to Hinduism, Jainism, Buddhism, or even Islam, Sikhism is a young religion. It was founded by Guru Nanak, born into a Hindu family in 1469, a time when northern India was ruled by an Afghan Muslim dynasty, the Lodis. A charismatic visionary, Nanak advocated a new faith, based on love, egalitarianism, and belief in a nonincarnate divinity. His preaching accommodated both the Islamic idea that the goal of religion is union with God, and the Hindu notion that through meditation and good work, the devotee could purge himself of impurities and achieve freedom from the cycle of rebirth. For his followers, however, peaceful coexistence with these two major faiths was rudely disrupted in the seventeenth century, during the reign of the Mughal emperor Jahangir, who punished them for what he perceived to be a rejection of Islam. Through the subsequent years of the Mughal Empire, Sikhs were subjected to intolerance and harassment, which had the effect of transforming them into a martial community.

My meager knowledge about the Sikh faith only added to the mystique of Amritsar, as did an unexpected friendship I had formed in the late eighties with one of India's most eminent Sikhs, Khushwant Singh—journalist, parliamentarian, and author of many books, including the magisterial *History of the Sikhs* and the wrenching novel *Train to Pakistan*. I was working as a journalist and translator in Calcutta when I met him, having returned to India after nineteen years spent in the United States and in Bangladesh, where my first marriage, to a Muslim, had foundered. In my hometown, I found myself to be a woman with a past, the subject of veiled disapproval in some quarters. Rebuilding a

life and friendships proved difficult, something that Khushwant understood all too well. He encouraged me to focus on work. "Write well,
and you will find everything you are looking for," he advised. Assignments often took me to Delhi, and I made sure to visit Khushwant and
his beautiful wife, Kaval, each time.

He used to laugh about the Bengalis' obsession with food, especially
about their passionate opinions about the best way to make the region's
signature dish, the fish jhol. Although he had grown up in Lahore (now
in the Pakistani part of Punjab) and Delhi, Khushwant had also spent
some time in Bengal as a student at Shantiniketan, the university
founded by the poet Rabindranath Tagore. On his first night there, the
young Punjabi boy had to eat his rice with the utterly unfamiliar fish
jhol. When I told him in 1989 about deciding to write a book about life
and food in Bengal, he made some friendly jibes about whether any
book would be long enough to suffice. Bengalis, for their part, tend to
write off Punjabi food as limited in variety and lacking in subtlety. But
what I learned from my visits to Khushwant's home was that the hospitality of a Sikh is unstinted. The food was always tasty, and both Khushwant and his wife urged guests to eat well. When I decided to leave
India again in 1990 and immigrate permanently to the States, Khushwant Singh was deeply disappointed and said so. To him, it must have
seemed that I was giving up too easily on the struggles of resettling in
India. Maybe I was.

Despite visits to Calcutta and Bombay, I had not managed to get
to Delhi since that time. My correspondence with Khushwant was also
rather sporadic, but it was never difficult to get news about a man as famous and controversial as he was. After his wife died of Alzheimer's,
Khushwant wrote poignantly about their difficult though enduring relationship, and about now becoming a recluse who focused only on his
work. When I planned the trip to Amritsar, I knew my first stop would
have to be Khushwant's house in Delhi. Renewing the rare friendship
that had been his gift would give meaning to my pilgrimage to a Sikh
temple.

The visit was the perfect prelude to Amritsar. Khushwant has always claimed he is not a particularly religious person, although his writings are full of references, learned and emotive, to the poetry and philosophy of the Sikh faith. He had visited Amritsar and the Golden Temple in the past and commented on its extraordinary atmosphere of serenity. However, he had never eaten in the langar.

"I didn't think I could eat properly while sitting cross-legged on the floor, I'd get all the food into my beard," he said, laughing. "And the food is nothing special; it's just your basic rice, bread and dal, not an elaborate Bengali meal."

That didn't discourage me; instinctively I knew that eating in the langar was about more than the food. Besides, as he pointed out, serving everyone, rich and poor, with the same food, enforces the ideal of equality. To me, coming from caste-ridden Hinduism, it was an attractive notion.

We talked some more about his native state and its postindependence prosperity. Spending a fortune on frequent multicourse banquets—a notorious weakness of Bengalis—is not the Punjabi way of showing off newfound wealth. They expend their resources on the more durable acquisitions of property and business. And for ordinary people, especially in the rural areas, cuisine is still limited. From October to May, Punjabi farmers subsist on mustard greens, rice, bread, dal, and a halvah made from carrots. Perhaps this spare yet healthy diet accounts for the continued hardiness of Punjabis, their ability to succeed even in new or hostile locations.

After an hour talking over old times, I left Khushwant's house. He saw me off with the promise to organize a dinner at his house after my return from Amritsar. "Bring your friends, anyone you know," he said with the magnanimity I remembered from sixteen years ago.

After checking into the hotel in Amritsar, I had a light dinner, and fell asleep to the sound of cars whooshing by. I woke very early in the morning. Having made a cup of tea with the aid of the electric kettle and tea bags provided by the hotel, I drank it standing by the window, watching the morning mist dissipate. Directly opposite was an enormous building with expansive grounds. A large sign on the gate said, Khalsa College International Public School. Soon enough, auto-rickshaws began driving up and depositing groups of schoolboys, most of whom sported Sikh turbans. The Amritsar morning had begun. It was time for me to start on my pilgrimage.

The Golden Temple is located in the old part of Amritsar, where the congested lanes were already aromatic with coal smoke, hot milk, and fried goodies. I stopped in front of a sweetshop. Saffron-colored jilebis, looking like sunflowers in a dark field, were being fried in oil prior to being coated with syrup, watched by an eager queue that waited to buy them. Moving on, I noticed with delight that the frequency of sweetshops here almost paralleled that of my city, Calcutta. But what was very different in Amritsar, according to many accounts, was a culture of eating out, probably stemming from a long-established rural tradition of women preparing their dough at home and taking it to communal, open-air village tandoors to be made into bread. Even early in the morning, the dhabas (roadside eateries) in Amritsar were doing brisk business. And the clients were not merely itinerant truck drivers who had stopped for a bite. Comfortable, middle-class men and women happily dug into kulchas (a type of stuffed bread) served with a spicy chickpea concoction. Amritsar's kulchas, eaten only at breakfast or brunch, are considered unique. The plump, soft breads made with refined flour are stuffed with potatoes, onions, chilies, black pepper, cumin, and pomegranate seeds, and baked in a tandoor. Lashings of butter on the outside create the delightful contrast of a crisp exterior. Nowhere else in Punjab can you find such kulchas. As I walked past one of the dhabas, I saw a turbaned young man dipping a portion of kulcha into a chutney that looked to be an enticing combination of tamarind, mint, and green chilies.

This was a world far removed from Bengal, where people prefer waking up to homemade tea and breakfast before they face the world, even if facing the world means only a short trip to the market for the daily purchase of fish and vegetables. I remembered the leisurely Sunday mornings of my youth when my mother made luchis to be eaten with a potato–onion–green chili bhaji (fried vegetables), followed by either halvah or payesh. The halvah was usually made with semolina, sugar, and ghee. The payesh was a sweet pudding, consisting of rice or vermicelli cooked in evaporated, sweetened milk. Both were scented with cinnamon and cardamom. To the Amritsar housewife, the idea of so much kitchen labor in the morning must seem insane when you can simply step out and get your fill of kulchas, jilebis, and hot, milky, spice-scented tea. Some people even arrange to have their breakfast kulchas delivered at home, along with the morning paper. Perhaps this tradition of eating out instead of obsessing in the home kitchen has some bearing on the fact that first-generation Punjabi immigrants in Britain created the "curry houses" that became a fixture on the British culinary landscape. Indian food, served by restaurants in the West, is still mainly Punjabi food.

Punjab's overall prosperity is rooted in the so-called green revolution of the sixties. The fertility of the land, the industry of its farmers, and their willingness to adopt modern ways of farming have all combined to transform it into the granary of India. Aside from huge quantities of wheat, the state also produces basmati rice that is exported worldwide. The Sikhs are the dominant community here, but their presence has a reach well beyond state lines. Sikh entrepreneurs have built successful businesses in India and abroad, and Sikhs figure prominently in the Indian armed forces.

The Golden Temple complex, built in the sixteenth century during the tenure of the fifth Sikh guru, Arjan Singh, is supported and maintained by the contributions of an affluent community, many of whom work there as volunteers. The temple's name derives from the gilded exterior of its central edifice, the Harmandir Sahib, where the Sikh holy book is housed during the day. A reminder of the martial nature of the Sikh faith stands right beside the temple—a shop called Bharat Kirpan Factory, which manufactures the swords that every Sikh male has to acquire and keep as one of the five sacred items that define him as a Sikh. Inside the temple, however, the atmosphere is anything but martial. As soon as I entered the outer gates, I heard hymns performed by raagis (singers) being broadcast through a sound system. The noise and ruckus of the city outside and the clutter of my thoughts inside, all seemed to fall away.

Having taken off my shoes, washed my feet, and covered my head, as required, I spent the morning wandering through the complex. At different points, water channels had been cut into the marble walkways for further automatic cleansing of the feet. I looked at the Sikh men and women around me and wondered if such ritual gestures could ever wash away all memories of the greatest crisis weathered by the Golden Temple and India's Sikh community. The marble walls were not only inscribed with the names of donors and Sikh soldiers who had died in the two world wars and in India's wars with China and Pakistan, they were also scarred by bullet marks from 1984, when Prime Minister Indira Gandhi ordered the Indian Army to attack the temple where Sikh separatists had stashed arms and taken shelter. The fateful decision to launch Operation Bluestar, as it was called, resulted in the assassination of Mrs. Gandhi four months later by two Sikh bodyguards, and consequent nationwide riots in which thousands of innocent Sikhs were killed by irate Hindu mobs. In protest, Khushwant Singh, who was a Member of Parliament at that time, returned his Padma Bhushan, a high honor given by the Indian government. But, I remembered, he also wrote appreciatively about my city, Calcutta, where not a single Sikh was killed.

I shook off these somber reflections when I came to the communal refectory, the Guru Ram Das Langar. It was lunchtime and people were going up the stairway leading to the langar. But just as I placed my foot on the first step, I found myself accosted by a stranger. "Wouldn't you like to see where they make the bread?" He was an elderly turbaned Sikh, his gray beard neatly packed against his face with a net. From his great height, he bent a friendly yet quizzical look on me, having somehow determined that my interest in food was both professional and personal. As I followed him, he asked if, by any chance, I was from Calcutta—my stumbling Hindi and Bengali features had often proved to be giveaways in other northern Indian locations. When I nodded, he told me that he had visited the city many times, as his son worked there as a cab driver. It was a bond of comfort; Sikh taxi drivers were considered emblems of honesty and reliability when I was growing up.

Despite all I had heard about the superachieving efficiency of Sikhs, I was quite unprepared for the sight of the cavernous hall where automation had replaced human toil. A complicated set of machinery mixed the dough, made little pellets, flattened them into disks, rolled them out into larger disks, and submitted those to an enormous oven for baking. The final step transported the bread along a conveyer belt into large bins that were then taken into the langar. The scene could well have been part of Chaplin's *Modern Times*. Earlier, I had come across some impressive numbers. The kitchen makes 112,000 chapattis per day and provides free meals for 30,000 people. As I looked at the awesome conveyer belt, I had no problem believing it.

Turning to my companion, I tried to find the right words to express my reaction. But he had no time to wait. "Come along, let's go and eat," he said, vigorously waving me ahead.

In the langar, as Khushwant had warned me, one had to sit cross-legged on narrow rugs spread on the floor. Before each person was a large steel plate and a steel tumbler filled with water. From one doorway, I saw the servers appear, each carrying a large basket from which they served the bread. But it was only when one of them came to a stop in front of me, that I understood my unthinking gaffe. The bread is not dropped onto the plate. You have to "receive" it, holding up both hands in which the server places the bread. It was yet another moving reminder of the beauty of the Sikh heritage, and how it had dispensed with the two evils of Hindu society—caste and untouchability. I noticed that some people in the row facing me were requesting and receiving multiple pieces of bread, some of which they neatly packed into plastic bags they had brought with them; provision for dinner perhaps, although they did not seem poor. The Golden Temple, as I had heard before, made no distinctions between the prosperous and the needy. Ask and ye shall receive, seemed the operating principle.

On the heels of the bread servers came others carrying steel buckets from which they ladled out large portions of "kali dal"—legumes that had not been husked. After that, came the rice, not plain boiled rice as we tend to eat in Bengal, but a pilaflike concoction glistening with ghee. Once again, the servers surprised me. Instead of using spoons or ladles, they simply took out handfuls of the pilaf from their buckets and deposited it on our plates. A tactile though indirect connection bound the giver with the receiver.

The meal had now been served—simple sustenance for a sturdy people. For a while, I was pleasantly amused by the quiet vigor with which people around me tore their bread, mopped up dal with the pieces, and chewed the mouthfuls. When I followed their example, the langar's bread tasted like a cross between a homemade chapatti and the naan bread one finds in restaurants. Its unleavened wheaty thickness was guaranteed to quickly fill the belly. But it was the dal that amazed me with its fragrance and its taste. I had eaten Punjabi "kali dal" many times, in restaurants and the homes of friends. This, however, was absolutely unlike the rich, buttery preparation I had previously encountered. There was hardly any detectable touch of fat. A faint echo of ginger and some other unidentifiable spice made it a dish of which multiple helpings could be consumed.

As I observed the quiet, almost silent contentment with which everyone around me ate their food, it occurred to me that religious sanctums that serve meals on a large scale are the last bastions of culinary authenticity and continuity in India. The material world embraces change, novelty, experimentation, and fusion with restless avidity, while food in many of India's temples, whether Sikh or Hindu, continues to be immutably rooted in the land. I thought of the daily meal cooked for devotees in the kitchens of the great Jagannath Temple in Puri, which I had visited as a child. What I didn't know then was that, as in that Vishnu temple in Calcutta, this was a place where non-Hindus are barred from entering—an exclusionary policy that, in my mind, casts a shadow over the beauty and grandeur of the place. Thankfully, however, the caste system does not hold sway there; thousands of Hindus freely come in and share the sanctified vegetarian offering called Mahaprasad, which is made according to a recipe that has remained unchanged for hundreds of years. Many items are prohibited, including onion, garlic, potatoes, tomatoes, cabbages, okra, and green chilies. The reason is clear. They are either imports brought in by the Portuguese traders from the New World, and even Africa, or they are associated with the cooking of meat, especially by Muslims. The meal in Puri's temple today is likely to be exactly what was served to the deity when the temple was built in the twelfth century, just as the meal in the Golden Temple is what the Sikhs have eaten from the time of Nanak, the founder of their religion.

Once everyone had finished eating, we took our plates and glasses out of the langar and handed them to a waiting army of volunteers, men and women, who would dispose of the leftovers and wash up. A look backward showed me a new batch of people sitting down for their meal. I said good-bye to my chance-met companion before heading for the climactic eating experience.

In a separate kitchen, temple cooks prepare a halvah with semolina, sugar, and enough ghee almost to drip down your fingers to the elbow. People purchase the halvah to make their offerings to God. My small portion was handed to me in a bowl stitched out of dried shaal leaves, with a separate leaf placed as a cover. I followed the throng of devotees who circled the central temple, praying and singing hymns while carrying their offerings. Once again, I admired the orderliness of the Sikh crowd, and couldn't help comparing it to the mad crush that had overwhelmed me when I visited the Kali temple in Calcutta. At the end of the circumambulation, the halvah was considered consecrated food, accepted by God. On the way out, everyone donated part of their halvah back to the temple.

The concept and ritual of making offerings was nothing new to me; it is also part of Hindu religious practice. So I knew that the unusual lifting of my spirits was born not out of personal spiritual epiphany, but rather from taking part in a community's devotion without having to prove that I belonged. The effect, strangely, was that of a shot of confidence. Any debilitating memories of my last illness fell away; I felt expectant and capable, ready to move forward with my quest, with my life. Watching the red-gold fish swimming gracefully in the temple lake, I

ate the halvah with relish. Afterward, I made my way out to the earthly
realm of Amritsar's crowded streets.

There is enormous life and history (some of it violent) crammed into
this part of town, which presents a stark contrast to wealthy residential
neighborhoods with gardens, garages, and plush mansions, glimpses of
which were presented in the popular film *Bride and Prejudice.* An older,
grittier, survivor reality pervades the old city. Long before the 1984 Operation Bluestar, the Golden Temple had suffered multiple attacks, not
only from the forces of the Mughal rulers of Delhi, but also by the
Afghan raider Ahmed Shah Durrani. Close by is the Jallianwala Bagh,
the scene of an infamous massacre carried out by the British general
Reginald Dyer. On April 13, 1919, crowds had assembled in the bagh
(literally, garden) to celebrate the festival of Baisakhi that begins the
New Year. General Dyer marched his troops into the gardens and ordered them to open fire. The incident proved to be a defining moment
in India's freedom struggle.

I wandered in and out of the poorest, most congested part of the
city—shops crammed on top of one another, houses with doors and
windows made of cheap, garishly painted wood, handcarts filled with
fruits and vegetables, hole-in-the-wall eateries where laborers huddled
with their hot tea against a chilly breeze blowing in over the northern
plains. It reminded me of scenes from the novel *The Sari Shop*, by the
Amritsar-based writer Rupa Bajwa. But everywhere I went, I was aware
of an irrepressible, pulsing energy—productive even in the midst of
chaos or despair. The residents of this city were living up to the outsider's image of Punjabis; they did not while away the hours over tea,
samosas, and talk, as my fellow Bengalis loved to do. Had the Punjabis
always been thus, I wondered, or did this urban energy stem from the
bloody upheaval of the Partition of 1947, when Hindus and Sikhs from
the Pakistani side of Punjab came into India, while the Muslims did the
opposite? Certainly the immigrants who crossed the border and then
made their way across the state and into the nation's capital, Delhi, sig-

nificantly reshaped many aspects of life in that city. Eating out there, for one thing, was never the same again.

The westernmost section of India's Grand Trunk Road once linked Amritsar to Lahore, its sister city. Now, a mapmaker's line, darkened with blood and suspicion, reinforced by miles of barbed wire and desolate stretches of land, lies between the two. Lahore has become a stepsister, belonging to Pakistan.

It took me an hour to drive from Amritsar to the border checkpoint called Wagah. The end of the 1,250-mile Grand Trunk Road ran straight and smooth—bordered by ochre fields from which the wheat had already been harvested, alternating with enormous expanses glowing with the yellow flowers of mustard, one of Punjab's chief crops. No wonder Khushwant had commented that the Punjabi peasant practically lived on mustard greens throughout the winter. It remains, however, an oddity that mustard oil is an obsession in Bengal, so far away from Punjab. In the distance, I could see tractor trailers, busily reworking the land for the next sowing. On the outskirts of small towns, there were fat cows and water buffalo, lazily cropping at the grass or resting under rows of eucalyptus trees. Trucks overtook my car and passed by, loaded with logs. I wondered what kind of trees had been felled for them. Even small towns in Punjab were seeing a building boom, and groves and stands of trees were vanishing at an alarming clip. After a while, all signs of habitation and daily life fell away as the last bit of road cleaved through the zone of emptiness that lies between hostile nations. Although I couldn't see it, I knew that beyond the elaborate set of gates and barriers at the checkpoint, there was a stretch of grassland with a barbed wire fence—the real cleavage between the two countries.

The scene that greeted me when I got to the Wagah checkpoint around four o'clock, was, however, more like a carnival than a war zone. Trucks loaded to the hilt with all kinds of merchandise lined one side of the road. Porters clad in vivid blue shirts loaded and unloaded rice, wheat, dried fruits, blankets, and woolen clothes. Whatever the official degree of suspicion, the spirit of commerce was intensely active here, the only point between India and Pakistan through which people and traffic are permitted to pass.

Since 1948, the checkpoint has also been providing a tourist attraction at sundown—a ceremony called Beating the Retreat. It is a remnant of the subcontinent's colonial past, a bizarre combination of carefully orchestrated lowering of national flags on each side, and repeated gestures of mock aggression by the soldiers taking part in the ceremony. Hordes of visitors turn up on both sides of the checkpoint every day to watch the Indian Border Security Force (BSF) and the Pakistan Rangers go through a twenty-minute drill calculated to arouse a high pitch of nationalist fervor.

After the first set of gates on the Indian side of the border opened, we were herded into the visitors' gallery the BSF has built. From the shallow concrete tiers I looked across to the other side and saw that the Pakistanis had positioned their gallery better. It faced the flagpost around which the ceremony would take place, while the Indian gallery provided a side view. The soldiers on both sides had obviously been selected for their imposing height and bearing, a further indication of the importance of pageantry in this daily ritual. The Indians wore khaki, with colorful turbans; their Pakistani counterparts were dressed in dark green, with equally arresting headgear.

As the bugles sounded loud and clear, the ceremony began. Soldiers on each side marched up to their opposite numbers, goose-stepping deliberately, so that the bottoms of their soles were presented to the enemy—a somewhat insulting gesture in the Asian subcontinent. Chests puffed out like those of pouter pigeons, faces set in a fierce expression, they put on a seriocomic show of battle-ready vigor, while military commands were shouted through handheld megaphones. The crowd on both sides erupted into a frenzy of shouting. I heard the slogans "Jai Hind" (Victory to India) and "Vande Mataram" (the title of a patriotic song) all around me, while several young men leapt up and began waving the Indian flags they had brought with them. The Pakistanis were not to be outdone. Across the distance, through the din of commands, bugles, drum, and cheers, I heard the shrill voices of schoolgirls—a large group in white uniforms was clearly visible—shouting "Pakistan Zindabad" (Long Live Pakistan). Finally, the designated soldiers on each side lowered their flags, each of the commanding officers shook hands with his opposite number and, as they retreated to their respective domains, the gates clanged shut. The sunset showdown was over for the day. The soldiers could relax and the crowds could go home, all pumped up with patriotic zeal.

The twenty-minute ritual could be interpreted as either a perpetuation of hostility or an attempt at making a connection through impersonal, long-established rituals. For me, though, it was the experience of waiting at the checkpoint, prior to the ceremony, which left a lasting impression. A cluster of little shops has sprouted near the gates, and they do brisk business regaling the spectators with tea, coffee, bottled cold drinks, and a variety of freshly made savory snacks.

It was here that I discovered that the Punjabi pakora can be made with a very light touch, a far cry from the heavy-crusted, oily vegetable fritters that usually pass by the name of pakora in restaurants. Savoring narrow strips of potatoes and onions, encased in the lightest of batter, sipping from a glass (none too clean) of milky tea scented with cardamom, I watched my fellow Indians eat and drink with gusto. Although the brand names of the West—McDonald's or Subway or Domino's—had not reached this far, odd-shaped buns enclosing ground lamb and chicken were being sold as burgers, along with Coke, Pepsi, 7-UP, and their Indian versions. Sitting there, I began to feel the effects of the endlessly retold bloody history of Partition slowly begin to seep away. Beyond the gates of the checkpoint, lay the rolling fence of barbed wire, silently screaming "Keep out" at anyone who dared to come too near. But on this side, at the Indian end of the Grand Trunk Road, surrounded by a crowd of happy eaters, I felt strangely exuberant. Partition may never be undone; but in the interstices of war and anger, hands can stretch out and offer a pakora, a samosa, a sandwich, even a whole plateful of rice, bread, dal, vegetables, and meat. As long as food can be enjoyed and exchanged, we can all be pilgrims of a sort, and hope to survive as a species.

The lingering effect of that hopefulness added zest to what I later ate for dinner at a restaurant on Lawrence Road in downtown Amritsar. Called simply Amritsari machhi, it was pieces of freshwater fish, from the nearby Beas River, coated in a batter infused with the muted pungency of powdered ajwain that had been liberally used to season it. While I ate, I observed the families of Amritsar crowding the restaurant. The food on their plates was relatively simple—chicken, meat, and fish, marinated and cooked in the tandoor or fried in batter; chicken and meat in a rich sauce that incorporated yogurt, powdered almond, and ground-up fried onion. There were several types of bread, including the makki ki roti, made with coarse-ground corn flour; bowls of thick dal; and of course, sarson ka saag (mustard greens) stewed with ginger and ghee. Perhaps, at the end of the meal, some would order the other winter staple that Khushwant had mentioned, a rich halvah made with grated carrots, ghee, sugar, and dried milk. But I didn't stay to watch. I had to make an early start the next day and go back to Delhi—to see Khushwant again, and explore the culinary mosaic of a city that has played host to ruler and ruled for many centuries.

"So, how was Amritsar; did you go to the temple?" Khushwant asked me when I arrived at his house for dinner the next evening. He gestured towards the predinner spread on the living room table—smoked salmon on toast, spicy potato chips, a bowl of nuts, a bottle of wine. I helped myself and described my meal at the langar. Though he laughed at the extent to which I was willing to go in search of a new eating experience, I could see he was also touched by my admiration of this aspect of Sikhism.

Dinner, served notoriously early by Indian standards ("we eat at seven thirty and retire at nine," Khushwant always tells his guests, without exaggeration), was simple but delicious. His daughter, who lives next door and supervises his housekeeping, had made sure of it. There was the traditional Punjabi pilaf but, unlike the one served in the temple, this was enhanced with expensive spices and nuts. A delicate yellow dal and a spicy dish of green peas presented a pleasing contrast. The final item was an enormous bowl of hariyali murgh—chicken in a gravy green with pureed cilantro, spinach, and fenugreek leaves, its taste delicate yet tantalizing. The small group of guests happily dug in, but I noticed that Khushwant himself did not touch the chicken. He preferred eating light at dinner, he said, spooning some yogurt over his rice and vegetables. When lychees and ice cream were served for dessert, he contented himself with a small portion of ice cream.

Throughout the meal, Khushwant made many references to his childhood in Lahore and to the home village in Pakistan. He was a survivor of the Partition. The border and the barbed wire I had seen only a couple of days earlier had cut into his life and memory in a deeper way than I would ever really understand. Yet there was no trace of bitterness or bigotry in him. The loss of part of his country had saddened him, but had neither made him intolerant, nor dented his faith in his fellow man.

Under cover of conversation that occasionally bordered on the ribald (Khushwant has always been notorious for his lack of inhibition), I watched him carefully. The gnarled hands with which he mixed his food displayed their knuckles and veins more prominently than I remembered. But even at ninety, he continued to have a robust enjoyment of life. He loved his evening glass of whiskey and relished his meals, however modest his chosen portion. And he continuously exhorted his guests to take more, to eat well. From my previous visits, seventeen years ago, a woman's voice also sounded in my ears—"Come, beta [child], help yourself," she had said as she held different dishes for me. Were she present, she would approve of the way her husband was looking after his guests, as would the spirits of the Sikh gurus who had created the Golden Temple.

My pilgrimage was a success. I knew I would not let myself be haunted by undue anxieties about getting sick again. No matter what my future travels portended, whatever disappointments I faced, I knew that a few gratifying meals like this could give me the energy to deal with them. I left the table replete with the savor of renewed connection, of the triumph of love over time.

Chapter Seven

BANQUETS OF THE IMPERIAL
PALACE—MUSLIM STYLE

It is often easy to forget that the arrival of the Muslims was the first major external influence to radically reshape cooking and eating in India. The country's haute cuisine—which, for a thousand years, has been Islamic imperial cuisine—was born in Delhi and developed to a point of exquisite, almost overblown refinement. From there, it branched into two distinctive offshoots in two other centers of Muslim power: Lucknow, the capital of Uttar Pradesh, and Hyderabad, capital of the southern state of Andhra Pradesh. The long history of Muslim rule—going back to the eleventh century when the invading Turks from Afghanistan descended on India, and ending in the nineteenth century when the British exiled the last Mughal ruler from Delhi—helped to consolidate the union of foreign and indigenous influences in India. It is a story of violent impact, slow, begrudging exchange, and eventual integration. Although the sultans, badshahs, nawabs and nizams—the titles of Muslim royalty in India—have long been replaced by other powers, they have left behind a courtly redolence that enchants both palate and imagination.

Growing up in a middle-class family, I was prone to indulge in gilded fantasies that included the image of an imperial couple (nameless, but clearly resembling the schoolbook portraits of the most romantic Mughal ruler, Shahjahan, and his immortal beloved Mumtaz Mahal) seated on a plush carpet before an array of gold and silver plates loaded with exotic meats, breads, pilafs, and desserts. In the twenty-first century, I did not expect to meet any members of royalty, but the prospect of tracking down a reasonably authentic reproduction of the dishes that used to be made in their kitchens was exciting. Delhi was the obvious starting point, and the day after my memorable dinner with Khushwant, I began my explorations. Later, I planned to travel to Lucknow and Hyderabad.

It is in the older sections of Delhi that the receptive nose is more likely to pick up the aromas of the pilafs, biryanis, kebabs, koftas, and a host of other dishes that the Muslims brought to India with them, and which India enriched with her spices and flavors. The centerpiece of the imperial spread was the dish that still carries a primarily Islamic aura—the pilaf (*pulao, pilav, pallao* in transliterated Persian and Arabic), rice cooked with ghee and spices, sometimes with meat. As with so much in India, there are conflicting opinions as to the authenticity of pilaf as an original Muslim creation, since some ancient Hindu texts, written in Sanskrit, describe a similar dish. Even more confusing, the word *biryani*, which we now think of exclusively to mean rice cooked with meat, was used interchangeably with *pilaf* as late as the sixteenth century. Whatever the authentic origins, the exquisite refinement of a well-made pilaf or biryani today is the product of many influences. India's first Islamic rulers or sultans, the Turkish conquerors from Afghanistan, were certainly not noted for sophisticated cooking and eating. Like all martial and nomadic races, they were used to quick-grilled meats, cheese, yogurt, bread, and rice, supplemented with whatever fruit or produce was locally available. Once settled in their new realm whose wealth and resources must have seemed boundless after the starkness of the mountains and grasslands of Central Asia and Afghanistan, they probably imported sophisticated pilafs and other delicacies befitting royalty, from Persia (modern Iran), which already had a well-established, cultivated culinary tradition. As Delhi became a flourishing Muslim city under the Turkish sultans, many foreigners migrated there in search of opportunities. Among them were gifted chefs whom the sultans happily welcomed to the royal kitchens. One of the great travelers of all time, Ibn Battuta of Tangiers, Morocco, visited sultanate Delhi and ended up staying for twenty years. His detailed, witty observations not only paint a fascinating picture of the whimsical largesse of the ruler, they also hold up a mirror to the culinary and social mores of the times.

The second wave of Muslim rule came with the Mongol (or Mughal, as we say in India, following the mispronunciation of the British; the U.S. spelling is Mogul) conqueror Babur when he marched into Delhi after defeating Sultan Ibrahim Lodi at the battle of Panipat in April 1526. Although Babur was no epicure or sybarite, one of the few times he mentions the details of a meal in his famous autobiography, the *Baburnama*, indicates that the Persian influence was already at work in the royal kitchen. An attempt on his life was made by the mother of the dead Sultan Ibrahim. She bribed a cook to poison a dish served at dinner, described by Babur as "thin bread" on which the powdered poison was strewn and covered with a layer of "meat dressed in oil." But before touching this, Babur ate "a lot of rabbit stew and had quite a bit of dressed saffroned meat." Cooking meat with saffron was very much an Islamic, Persian custom. Fortunately for Babur, he survived the attempted assassination because, stuffed with other dishes, he ate only a tiny bit of the poisoned food. But the story is a reminder of the intimate connection between food, poison, and power in the history of great kingdoms. Lucrezia Borgia is by no means an anomaly.

It was with Babur's descendants, particularly his grandson Akbar, who consolidated Mughal power in northern India, that the refinement of food and culture in the imperial court took a quantum leap forward. A historical document glorifying the reign of the emperor Akbar, the *Ain-i-Akbari*, written by Abul Fazl, describes pilaf made with rice, minced meat, tons of ghee, and seasonings that include onion, ginger, pepper, cumin seed, cardamom, and cloves. Another pilaf, called navratan (nine jewels), was created by an imperial chef in honor of the nine great intellectuals at the Emperor's court. We can be reasonably sure, however, that the rice used in these pilafs was not the aromatic basmati we are so familiar with today. Basmati (or an ancestral cultivar) is said to have been brought to Dehra Dun in northern India much later by Dost Mohamed, an Afghan ruler who was deposed by the British in 1840. The aristocrats among the rice crops of ancient and medieval India were the "shali" rice strains that grew in a wide variety of terrain and, when cooked, became soft and fluffy even while the grains remained completely separate— ideal for a pilaf. The "sticky" rice varieties favored in Chinese and Japanese cooking or in the Italian risotto have not had much currency in India.

Meals, whether in the royal palace or the poor man's hovel, whether in a Muslim or a Hindu household, were traditionally served either on a cleaned floor or on a very low platform, prior to the popularization of chairs and tables used by Europeans. In the Mughal palace, the diners sat on rich carpets, which were covered by clean white sheets at mealtimes to avoid their being stained by the food. After rinsing their hands with perfumed water poured by servants, the royal family chose their favorite items and ate off jade plates—a safety measure, since jade was supposed to change color if it came into contact with most of the known poisons of the day.

Akbar, possibly the greatest of the Mughal emperors, liked to regale his guests occasionally with banquets serving as many as five hundred dishes, but was abstemious when it came to addictive substances. His son and grandson, Jahangir and Shahjahan (the builder of the Taj Mahal) respectively, enjoyed alcohol and opium and further encouraged development of the luxuries of courtly life. The numerous items served in their banquet halls included dishes richly doused with ghee and cleverly seasoned with spices. A huge variety of game birds, fish, beef, and lamb were cooked in an equally varied style. Marinating meat in yogurt and cooking methods like dum pukht, whereby the meat was sealed in a pot and cooked very slowly over a low fire, produced delectably tender meat.

Aside from spices, the cooks in the Mughal imperial kitchen used dried fruit in their meat and rice dishes, a custom inherited from the culinary practices of Turkey and Iran. Mughal rulers from Babur onward were extremely fond of formal gardens, and planted fruit trees all over the territories they conquered. From the fertile orchards of Kashmir, they also imported fruits of the temperate zone—peaches, plums, grapes, apples, apricots, pears. In and around their palaces, they promoted the cultivation and cross-breeding of many strains of India's native mangoes. Later, as European traders, most notably the Portuguese, brought in different fruits and vegetables from the New World, the Mughal chefs adapted their cooking to include these items. By Shahjahan's time, the chili pepper was a familiar ingredient, supplementing or supplanting the indigenous black pepper. Overall, however, surviving recipes from the royal kitchen indicate a surprisingly limited use of spices in the pilafs and biryanis produced. Cinnamon, cardamom, clove, black pepper, coriander seeds, fennel seeds, and fresh ginger were the common ingredients. Flavor was enhanced with the use of yakhni, a stock made by cooking meat and spices and straining the juices through muslin. The Mughals also seemed to have had a predilection for sweet-and-sour tastes, which the chefs created by adding sugar and lemon syrup to the pilafs.

The enormous scale and richness of Delhi is a far cry from Amritsar, which I had visited only a few days earlier. Of all the Mughal emperors, it is Shahjahan who has left the greatest imprint on the city. Although we tend to think solely of the Taj Mahal in Agra when Shahjahan is mentioned, he is responsible for many magnificent edifices, including Delhi's Red Fort and the Jama Masjid. One evening, shortly after the call for Maghreb prayers had died away under a blue-black sky,

I found myself in a lane near the Jama Masjid, reliving my schoolgirl fantasies about the emperor and empress sitting down to dinner in the fort's zenana (women's quarters). I visualized all the different pilafs being served on the dastarkhwan, the medieval Islamic equivalent of a tablecloth. Samosa pilaf might have been one of them. Like all fancy pilafs, it consisted of rice, meat, stock, ghee, and spices, but the distinctive touch came from tiny, delicate meat-filled samosas that were strewn over the pilaf just before serving. A recipe for samosa pilaf, outlined in a Persian cookbook called *Nuskha-e-Shahjahani*, translated into English by Salma Husain, includes instructions for samosa-making that require both finesse and patience:

> Make a mince of the remaining meat. Cook with ginger, onion, and garam masala. When cooked, cool and grind to a fine paste. Knead flour with roasted gram flour, white of an egg, and a little ghee. Roll pooris as thin as a betel leaf. Put cooked minced meat in the center, cover with another poori, place a betel leaf on the top. Repeat the process ten times. Seal [samosas] from all sides. Boil water in a pan, cover the pan with a muslin cloth, place samosas over it and steam. Make small cuts on three sides, leave one side intact, remove betel leaf from samosas, and deep fry them.

I tried to imagine rolling out a sheet of dough to the fineness of a betel leaf in my own kitchen and decided it should remain in the domain of fantasy. For a modern taste of the imperial food of the past, I was better off going to a restaurant called Karim's, a Delhi institution with an impeccable Mughal pedigree. Like the food it serves, the restaurant has its own mythology. Karim's was founded in 1913 by Haji Karimuddin, whose ancestor is supposed to have come to India from Arabia in the sixteenth century as a soldier of fortune who found employment in Babur's army. Some of his descendants became chefs in the Mughal imperial kitchen and continued in this hereditary post until the last ruler, Bahadur Shah Zafar, was exiled by the British. The courtiers and staff in the imperial palaces also had to leave the city. But many of them gradually came back and created new lives in a British-controlled city, among them the man who founded Karim's restaurant, with the purported aim of serving royal cuisine to the common man. Since then, Karim's has maintained its undisputed status, as one of Delhi's finest, and branched out with another restaurant in a New Delhi neighborhood called Nizamuddin.

The menu is predominantly nonvegetarian, as one would expect, and some of the dishes are named after the emperors—Akbar, Jahangir, and Shahjahan—and even after Anarkali, a dancing girl Jahangir was enamored of when he was a young prince. Business being business, the menu also includes the ubiquitous Punjabi dishes like butter chicken and chicken tikka. It is, however, the simple items that revive the memory of past greatness, as I realized once I dipped my spoon into a bowl of Mutton Yakhni. Soup has never been a very important part of the Indian meal, Hindu or Muslim, as the British found to their chagrin. But Karim's yakhni, whether you call it stock or soup, caresses the tongue and slides down the throat with a flavorful delicacy that is beyond words. It promises the consumer a range of other dishes made with the same kind of selectivity of spicing and technique that is documented in seventeenth-century cookbooks, even though the quantities of ghee have been minimized, and sometimes substituted with oil. Eating Karim's Murgh Biryani Anarkali, I remembered the tragic legend of Anarkali. Her beauty was so great, her hold over Jahangir (then the crown prince) so strong, that the emperor Akbar considered her a threat to the kingdom. Convicted on a trumped-up charge, she was supposedly given a particularly brutal death sentence—being walled up alive. Not a story to stimulate the appetite, but then who said the glory days of empire, any empire, were free of gratuitous cruelty? As I ate, the resonance of the past was reinforced by the growing animation of the conversation from a neighboring table. A large group of men were eating with gusto, their table so full of items they had ordered that their dinner plates were precariously balanced on the edge. I did not understand their words, but their language riveted me—Farsi, once widely used in India as the official language of

the Mughal court. Visitors from Iran, I learned from my waiter, not rein-
carnated figures from a bygone era. But I was grateful for the ambience
they added to my meal.

Despite Delhi's long history with the Muslims and the extensive architectural remains they have left behind, many Hindu historians like to focus
on a far older past, when Delhi was supposedly the site of an ancient capital city, Indraprastha, mentioned in the *Mahabharata*. To me, those accounts confirm not only the longtime significance of this bit of real
estate, but also the duality of the Hindu-Muslim identity that has shaped
India over the past thousand years. Power can be both real and illusory,
and the story of Indraprastha, the chief city of a kingdom ruled by the
five Pandava brothers, is rich with intimations of illusion, grandeur, envy,
and conflict. According to the *Mahabharata*, the Pandavas' royal palace, an
extravaganza of glittering gems and crystals, of extensive grounds laid out
with lakes and gardens and arbors, was built with magical materials by a
demonic architect, himself a master of illusions. When the rivals of the
Pandavas, their wicked cousins of the Kaurava family, were invited to see
the palace, they were burned up with envy and hatred, for they knew that
such a palace could never be theirs.

To make matters worse, the eldest Kaurava prince, Duryodhana, suffered repeated public humiliation as he failed to distinguish between glass
and water, between emptiness and solidity. Mistaking a large crystal plane
for water, he started undressing for a swim; sometime later, he fell into a
lake, thinking it was solid glass. In another part of the palace, he tried to
walk through a glass wall and banged his head painfully, and later, pushing
open what he thought was a glass door, fell forward through an open
space. The seeds of anger, sown by such experience and bolstered by existing jealousies, ripened into the fatal hostilities that led to the war to end
all wars, as described in the epic.

The power food served that day by the Pandava brothers to the Kaurava guests consisted of an elaborate spread that included fresh fruits
(India's glorious mangoes, her native jewels, must have shone on the
plate), sesame-studded rice, opulent platters of venison and boar meat,

and rice pudding mellow with ghee and sweet with honey. But as human history has shown so many times, when hospitality is a mere mask for antipathy, even the most glorious food only fuels the negative energy, the kind that can lead to war and destruction.

Contemplating the connections between food and power was seductive up to a point, but finally I needed a break. I felt the need to explore Delhi as a city of commoners, not royals. Like any capital city, it is a harlequin mixture of natives and foreigners, but it was impossible not to wonder whether it had overall become an overwhelmingly Punjabi city. The sight of turbaned Sikh men on the streets, and the voluble exchanges in Punjabi (identifiable to me, if not understandable) I heard in shops and on street corners, continued to remind me of the enormous, catastrophic migration of Sikhs and Hindus that had taken place from Punjab after Partition. To what extent had the moving finger of history rearranged the items on the ordinary person's dinner table after such an event? Had the bold strokes of the Punjabi dhaba obliterated the smaller identifying nuances that characterized the foods cooked by migrants from other states? And then there was the perennial question posed by a megacity—what was the future of domestic cookery in an age of intolerably long commutes, growing numbers of working women, frequent eating out, and the acceptability of entertaining guests with take-out fare brought in from neighborhood restaurants? One thing was evident. Even if the Punjabi influence was homogenizing Delhi's restaurant industry, the food with which it enticed the consumer was neither the exquisitely simple rice-dal-bread meal I had eaten in Amritsar, nor the sturdy chapatti-greens-panir-dal-halvah fare of the Punjabi peasant or laborer. In today's prosperous Delhi—and oddly, the smell of money is more blatant here than in a commercial hub like Bombay—the menu of the Punjabi dhaba boasts a range of breads and kebabs reminiscent of the rugged Northwest Frontier (an area now in Pakistan), supplemented by concoctions with a high lipid factor. Meat, fish, and vegetables, all are lush with oil or ghee. The meat sauces are richly laced with yogurt, cream, or pounded nuts, all of which have been part of Islamic Indian cooking, or tomatoes, which were imported by Europeans and popular-ized by the British.

One of the things that particularly struck me was the insistence with which people kept saying that I couldn't possibly leave Delhi with-out tasting the famous "butter chicken." The mere name sounded in-congruous in an Indian city. After all, it is ghee, rather than butter, that has been the preferred cooking medium from ancient times. Yet, mod-ern Delhi swoons over its butter chicken, an apt epitome for a city where, during the last half century, all the old rules of success have been rewritten. Butter chicken happens to be the brainchild of Kundan Lal, an enterprising post-Partition refugee from the Northwest Frontier, who started a restaurant in Old Delhi called Moti Mahal. The chicken is first grilled and then cooked in a sauce, but what makes it stand out is the near-heretical combination of ingredients—yogurt, garlic, and gin-ger, a variety of ground spices, tomatoes, and, of course, butter. Once it became a hit with the public, hundreds of restaurants and roadside joints started dishing up butter chicken themselves.

I had the opportunity to eat some one evening when I joined my cousin Benu and his family for his birthday celebrations. The butter chicken, Benu assured me, had not been made at home, but brought espe-cially for me, from an "authentic" Punjabi dhaba. Dutifully, I tasted it. An undertone of fenugreek lingered beyond all the other spices in the yogurt-tomato-butter sauce. The overall effect, even for a spice-loving Indian, was a confusion of the taste buds. Again I found myself remem-bering the simplicity of the ginger-scented dal of the Golden Temple. That was not available, but there was more than ample compensation in the dish of large prawns that Benu's wife, Shukla, had cooked in the clas-sic Bengali style. Both Benu and Shukla are expatriate Bengalis, raised in Delhi by immigrant parents. So I was not surprised that at the end of the meal, several kinds of Bengali sweets were brought to the table. As they both like to say, the confectioners in Delhi's Bengali enclave, Chittaranjan Park, can give the ones in Calcutta a run for their money.

The Bengalis became a significant presence in Delhi when the British relocated the capital from Calcutta in 1911. The huge army of clerks and government workers in Calcutta had to shift their residence—however disgruntled they might have felt about it—to keep their jobs. Soon enough, they developed a reputation for being obsessed with food and cooking. The story goes that smoke from the cooking fires in Bengali homes started coming out at four in the morning and did not die down till midnight. There is no smoke from cooking fires in this age of gas, electric, and kerosene stoves, but the Bengalis still retain their epicurean tendencies. The enormous fish market in Chittaranjan Park displays a large variety of fish as well as the crustaceans that Bengalis love: freshwater prawn, shrimp, and crab. As for Bengali confectionaries in Delhi, some of them have been around even longer than the K. C. Das eatery in Bangalore, and pleased the multiethnic palate well enough to have become landmarks in the city.

When I found my way to the famed Bengal Sweet House, located in central Delhi's Bengali Market area, I was momentarily distracted by the brisk business going on outside. Rows of bamboo gift baskets were laid out on the sidewalk, their eager vendor pouncing on anyone who showed the slightest twitch of interest. I studied the assortment of comestibles, native and global, that lay at my feet, wrapped in colored plastic. Each basket contained a couple of plump oranges and apples, two cans of soft drinks, slim Snickers bars, small bags of nuts and biscuits, and tiny containers of the after-dinner spice chasers collectively called mukhwas. But the most prominent item was on top, a finger in the eye of the beholder—yellow bags of potato chips bearing the logo Lay's.

After this, it wasn't much of a surprise to discover that the Bengal Sweet House was owned by a man from Rajasthan. The original Bengali proprietor had sold off the business many years ago. I looked around the enormous interior, at the gaggle of customers eating away. Their plates contained a bewildering number of items that did not in the least resemble Bengali sweets. The menu advertised South Indian dosas, French fries, Tibetan momos, Mumbai bhel puri, sugar-free kulfi, aloo chat. But the Bengali sweets were also on the list. I asked for a serving of rosomalai with some trepidation. Rosomalai consists of disks of sweetened cottage cheese cooked in a sauce of evaporated milk. Like many Bengali desserts, it sounds simple but is hard to make well. Tasting the rosomalai out of the little plastic bowl, I was delightfully surprised by its spongy texture and the delicate saffron flavor of the milky sauce. Here, within four walls, was a microcosm of evolution. Time, demand, and new ownership had changed a regional confectionary into a multiethnic food court with an essentially Indian character. The place bore no resemblance to the gleaming new food courts elsewhere in Delhi and in other major cities, where the logos were mostly those of Western fast-food chains, where "American sweet corn" was a surefire attention getter.

Before leaving for Lucknow, I was fortunate enough to meet Rahul Verma, a food critic and writer who knows Delhi, old and new, like the back of his hand. Tall and bespectacled, Rahul has a look of inner focus that seems to ignore the world outside—an impression totally at odds with the wealth of minutiae about India's many food traditions with which he regales you. When Rahul suggested going to one of the best-known food locales of Old Delhi, the Paranthewali Gali, I decided it would be folly to miss the opportunity. The Paranthewali Gali (literally, the alley of paratha makers) is a tiny stretch of restaurants within the maze of lanes that form Chandni Chowk, a market dating back to the Mughal era. An atmosphere of medieval commerce still lingers in the Chowk. Its narrow lanes were impenetrable to soldiers and horses alike, thus allowing the area to escape much of the major devastation visited on the city by rampaging invaders of the past. And the parathas (fried flat breads of many kinds) sold here have been a magnet for hungry eaters for half a century or more.

Trekking by road from New to Old Delhi used to be a time-consuming endurance test, given some of the traffic bottlenecks. But the spiffy new subway system, built with the help of Russian engineering expertise, has made things easy for the food pilgrim. Following Rahul, I hopped on the train at the Press Club station, and before I could finish admiring the comfortable, roomy seats, the clear-as-a-bell enunciation of the electronic announcements (what an improvement over the barely intelligible blaring on the Boston subway system), the muted gleam of the metal fixtures, it was time to get off. Before going into the Gali,

Rahul stopped at a tiny shop—little more than a stall—proudly bearing the name Natraj Café.

"They make the best dahi-vada in Delhi," he said. "You've got to sample some."

Dahi-vada, or fried lentil buns immersed in a yogurt sauce, is to India what the falafel with tahini is to the Middle East. However, I've never been able to acquire a taste for it. I hesitated to spoil my appetite when the lure of the Gali's parathas glimmered on the other side of the street. But I didn't want to appear either ungracious or unadventurous, especially in the eyes of a food enthusiast who had generously taken time out on a Sunday afternoon to be my guide. So I agreed, and portions of dahi-vada were dished out on small steel plates. The yogurt sauce covering the lentil cake received a dash of tamarind syrup before the plates were handed to us. I took a cautious spoonful, then immediately a much bigger one. If one had to eat a dahi-vada, this was the one, with its perfect balance of sweet and sour and its soft, granular texture. The owner, who seemed to be on friendly terms with Rahul, grinned at the surprise on my face. Even the face of the dancing Shiva (Natraj), painted on the business card the owner thrust at me, seemed amused.

Appetite stimulated, instead of spoiled, I crossed the street with Rahul and followed him down some tortuous lanes. A spicy-sharp aroma floating out to my nostrils announced the presence of the Paranthewali Gali. The restaurant Rahul chose was called The Power of Paratha. Entering, we were greeted by a pictorial demonstration of the power—a large framed photograph of India's first prime minister, Jawaharlal Nehru, his sister and daughter beside him, eating a vegetarian meal with utmost concentration. A closer look revealed a speck of white, possibly yogurt, on Nehru's upper lip. It gave the aristocratic Kashmiri Brahmin a kind of humanity I had not imagined possible.

The restaurants of the Gali are not designed for aesthetics or ambience. This one had walls tiled with rather dingy white marble. The straight-backed chairs and benches did not encourage leisurely, lingering meals. The clientele was a mixture of working-class and middle-class families, out for their Sunday lunch. Large black lettering on a yellow board listed the eighteen different kinds of parathas on offer. The real action, however, was in the front of the shop, where the cooking was being done on a raised platform. Enormous quantities of dough had been kneaded. The cook tore off lumps from it, rolled them out as parathas, put in the required stuffing, and deep-fried them. A collection of large aluminum pans contained several vegetable dishes to be eaten with the parathas—this was a strictly vegetarian joint. There was also a large metal tray heaped with hot samosas, catering to transient customers who walked up from the street or stopped their rickshaws, bought a clutch of samosas, and left.

Within a few minutes, a waiter arrived and put down large steel plates on our table. In three sections separated by metal ridges, there were pickles, green chilies, a serving of dal, and two kinds of vegetables. The parathas, once you chose the kind of filling you wanted, would be made right before your eyes—one of the attractions of the Gali. Leaving Rahul to do the ordering, I looked around the restaurant and noticed another big sign proclaiming, "Pure ghee used." No need to worry about trans fats here, only cholesterol.

Paratha, parantha, or prantha (as the restaurant menu spelled it) has probably been around in some form or other since antiquity and has many incarnations. Dough (made either with whole wheat flour or refined white flour) is usually rolled out in several layers, each brushed with fat, folded into triangular, square, or round shapes, and fried in a pan. While we associate the paratha mostly with Punjabi and northern Indian cooking, some believe that the poli of Maharashtra and Gujarat is a close cousin. The Mughal rulers and nobility were fond of parathas, which have been a big part of Muslim cuisine throughout India, going all the way to Bengal. The famous Dhakai paratha (named after Dhaka, the capital of modern Bangladesh) is a work of art, multilayered and flaky, like a dinner-plate-size millefeuille.

The Punjabi Hindu tradition, as evident in the shops of the Paranthe-wali Gali, has left its own mark on the paratha, using a variety of stuffings instead of making multiple layers, and then deep-frying the filled bread. Potatoes, radish, green peas, dal, cauliflower, tomatoes, carrots—parathas can be stuffed with any of these. Among the more exotic elements for stuffing that this restaurant offered were mewa (solidified milk), khurchan (the layers of skin that form on hot milk, skimmed off, pressed together, and dusted with sugar), cashews, chickpea flour, even sugar. Of the ones we tried that afternoon, the best was the paratha stuffed with fried pieces of pappadam. Our waiter, having stumbled on to the fact that I had come all the way from America, urged me to continue the meal even after I felt like a stuffed paratha myself.

"Go on, eat, let me give you some more of the pumpkin dish or these asafetida–flavored potatoes, and maybe you can try a paratha with the mixed vegetable stuffing, which you haven't tasted yet," he babbled excitedly in a mixture of Punjabi and Hindi. "You'll never have a meal like this in America. Who will feed you with so much love in that cold, rich country?"

An unanswerable question.

Two days later, I traveled to Lucknow, a little over five hundred miles from the nation's capital and itself the state capital of Uttar Pradesh. Like Delhi, this city has a long pedigree, stretching back to Hindu antiquity and later acquiring the patina of Muslim royal culture. The name derives from that of Lakshman, younger brother of Rama, protagonist of the *Ramayana*, India's oldest epic. The story goes that when Rama came back from a fourteen-year exile to his father's kingdom of Ayodhya (the etymological parent of the later names, Avadh and Oudh), he decided to give this part of his domain to Lakshman as a reward for faithful companionship in exile. The more recent history of Lucknow documents the city becoming one of the principal centers of the province of Avadh when Emperor Akbar divided his realm into twelve provinces, around 1590. But it was under a dynasty of nawabs (viceroys appointed by the Mughal emperor), starting in 1722 with Burhan-ul-Mulk and lasting for more than a century, that Lucknow became the epitome of courtly refinement in architecture, art, crafts, etiquette, and food. In 1775, Lucknow became the capital of Avadh. The nawabs belonged to the Shia sect of Islam and the city remains an important center for Shiites.

At first sight, Lucknow, rising on the bank of the Gomti River, seemed to lack the bustling activity of many capital cities. As I traveled from the airport, I had the sense of a measured lifestyle that evoked the gentle courtliness of its royal past. In medieval times, Avadh was a fertile province that supplied much of imperial Delhi's food—notably during a famine in the middle of the fourteenth century. Now things are reversed. While parts of Lucknow are very green with large parks and tree-lined boulevards (many laid out by the British), the area does not grow much by way of fruits and vegetables, most of which are imported from Delhi. The one notable exception is the mango. The state of Uttar Pradesh produces some of the most memorable mangoes of India, fruits that carry names like Dusseri (from the village of Deshehari near Lucknow), Chausa, and Langra. In the spring, the mango trees lining the streets bloom with tiny, greenish-white flowers and infuse the breezes with a sweet intoxication. Even outsiders critical of India (the first Mughal emperor Babur was one) could not resist the spell of the mango. In the eighteenth and nineteenth centuries, the British, even as they cursed the hot, humid weather, the relentless monsoon rains, and the many tropical diseases that afflicted them, would generally concede that eating mangoes was a fair compensation for these travails. The nawabs of Lucknow devoted considerable resources to the development of huge mango orchards and the cross-breeding of different varieties.

It was in the older areas of town, not in the green, open areas or modern residential districts that I had to seek the remnants of the nawabs' banquet. Here, one can easily get lost in a maze of lanes and bazaars, crowded with people, shops, animals, vehicles, and houses. A ghostly glamour lingers in the air, for these were the neighborhoods inhabited in nawabi days by Lucknow's legendary courtesans who, like the geishas of Japan, entertained clients noble and common with singing, dancing, and even poetry recitals. One of the classics of Urdu literature, a nineteenth-century novel titled *Umrao Jan* by a Lucknow writer named Mirza Ruswa (made into a Bollywood hit in the seventies, starring the legendary film star Rekha) depicts the life of a courtesan named

Umrao Jan, who could not avoid heartbreak despite her charisma and her gifts.

Many of the city's historical landmarks—the Bara Imambara, the Gol Gambaz, the Macchi Bhaban (destroyed by the British, but its remaining walls still decorated with an elegant fish motif), the Rumi Darwaza, and others—are the architectural gifts of the hundred-odd years of nawabi rule. Despite the common Muslim elements of domes and minarets, they do not resemble the Mughal monuments in Delhi. A less severe, more fanciful imagination seems to have been at work behind these structures. And the cuisine of the nawabs' court, likewise, though it had many similarities with that of Delhi, had a distinctive touch that is still apparent. Part of the reason for this innovation may have been the sheer extent of self-indulgence that marked the lives of the nawabs. One had his food prepared in and served from six different kitchens. Aside from homegrown talent, renowned chefs from Delhi were hired at astronomical salaries and encouraged to give full rein to their fancy. For the royal family, as well as the elite, innovation was prized as much as the actual taste of the food. Playful deception was often the hallmark of a great rakabdar (chef), many of whom were capable of temperamental excesses on a par with those of the archetypical French chef.

Nawabs and noblemen encouraged their chefs to compete with each other in the art of culinary masquerades. The last nawab of Lucknow, Wajid Ali Shah, once invited a prince who had recently moved from Delhi to Lucknow. When a fruit conserve was served, the guest discovered, much to his consternation, that it was sweetened meat made to look like preserved fruit. Some time later, the prince invited the nawab and presented him with a lavish spread of many kinds of rice, bread, meats, and pickles. Upon tasting these, however, the nawab found that everything was made of sugar. Another chef is credited with fashioning small birds out of meat and using it in a pilaf without damaging the bird shapes. When the pilaf was served, it looked like a platter of rice on which birds were pecking. Perhaps the best instance of this kind of deception was the dessert served by a legendary chef, Pir Ali, who worked in two centers of imperial cuisine—Lucknow and Hyderabad. He served what appeared to be a whole pomegranate. On inspection, it was revealed that the seeds were made of jellied pear juice with almond kernels inside, while the thick outer rind, as well as the delicate membranes between the seeds, was made of sugar.

I was, however, most intrigued by the descriptions I had read of shirmal, a bread that Lucknow claims as its unique product. And the place to get the best shirmal, according to those who know, is Lucknow's legendary downtown eatery, Tunday Kababi. As I made my way there one evening, I did a mental inventory of northern Indian breads I had tasted. The baked, stuffed kulchas in the Amritsar dhabas and the thick, substantial chapattis at the Golden Temple; the garlic butter–lashed naan bread served with kebabs at Delhi's Bukhara restaurant, whose Afghan-style food was such a hit with President Bill Clinton that the restaurant now has a special menu called "The Presidential Platter"; the thin wheat phulkas or chapattis, puffed up with air, that I ate at my friend Gayatri Acharya's house; the deep-fried stuffed parathas of the Paranthewali Gali; the delicate, paper-thin, folded romali roti (handkerchief bread) at Karim's—each had its unique appeal but, by every account, the shirmal of Lucknow would surpass them all in delicacy and malleability. The dough for shirmal is made without any water. Only ghee and milk are used. The result is a melting-in-the-mouth softness that lingers like a caress even after the shirmal has been eaten. In the old days, a nawab's kitchen had many grades of ghee for cooking different dishes, the most prized being metha ghee, which had a sweet taste because of a special processing technique.

Tunday Kababi's shirmal, flavored with saffron, certainly lives up to its reputation, as do the kebabs and rich dishes like Shahi Chicken Masala. The restaurant faces a bazaar, and the cooking is done in the open air (though not during the monsoon). Customers order their food, then go inside and get their tables. Here, as in the Paranthewali Gali, one should not look for décor or ambience. The tables are set close to one another, and the decibel level of adult conversation and crying children can be distracting. But only till the food arrives. The restaurant serves many specialties of the courtly cuisine of Avadh/Lucknow. Two meat items that melt in the mouth as readily as shirmal are Gelavat and Kakori kebabs. Both exude a complex, entrancing fragrance of spices and kewra (screw pine blossom) water; both are entwined with stories, though the connection may be mythical. A Gelavat kebab, which is a flat, medium-sized patty of lamb, is the softer of the two, and the story goes that a chef created it to please a nawab who had lost all his teeth, but not his appetite for richly cooked meat. For a Kakori kebab, the meat is ground, mixed with spices, and wrapped around a skewer before being gently roasted on a flame. What makes it different from any other seekh (skewer) kebab is its supposed commemoration of the Kakori Train Robbery of August 9, 1925, during which Indian freedom fighters looted British treasury funds from a train going from Shahjahanpur to Lucknow. They were eventually caught, and four of them were later executed. But the kebab lives on, its texture softened with the extract of green papaya, its aroma enriched with expensive spices and the heady scent of liberation.

Over the past couple of decades, there has been a conscious effort on the part of many hotels and restaurants in India to revive the different branches of fine cuisine and popularize them. The cuisine of Avadh is, naturally, one of the prime targets of this effort. It easily transcends the barrier of regional preferences because of its mild taste and tempting richness. One of the characteristics of this style of cooking is the very fine pureeing of the ingredients for sauces and gravies. Sometimes, items like onions are first roasted or fried before being pureed and then strained, the objective being the smoothest possible gravy. As in all Muslim cookery, ghee and pounded nuts, such as cashews, are lavishly used. Kewra (screw pine) water and saffron are two other important elements, making the food more aromatic than that of Delhi's Muslim cooking. Among the more unusual creations surviving from the nawabs' kitchens are Tingri Dolma, mushrooms stuffed with minced meat; Sevian ka Muzaffar, which is made of fine strands of noodles; and Lasoon ki Kheer, a rich, custardy concoction made with garlic and evaporated milk, in which the garlic totally loses its identity. One example of a common, even throwaway item being transformed into something rich and strange is the dessert called Shahi Tukra (a royal tidbit). Again, there is an anecdote behind the dish. One of the nawabs, in his charitable moments, used to throw pieces of stale bread to the poor during his progress through the city. One day, a creative cook decided to gather some pieces, deep-fry them in ghee, steep them in syrup, and serve them with a garnish of thick evaporated milk—creating a new dessert

I learned these mouthwatering details from Nagendra Singh, a chef at the Taj Mahal Hotel in Lucknow. As marvelous as these dishes sounded, I still wondered if the nawabs did not occasionally hanker for a taste of fish and vegetables. He assured me they did. Several kinds of freshwater fish were very popular and still are. The passion for kebabs extended to the famous hariyali kebab, made with lentils and spinach. Even the humble dals were made into rich specialties like Shahi Dal, in which each grain of urad dal remained separate even after being thoroughly cooked, or Dal Sultani, in which the larger grains of arhar or toor dal (pigeon peas) were flavored with garlic, cream, and lemon.

Lucknow also has a surprising variety of sweets that can either be served as dessert, as an occasional snack, or even a late-morning amuse-bouche, stirring the gastric juices for lunch. Most of them are made either with solidified evaporated milk or lentils ground to a paste and ghee. The confectioners in Lucknow also make a few items out of chhana (cottage cheese), which they have probably learned to make from the Bengalis, but their sweets have variations in texture that are not to be found in Bengal. A legendary sweetshop, Ramasrey, which has been doing business since 1805, presents a range of sweets that illustrate the relationship between culinary trends and social conditions. The dry sweets, such as pedas, were prized by the soldiers and ordinary citizens of the Mughal Empire because of their durability in times of war. The courtly tradition, originating in the Islamic world that included Persian, Turkish, and Arabian kingdoms, is reflected in the lavish, halvahlike sweets that require profuse quantities of ghee and nuts. Lucknow's own delicate refinement is seen in items like malai paan, made with pressed layers of cream filled with sweet nuts and spices, and rolled like a betel leaf.

However, the signature dishes of Avadh's royal cuisine were indisputably the varied pilafs and biryanis that the nawabs inherited from the Mughal court and enhanced with their own extravagant touch. Aside from nuts, raisins, and many kinds of dried fruits, these rice dishes were also decorated with edible gold and silver foil. The names of different pilafs indicate the artistry that went into their preparation—the pearl, the garden, the cuckoo, the jasmine, and the light. I read about the technique for making pearl pilaf—simple to the point of greatness—in a collection of essays by a veteran Lucknow journalist, Abdul Halim Sharar, written in the early part of the twentieth century. Carefully measured amounts of gold and silver foil were beaten with an egg yolk and stuffed into the gullet of a chicken already cleaned and ready for cooking. After being kept in the oven for a while, the chicken was taken out and sliced open. The yolk and the foil had by then formed perfect, radiant globules—no less beautiful than natural pearls. These were added to the pilaf before serving. Sadly, I could not find anyone who could duplicate this creation.

Chewing paan at the end of a meal, to aid digestion and freshen one's breath, is a common habit in all parts of India even today, and the courtly culture of Lucknow endowed it with a special aesthetic. In some specialty shops, I discovered that one cone of betel leaf stuffed with special ingredients can cost as much as two hundred rupees. In the nawabs' time, the elite and members of the royal family also frequently chewed cardamom pods throughout the day, as a mark of sophistication. The Mughal court in Delhi already had the custom of offering guests a few seeds of cardamom as a mark of welcome and favor. The courtiers of Lucknow went one better in their obsession with this magic pod: They chewed cardamom seeds that had been taken out of the pod, covered in gold and silver foil, and dipped in tobacco-laced rose water—a simultaneous gratification of taste and addiction. Like the jeweled snuff boxes of Regency England or the sumptuously decorated Fabergé eggs made for a Russian czar, exquisite miniature caskets of gold and silver were made by the court jewelers of Lucknow so that the nobility could easily carry around a supply of cardamom seeds, with or without nicotine.

The practice of chewing gold- and silver-coated cardamom seeds survived well beyond the age and milieu of nawabs and princes, as I can testify. Growing up in a household of adults who loved chewing paan with its many accompaniments (including zarda [scented tobacco]), I often went with my mother to a specialty shop that provided tobacco, areca nuts, and cardamom seeds processed in a variety of ways. This was a jaunt I enjoyed, unlike the excursions to the fish market, for I knew that, at the end, I could expect a treat. Patiently, I watched the shopkeeper mix shredded tobacco in a brass bowl. Even as a child, I realized this was an art. Tiny amounts of mysterious liquids from a series of bottles were shaken into the tobacco bowl and, after each addition, the tobacco was vigorously stirred with his fingers. Strange perfumes filled the air around us, almost to the point of knocking me over. But I held on to a brass rod that ran in front of the counter, inhaling more and more deeply, enjoying an unreal sensation, determined not to pass out. Finally, the tobacco mixed to his satisfaction, the man poured it into shiny aluminum boxes, their lids engraved with the name of his shop. Once this important business was concluded and my mother had paid, he would give me a conspiratorial smile. In response, I would stretch out my palm into which he poured a large thimbleful of perfumed, silver-coated seeds of the large black cardamom. All the way home, I chewed on the seeds, a few at a time, enjoying their texture, fragrance, sweetness, and the sharpness imparted by a dash of peppermint oil. That shop has now vanished, as, I fear, has the art of mixing tobacco to satisfy individual preferences. Indians wanting perfumed tobacco in their paan now have to buy it prepackaged from big companies.

I might as well confess here that of all the Islamic courtly destinations in India, I've always had a particular fascination for Lucknow, because of the sad connection between the last nawab, Wajid Ali Shah, and my hometown, Calcutta. It is a historical denouement in which native authority was brazenly overwritten by a foreign commercial entity that had no mandate whatsoever, democratic or royal. It is also an outcome that allowed the residents of Calcutta, hundreds of miles from Lucknow, the opportunity for a close-up look at the cuisine and culture of the nawabs.

During the heyday of the nawabs, the British East India Company had already established a stronghold in the province of Avadh, doing brisk business in sugar, indigo, and calico. Far away to the east, the British had defeated the last nawab of Bengal, Seraj-ud-Daulah, at the Battle of Plassey in 1757. Over time, they also began to flex their political muscles in Avadh, trying to acquire influence, power, and territory. A series of political maneuvers and the 1764 victory in the Battle of Buxar (where military forces of both Bengal and Avadh united against the British), allowed the British to negotiate extraordinarily exploitative terms with the nawab of Avadh. However, not content even with such extreme accommodation, the British governor general in India, Lord Dalhousie, formally annexed the province of Avadh (or Oudh, as they called it) in 1856, the supposed grounds being mismanagement of the state's governance, the real objective being total control of the state's considerable resources. With hindsight, the annexation of Avadh seems as significant an indicator of the colonization of India as Hitler's *Anschluss* was of Nazi domination. Nawab Wajid Ali Shah was exiled to Calcutta, lest he rally his people around him and make trouble for the British. Although self-indulgent and effete to a fault, the nawab was also a gifted poet and musician; one of his songs, "Jab chhor chali Lucknow nagari" ("When I left the town of Lucknow"), is a piercing lament over his fate.

The nawab's entourage included not only his wives, mistresses, dancing girls, and courtiers, but also many of the royal chefs. In Calcutta, where the courtly lifestyle was limited by comparatively meager finances, the chefs had to use their ingenuity to feed the nawab the way he was used to. In a curious historical irony, the British predilection for "meat and potatoes" came to figure on the nawab's plate as well, but purely out of frugality. The potato, a foreign tuber that was slowly gaining acceptance in Indian kitchens, was liberally added as filler to biryanis and gravy-based meat dishes to reduce the expense of meat. It is a tradition that still prevails in Calcutta, when Avadh-style biryanis are prepared.

Neither Wajid Ali Shah nor the British could foretell the outcome of this ruthless expulsion. Within a year, the sepoys, or native Indian soldiers in the British army, rose up in rebellion. The legend behind this uprising—originally labeled the Sepoy Mutiny of 1857, later amended to the First War of Independence—was that both Hindu and Muslim soldiers were furious at discovering that the cartridges of their new Enfield rifles, which they had to tear open with their teeth, were greased with fat from pigs and cows. Since pigs were forbidden to Muslims and the cow was sacred to Hindus, the two communities were equally outraged and rose up together in mutiny against an insensitive foreign power. Of course, the greased cartridges were not the sole cause of a large-scale rebellion; the soldiers had already begun to fear that the British would destroy their religion and culture, and the ruthless annexation of provinces like Avadh and the deposition of the traditional ruler added to their disquiet. In any case, the uprising was surprisingly well orchestrated across the cities of northern India, and here, too, there is a food-based legend. Wheat-flour chapattis with messages concealed inside were supposedly distributed hand to hand to coordinate the time and place of action.

The besieged British Residency in Lucknow saw some of the bloodiest action of the uprising between June and November of 1857. The property has been preserved as a ruin, in memory of those who lost their lives, its walls scarred with cannon shot, its slender bricks scattered here and there, its grassy graveyard eloquent with mute headstones. Walking around the grounds, I came face-to-face with a large placard saying "Banquetting [sic] Hall," planted in front of a large building. Inside, the remains of the fireplace are still extant, and through the gaping holes that once were windows, you can hear pigeons cooing loudly. I wandered into a small room leading off from the main hall and came upon a pair of very young lovers kissing each other. Seeing me, they sprang apart in embarrassment. Equally embarrassed, I retreated hastily, but not before I had seen the half-eaten chocolate bar in the boy's hand. Had he been feeding her chocolate and then taking his share from her mouth? It was at least an image that obliterated some of the sadness of the place.

There is nothing like Lucknow's elegiac mood about Hyderabad, the capital of the southern state of Andhra Pradesh, a part of the Indian

South where several Muslim kingdoms flourished over a period of five centuries, first under the Bahamani sultans, then under the Qutb Shahi dynasty, and later under the nizams. Hyderabad not only has a rich past, it is also an up-and-coming city, brashly vying with Bangalore as a technology hub. Medieval monuments and palaces coexist happily with the gleaming glass and concrete structures of what is billed as "cyberabad."

Carved out of the rocky Deccan plateau, the massive Golconda Fort on the outskirts of modern Hyderabad is a testament to the grandeur of the past. Originally attributed to a Hindu king, the fort is permanently associated with a Muslim dynasty of Turkmans from Persia called the Qutb Shahis, who made it into a luxurious palace invested with all the comforts that contemporary art and technology could provide. The name comes from two local words: *golla*, meaning "shepherd," and *konda*, meaning "hill," and seems to fortuitously foreshadow the growth of a cuisine which centers on meat, meat, and more meat, most of it lamb. The seven rulers of the Qutb Shahi dynasty ruled the area for nearly 170 years, from the sixteenth to the seventeenth centuries. As the Shiite nawabs of Avadh had done in the north, the nizams of Hyderabad oversaw the development of a unique Muslim culture in the south, on which their adherence to Sufism left its imprint. Golconda Fort is a reminder not only of a medieval past, but also of the stony obduracy with which the old city defied the huge army of the Mughal emperor Aurangzeb who marched here from Delhi and laid siege to the fort, determined to conquer the Deccan. It took the Mughals eight months of waiting, during which time they were almost on the verge of starvation, before Golconda fell in 1687. What neither the besieged occupants of the fort nor the victorious Mughals could know was that the enforced period of siege was the gestation time for the birth of Hyderabad's unique cuisine as we know it today, a cuisine that is distinct from that of the rest of Andhra Pradesh. For, out of desperation, the Mughal army cooks foraged in the land around the castle and learned to use the local herbs and vegetables in the meals they cooked for the soldiers.

Like all conquerors from Alexander the Great onward, Aurangzeb eventually had to go back to his home base, leaving behind a deputy to administer the Deccan. In 1724, the administrator declared the region to be independent of the Mughal Empire. There was no protest, since Aurangzeb had died in 1707 and his successor had no stomach for another long march to this southern realm. Under the title of Nizam-ul-Mulk, a powerful minister at court, Asif Jan, installed himself as the ruler of the province. His descendants proceeded to govern a prosperous region for nearly 224 years. One of the secrets of their long survival (there was a nizam as recently as 1948, when India had already become an independent democratic nation) was to work out a cleverly amicable arrangement with the British, who stationed a Resident at the nizam's court, as they had in Lucknow. The nizams also successfully played off the British against the French, who were trying to get a foothold in southern India.

It was in the kitchen of the nizam's palace that Lucknow's famous chef Pir Ali performed some of his miracles. On one occasion, he delighted the nizam's distinguished English guests by presenting a gigantic pie that contained tiny, live birds, which flew away when the piecrust was cut open. Reading the story, I wondered whether Pir Ali's opus could have had some strange, convoluted connection with the English nursery rhyme, "Sing a song of sixpence, pocket full of rye/Four and twenty blackbirds baked in a pie."

While the elite cookery of Delhi and Lucknow still demonstrates its Persian–Afghan–Central Asian roots, not merely in the techniques of preparing pilaf or meat, but also in the selection of ingredients, Hyderabad's Muslim cuisine has a strongly Southern identity. Aside from the famed pilafs and meat dishes, the cooking of vegetables also demonstrates notable flare and ingenuity. The flavors of mustard seeds, kari and ghungura leaves, hot chilies, peanuts, tamarind, and coconut milk merge into a flavorful entity that is found nowhere else.

However, as any Hyderabad resident will tell you, this is a cuisine in which meat rules. The city is like an island where, despite the significant presence of vegetarians all around, the residents cannot imagine a meal without meat. This goes for both Hindus and Muslims. Even breakfast, which for nonvegetarian Indians elsewhere generally means eggs, becomes here a meal of tiny samosas filled with meat, or bread with nehari, a rich soup made out of lamb trotters. For weddings or other celebrations, even the poorest person will somehow scrape together money to buy basmati rice, ghee, meat, and spices to make biryani for the guests. So ingrained is the notion of biryani being the food of festivity that Hyderabad's Hindus will even eat biryani to celebrate the great annual festival of Diwali, which, in other parts of the country, is usually the occasion for a vegetarian feast. Another sturdy meat concoction, which came to India from the Middle East and was enjoyed by both the sultans and the Mughal emperors, became a renowned delicacy in the hands of Hyderabad's chefs. Haleem (if it is made with lamb) or harees (if made with chicken) is a substantial pottage that combines meat with five kinds of dal and cracked grains of wheat, all of which are cooked in milk and then pounded to a pulp with wooden mallets. Afterward, the mash is cooked in ghee with fried onions, chili peppers, coriander, and cream. The entire process can take quite a few hours. In medieval times, this was a convenient one-dish nourishment for soldiers in the Mughal army. In modern Hyderabad, the aroma of the dish suffuses the air mostly during the abstemious days of Ramadan. After the day's arduous fast, it becomes a nourishing and tasteful evening meal.

I arrived in Hyderabad with one overriding mental assignment—to taste the biryani and find how distinctively different it was from its counterpart in northern India. I remembered Rahul Verma in Delhi telling me that he much preferred the Hyderabad biryani over Avadh's dish. But in Calcutta during my childhood, there was much greater mystique attached to the biryanis and pilafs of Avadh, especially because of their exquisite aromatic signature. The nizams of Hyderabad were better known to us for their fabulous wealth than for their inventive kitchens.

One of the important differences in the two biryanis is that, in Hyderabad, the meat is not precooked when it is added to the rice—an apparent conundrum, since meat takes far longer to cook than rice. Even more surprising, no water is added to the pot. The juices released by the meat are supposed to provide just the right amount of moisture. And as I discovered for myself, both are cooked to perfection. The secret lies in the selection of only the most delicate portions of young animals, in the ingredients used to marinate and tenderize the meat, in the length of marinating time, and, finally, in the sealing of the pot in which the biryani is cooked. Surprisingly, the cooking doesn't take more than half an hour, at most. Even more surprising, the biryani is often served with a thin stew in which long, fat, green chilies have been simmered in a tangy broth. The ingredients of the broth include copra (dried coconut), sesame, whole coriander, whole cumin, and peanuts, which are all roasted and ground together before going into the broth with tamarind and brown sugar. This mirch ka salan is poured over the biryani, and the two are eaten together. Although the chilies look fearsome, they are quite mild, like Italian peppers. *Salan* is the generic name for a stew; when you get tired of the large peppers, other vegetables can be used to make the salan accompanying the biryani.

The spicier register of the biryani, the thinness of the pieces of meat, and the addition of the salan—all added up to a novel eating experience, but did not dislodge the Avadh biryani from its superior position in my mind. Could this be rooted in some peculiar fascination for the hapless nawab Wajid Ali Shah, living out his days as an exile in my city, eventually dying in London? I think not. The best-known portrait of the nawab shows a grossly overweight person, done up in the jewels and regalia of the day, his upper lip overshadowed by a thick, well-curled mustache, his hair drooping to his shoulders like grape clusters, one nipple bared through the loop of his dress, as decreed by fashion. Not the kind of figure to arouse romantic visions in my head; only a rather pathetic symbol of India's failure to resist the voracious appetite of the British.

Biryani aside, however, Hyderabad has a whole slew of delightful dishes that any region could be proud of. Take pathar ka gosht: Scallops of lamb, cut very thin, are marinated for eight to ten hours with the juice of green papaya, garam masala, and crushed green chilies. They are then grilled on the pathar (stone), a two-inch-thick slab of granite that is heated over a blazing charcoal fire. My friend Shermeen Ahmed, who grew up in Hyderabad before moving to Dubai with her husband, once told me that these stones are heirloom pieces, passed on from mother to daughter. They are never washed, only rubbed clean after each use. Another special Hyderabad concoction, chigur ka gosht, was one of her childhood favorites. It is a springtime dish, when the tamarind is in bloom, and the tiny flowers are harvested and cooked with boneless mutton, adding both fragrance and flavor. The renowned dum ka murgh is an example of a courtly dish enlivened with local touches. Almonds, cashews, and chironji (lentil-shaped, mildly almond-flavored nuts) are ground up with dried coconut, green chilies, and fried onions to form the basis of the gravy in which a chicken is cooked.

Along with their rapturous descriptions of meat dishes, however, a number of people reminded me that the cuisine is not really one-dimensional. Legumes and vegetables do have a role and are transformed by using typically Southern ingredients. Dalcha is one example. As Rajarshi Guriya, the executive chef at the Fortune Katriya Hotel, told me succinctly: "Dalcha *is* Hyderabad." Two kinds of dal, toor and chana (chickpeas), are cooked, pureed fine, and tempered with ghee, mustard seeds, and kari leaves. Tamarind pulp and brown sugar are added for a sweet-and-sour taste. The versatility of dalcha is demonstrated by its different incarnations. Different types of vegetables, or even meat, can be added to dalcha for seasonal flavors or richness of taste.

No cuisine in post-medieval India could have developed ignoring potatoes and Hyderabad is no exception. William Dalrymple's *White Mughals* is a magnificent reconstruction of life in eighteenth-century Hyderabad, with all its political intrigues and maneuvers of colonial and imperial power. He quotes from a letter written to a friend in Calcutta by James Kirkpatrick, the British Resident at the court of the nizam. Hankering for the vegetables to which his Western palate is accustomed—peas, French beans, lettuce, endive, celery, cabbage and cauliflower—Kirkpatrick laments that the only thing available in Hyderabad is the eggplant. What he really longs for is "a good supply of potatoes, being a vegetable I like much but have not tasted these two years and more."

Two centuries later, the popularity and ubiquity of potatoes in the

Indian meal demonstrates the conquering power of this magic tuber. The cooks of Hyderabad can be credited with using it to make a dish called veppudu, to which even a Bengali like me might be willing to concede equal status with the dam and chachhari and bharta we make with potatoes. It is a dry and spicy dish in which baby potatoes are peeled, boiled, and then fried with onions, ginger, and roasted and ground spices such as turmeric and coriander. The oil in which the potatoes are fried is first tempered with whole red chilies, mustard seeds, and tiny portions of yellow split peas and urad dal. A final garnish of chopped kari leaves and mint leaves adds freshness and fragrance.

As for the humble eggplant so derided by James Kirkpatrick, in Hyderabad the vegetable has as mystical a status as in Turkish or Middle Eastern cuisine. It is impossible to overstate its significance in India's food, given its long availability as an indigenous vegetable. Every regional cuisine in India has developed its own array of eggplant recipes, but in terms of richness and delicacy of preparation, Hyderabad is the winner every time. Baghare baingan is almost as famous as Hyderabad's biryani, and has titillated the palates of both nizams and commoners. It is not just Indian bias that makes me say that it outdoes the Turkish *imam bayaldi* (literally, the imam fainted—a stuffed eggplant dish) in its potential to make the consumer faint with pleasure.

One sunny morning, I decided to drive out of the city to Golconda Fort, wanting to savor the atmosphere of a hardier, simpler era when biryanis and luscious meats might not yet have fully developed their opulent potential. As the streets narrowed and the density of population and transportation decreased, I noticed a small Hindu temple standing right next to a butcher's shop filled with caged chickens and hanging animal carcasses. I was amazed. The South has a reputation for being dominated by Brahminical Hinduism, which advocates strict vegetarianism; its temples are barred to Muslims. Yet, in this undistinguished neighborhood, I saw a series of worshippers entering the temple and performing their rituals absolutely unfazed either by the contiguity of the shop or the Muslim name on the signboard. I doubted that I would see such close coexistence even in my state of West Bengal, which has a reputation for communal tolerance. I thought about the terrible religious rioting that had recently torn apart the state of Gujarat, where the nonviolent religions of Buddhism and Jainism had once flourished. I remembered the even worse trauma of the 1992 riots in Uttar Pradesh, when a mosque had been destroyed by Hindu religious fundamentalists on the grounds that a Muslim emperor had built the mosque after destroying a temple honoring Rama. Would it be possible to construct a different history if we learned to tolerate or even simply ignore each other's food?

Inside Golconda Fort, there is an echo that sounds from the entrance all the way up to the royal chambers at the top, as tour guides will tell you. The diamond-shaped niches in the dome of the front portico trap sound and transmit it upward—a clever way for a ruler to know who was coming near him. Hearing all the visitors happily clapping away and pausing to listen to the echo filled me with a sudden sharp awareness of the continuity of Indian history. However, by the time I had climbed all the way to the top of the fort and made my way down, my feet sore from stumbling over broken, unstable rocks and uneven grassy surfaces, my face burning in the heat, my eyes dazzled by the southern sun to the point of hallucinating, I was ready to walk out on history and seek more edible experiences.

Small things are big indicators of cultural predilections. And two shops in Hyderabad provided me with an example. This is a city with an inordinate passion for baked goods, probably even more than the centers of European dominion like Goa or Calcutta. In shops like Karachi Bakery or Sarvi Bakery and Café, large batches of cookies, cakes, and "puffs" (flaky pastry stuffed with chicken, meat, or vegetables) vanish from the glass cabinets at record speed. Bakeries flourish here with the same assurance as sweetshops in Calcutta. According to Pradeep Khosla, executive chef at the Taj Krishna Hotel in Hyderabad, hard-baked crackers, cookies, and meat-filled pastries called tutaqs were part of Mughal army rations. During the eight-month siege of Golconda Fort, when the Mughal army had to camp out for eight months, a two-way exchange of food and culinary habits began to flourish. The locals acquired a taste for these baked flour products and, in the absence of familiar ingredients, the emperor's officers, commanders, and soldiers learned to recast their Delhi-style cooking with the spices, herbs, vegetables, and grains that grew on the rocky plateau of the Deccan. Over time, under the patronage of the nizams, gifted chefs came up with specialties that have now joined the endangered species list. I remembered Shermeen Ahmed's rapturous descriptions of the courtly descendants of the soldiers' biscuit. One, called badam ki jali, is made with marzipan shaped in floral molds; two flowers are put together with a layer of edible silver foil in between, and baked. Another, called ashrafi, is made of marzipan mixed with ground saffron, and is a sweet replica of the old coin of the nizam regime. As with so many delicacies, only a handful of families still know how to make these items, and they are likely to take their secrets to the grave.

At eleven thirty in the morning, Sarvi Bakery was already full of young people eagerly buying up their chosen goodies, some taking them away in boxes, others standing in the shop and devouring them with gusto. Most of them seemed to be college students or young professionals, very probably working in the call centers and software companies that are rapidly multiplying in Indian cities. I watched them with envy. The capacity to demolish large quantities of rich, filled pastries and still be able to eat lunch is a gift that only comes with youth.

My young friend Ananya, who had accompanied me on this bakery jaunt, belonged to the category of software migrants. She and her husband had grown up in Calcutta and gone to the States for higher education. Ananya's husband had started his own dot.com, sold it at a substantial profit, and then joined the buyer corporation, which had sent him to India to start their Hyderabad operation. They lived in a pleasant gated compound in the suburb called Banjara Hills, and their two children were growing up learning to eat rava (semolina) dosa, or paserattu (a thin pancake made with green moong dal paste) instead of toast, eggs, and cereal for breakfast. The daughter, who was old enough to go to the International School, had lost her American accent and inflected English

words in the Telugu (the language of Andhra Pradesh) way. Even as
Ananya and her husband enjoyed their life in Hyderabad, they knew that
in a few years they might have to retrace their steps back to the United
States. It was a pattern of repeated migration that their parents could
never have dreamed of.

After sharing one of the chicken puffs—deliciously flaky and
spicy—Ananya and I decided to find a tea shop serving Irani chai, another Hyderabad addiction. But though it was called Irani, it did not
taste any different from the cardamom-scented milky tea sold in northern Indian tea shops. At our next eating stop, Ananya insisted I have a
taste of another typical Hyderabad dish, though it has nothing to do
with Muslim royalty. Chicken 65, as it is called, is an upstart concoction,
consisting of pieces marinated in yogurt, and cooked with fresh kari
leaves and other spices. Mythmaking about food has not died out in the
modern age, and there are two versions of how Chicken 65 came by its
name. The more obvious one is that the chef who invented it used
sixty-five different spices in the marinade. The other, which tickles my
fancy more, is that the chicken used for this dish always has to be sixty-
five days old.

For dessert that afternoon, it had to be yet another oddity. Hyderabad, I learned, is famous for its ice-cream shops in the old town, near
the landmark that symbolizes the city—the Char Minar, an elegant
monument built by Mohammed Quli Qutb Shah in 1591. The slim
minarets soar up to 180 feet and provide a breathtaking view of the city
spread below. We made our way past the Char Minar into the old market area, where bangle shops displayed shelves filled with exquisite mir-
rorwork bangles, glinting under a blaze of neon. Women in colorful
burqas held out their bared wrists, and the male shop assistants squeezed
their hands and slipped on the bangles one by one by one—a peculiar
circumvention of the conservative Islamic taboos against touching between the sexes. The bargaining in Telugu was, however, vociferous and
utterly unromantic. Making one's way through this absorbed, unyielding
crowd was hot work and the prospect of ice cream or kulfi enticing.

Modern ice cream is an appropriate corollary of the medieval food tradition that gave India the kulfi, which was either brought in by the Mughals from their previous habitations in Kabul and Samarkand, or developed by them in response to the torrid heat of the upper Gangetic plain. Whatever the origin, the kulfi has remained remarkably un-changed through the centuries. It is named after the conical metal vessel in which a portion of khoa—obtained by boiling milk down to a solid form—is frozen. In Mughal days, probably an ice-salt mixture was used to freeze it.

The ice cream served in Hyderabad's shops today, as in the rest of India, is the product of interaction between East and West. Europeans, especially the ruling British, suffered even more than did Mughals in In-dia's tropical heat. In a curious quirk of history, the ability to supply ice on a commercial scale and the subsequent introduction of ice cream into India linked the world's oldest and youngest immigrant nations. It was an American, Frederick Tudor, who first successfully shipped ice from Boston to Calcutta in 1833. The event must have made the news in New England. Henry David Thoreau wrote in *Walden*, "Thus it ap-pears that the sweltering inhabitants of Charleston and New Orleans, of Madras, and Bombay, and Calcutta drink at my well . . . The pure Walden water is mingled with the sacred water of the Ganges." The same Frederick Tudor is also credited with introducing the technique of making ice cream to both India and Iran.

Sitting with Ananya inside the stark interior of Hyderabad's most famous ice-cream shop, I wondered what Frederick Tudor would think of the offerings listed on a board against the blue wall. Under the cate-gory of "Brick," which I took to mean large square blocks, you could have the following flavors: Mango, Pista (pistachio), Vanilla, Stabry (strawberry), Anjeer (fig), Dry Fruit (no further definition available), and Butterscotch. Questions elicited only enormous grins, not answers, from the man waiting on us. Another board carried illustrations of two items, the Chocobar, popular with kids, and the traditional Kulfi. A third advertised the Kasata, which was a pyramid sporting the colors of the Indian national flag—a reddish-orange strawberry, a white vanilla, and a green pistachio. Since the "brick" could be bought in quarters and halves, we ordered portions of mango and vanilla. The texture of the handmade ice cream and the intensity of the flavors were astonishing. As we spooned up the confection, the relief from the heat and humidity outside became more and more palpable. Unlike the Anjeer ka roll (fig cooked with sugar like a preserve and encased in a shell of solidified evaporated milk), which was introduced by a Turkish princess who married into the nizam family a hundred years ago, the ice cream has no association with nizams or nawabs. But as I ate, I felt convinced they would have relished this foreign invention even as they rued the foreign invasions that eventually unseated them.

The descendants of the nizams still live in the city and maintain homes in the countryside. One of them, Mehboob Alam Khan, is reputed to be both a connoisseur of good food and a gifted cook. At one of his dinners, he is said to have served forty dishes, all made with lamb, but each one different. Every Sunday, he indulges his love of cooking in the cause of philanthropy. He goes to his native village and prepares a substantial lunch for three hundred or so villagers. The menu consists of perennial Hyderabad favorites—pilaf, biryani, a variety of chicken dishes, a hot and sour fish stew, a salan of large peppers. Only when the villagers have been served do Khan and his family sit down for their own meal. *Noblesse oblige* is still a motto to live by in the new millennium.

Chapter Eight

BENARAS: FEASTING AND FASTING IN SHIVA'S CITY

Delhi and Lucknow may symbolize the patrician Islamic culture of northern India, but there is another city in the state of Uttar Pradesh (of which Lucknow is the capital) that faces the world as Hinduism's most sacred site. Varanasi, more familiarly called Benaras, is noted for its temples, ghats (steps leading down to a river), pilgrims, and funeral rites, as well as its music and street food. It is a peculiarly photogenic city where beauty asserts itself in spite of claustrophobic, malodorous lanes often blocked by the slow progress of a bull; the cloying smell of offerings and incense; and a river choked with urban waste and the detritus of human cremation. In

Benaras the business of death surmounts the business of worship, since Hindus have believed for centuries that dying here ensures freedom from rebirth and permanent salvation. As the river flows past the cremation grounds every day, you see flowers offered to the dead being carried by a current that has witnessed the unbearable and the unspeakable.

I was not interested in doing penance or finding salvation. I went to Benaras looking for its worldly side, the side that glories in the pleasures of food and drink, the side that has survived with hedonistic panache in spite of the overwhelming aura of sanctity projected by temples, priests, and worshippers. But the first thing that confronted me there made a far greater impact than either the sacred or the secular. It was a human tragedy I had always known about and yet pushed aside from the forefront of my mind. Benaras has been, for centuries, the final destination for Hindu widows, particularly young widows, packed off by their families to live out the rest of their days surrounded by holiness, while forced to endure nearly intolerable deprivation. Although widows from many parts of India, especially northern India, were regularly exiled to Benaras, probably no other state sent as many as my region, Bengal.

The life of the Hindu widow has always been the dark side of eating in India, and nowhere was it darker than in Bengal. Not only was the Bengali widow forbidden to remarry, as were widows from other regions, she was also expected to give up a large number of common foods permanently. In a fish-loving culture, she was forced to become a vegetarian, giving up fish, meat, eggs, and even lentils, onion, and garlic for her entire lifetime, which was also punctuated by frequent, rigorous fasts. Her husband's death was traditionally attributed to her misdeeds and unnatural appetites; a common word of abuse in rural Bengal translates as "husband-eater." Guilty of the sin of survival, she was considered a personification of disaster and bad luck, and as such, her presence was forbidden at any happy ceremony, particularly weddings. If she was allowed to stay with the family, her days were often spent in unmitigated drudgery. In times past, when very young girls were often married off to doddering old men, these deprived lives extended over many years— a dreadful experience of thwarted desire.

Many families banished their young widows to pilgrimage centers like Benaras for a variety of motives—to avoid scandalous possibilities like clandestine affairs and illegitimate pregnancies, or to appropriate the widow's property, or simply to not deal with any sense of guilt or compunction produced by her presence. Hundreds of miles away from home, these lonely exiles were expected to find sublimation in devotion. In reality, the sacredness of the city was small compensation for their isolation and deprivation. Most lived like penitents waiting for the end long before it was due. Others, unable to live on the meager pittance sent by their families, ended up as beggars or prostitutes. The pleasures of food, which might have partially compensated for the absence of a married life, were on display all around them, only to underscore the cruelty of fate.

As one might expect, widows from poor, rural, and uneducated families always fared the worst. They are the ones who still throng the temples and riverbanks of holy cities. But with urbanization and education, the custom is slowly dying. My personal experience of a widow's life was rather different. I watched my grandmother spend the last twenty-seven years of her life as a widow. There was no question of banishing her anywhere. Nor did anyone even dream of blaming her for her husband's death. Urban, middle-class families in Bengal had already moved into a different way of thinking. Yet, there was no escaping the sense of separateness that was imposed on her simply because of her widowed status. I saw her change overnight, from a bossy, middle-aged woman wearing a sari with a wide red border and bangles on both arms, into a silent, shadowy figure in white. No borders, no color, no jewelry. Later, as a teenager, I mostly noticed the strictures relating to food. How did she feel, I wondered, when the large serving dishes of meat cooked for Sunday lunch were brought in from the kitchen, filling the entire floor with its rich, spicy aroma? Or when we ate fish jhol, with tiny new potatoes and green peas bobbing up and down? My grandmother served the food, but never dined with us. Sitting away from everyone in a solitary corner, she ate her simple vegetarian meal. Dinner often was nothing more than some fruit, milk, and a bit of popped rice. At the beginning of the monsoon came three days in the Bengali calendar when it was forbidden for the widow's food to be touched by fire. My grandmother cooked enough food (with the exception of rice, which was not allowed) to last her for that time, but she could not reheat anything. Watching the cold, stale luchis on her plate almost put me off my favorite food. And then there were those days when she hardly ate a thing. Unsaid penance? Unthinking observance? I still don't know.

On the train to Benaras, however, I was not thinking about exiled widows. They had not yet resurrected themselves in my consciousness. It was the city's long history that occupied my mind. Even in a country filled with ancient legends, Benaras is remarkable. Although its beginnings are shrouded in myth and mystery, Benaras was already a well-developed settlement in 550 B.C., when Buddha came to preach his message. Rising on the left bank of the River Ganges, it was often referred to as Kashi, the City of Light, though unlike Paris, the evocation this epithet carries is entirely spiritual. In the course of history, the sacred city of the Hindus attracted the wrath of Muslim conquerors and rulers who demolished many of the temples and built mosques on some of the sites. The Mughal emperor Aurangzeb—the same who besieged Golconda Fort for eight months—was one of them. He built two of the city's landmarks, the Gyanvapi Mosque and the Alamgir Mosque.

But such destructive episodes are nothing more than the quiver of a frown line on the forehead of Shiva, the patron deity of Benaras. The city's most famous temple, the Kashi Vishwanath Temple, is dedicated to him, its gold-plated spire making it the Golden Temple for Hindus. In many ways, Shiva remains the most intriguing member of the Hindu pantheon. My early conception of him came from a framed portrait in our house. This was no phallic symbol like the countless ones you encounter in shrines, homes, and even street corners. It limned a serene face, half-closed eyes (including the all-seeing third eye in the forehead, a crescent moon underneath serving as a third eyebrow), a towering bunch of dreadlocks on the head, and a large snake coiled round the neck, rather like a feather boa. The portrait was neither a painting nor a photograph. My mother had embroidered it on canvas and displayed it prominently in the small room set aside for the gods. A teenager today, if he or she were to observe this image without preconceived notions of piety or disrespect, might easily find Shiva to be downright cool.

The myths and stories about Shiva that have grown over the centuries represent an astonishing amalgam of widely disparate imaginations. For one thing, despite being a god, he is perpetually high on bhang and ganja, hallucinogens extracted from the dried leaves and flowers of the cannabis plant. He is also pictured as the sole ascetic among a pantheon of deities who seem as desire-driven and power-hungry as humans. His utter indifference to material comforts has conferred on him the name of Ashutosh, he who is easy to please. In a male-dominated society, women prayed for a husband who would be as easygoing as Shiva, though more endowed with wealth and comforts.

The best stories about Shiva focus on love and marriage. In one, the princess Parvati, whose father was Himalaya, the king of the mountains, encounters this divine ascetic in the forest and falls madly in love. She woos him by leaving her comfortable home and spending eons living like an ascetic herself. In another story, depicting the more human side of Shiva, he marries Sati, the daughter of a king called Daksha. When her father insults Shiva, calling him a pauper and a junkie, Sati chooses to die—the ultimate act of protest. The serene Shiva goes mad with rage and sorrow. He picks up her body and whirls through the universe until all creation is on the brink of annihilation. At the urging of gods and men, Vishnu, the second powerful god of the Hindu trinity, cuts Sati's body to pieces with his magical whirling discus. With the loss of his wife's body, Shiva comes to his senses and the world returns to its normal state. In Bengal, where the great and powerful goddess Durga is worshipped for three days each autumn, she is perceived as the wife of Shiva, the mother of his four children, a royal princess who has given up all the trappings of wealth and gone out begging with her rice bowl to support her family—all out of love for Shiva. Whenever I heard these stories, expertly narrated by my grandmother, I was ready to fall in love with Shiva myself.

But then there was the other aspect of Shiva as Nataraj, the cosmic dancer, who starts the process of dissolution of the universe when it is old and decayed. It was hard for me to reconcile that image with everything else I had been told, particularly when I contemplated the serene image embroidered by my mother. As I grew older, the portrait made me think of Shiva as a center of stillness and detachment, a last court of appeal in the maze of dilemmas and traumas that made up life—an idea that seemed utterly ironic later, when I considered the exile of Hindu widows to Shiva's holy city.

The Ganges, India's holiest river, adds to the sacredness of Benaras. In Hindu mythology, she is a goddess who resided in the dreadlocks gracing Shiva's head. An ancient king prayed and fasted for a long time and persuaded her to come down to earth to purify and reanimate the remains of his ancestors. Although the Ganges flows through the central Indian plain all the way to the Bay of Bengal on the east, it makes a crescent-shaped detour in Benaras, changing its flow from south to north, as if longing to go back to its source in the Himalayas. The eastern bank, facing Benaras, has been left mostly undeveloped except for an ancient royal palace. The bare stretch on the other side can almost serve as a metaphor for the state of salvation, which entails the shedding of both the mortal coil and the material needs of life on earth. It further reinforces the Hindu belief about dying in Benaras to obtain salvation. For centuries, people have come to Benaras as they sensed the approach of death. Some were even taken to the riverbank by their families to await the end (for days if necessary), so that their last sight and sound would be that of the holy Ganges whose waters can wash away all sins. For the living, too, a daily dip in the Ganges has the same purifying effect.

After checking into a hotel, the first thing I did was to slowly make my way to the river, like any tourist. The afternoon light was strong; and there I saw them. Widows leaning out of ramshackle balconies, crowding in front of the temples, sitting on the concrete ghats by the river, standing waist deep in water and praying with their eyes closed, all dressed in dingy white, many with shaved heads, their somber faces lined with resignation that seemed worse than anger. Some sat on the steps with begging bowls into which people dropped coins, no doubt to further their chances of salvation. Others, after bathing and praying, gathered for sermons around priests and Brahmins who sat and read aloud from Hindu holy texts. One group of widows chanted hymns, rocking to a monotonous rhythm. What would they eat when they went home? A lump of cold boiled rice and a few vegetables, perhaps. Or maybe a couple of dry chapattis. Or a handful of puffed rice and some roasted chickpeas. Or it could be nothing. Perhaps only one meal was permissible and that had already been consumed.

Knowledge is inescapable. Ever since I had learned about the fate of Hindu widows, especially the fish-deprived Bengali ones, these women had inhabited my dreams, my awareness; but, like many uncomfortable truths, they had been pushed back into invisibility. Benaras paraded them before me in the garish light of a stuffy afternoon. In a country that boasts of hospitality to strangers, these daughters, mothers, and sisters were humiliated with unsatisfied hunger and desire, every single day. This was one of the many contradictions of India, even modern, youthful, up-and-coming India. Despite my lack of religious faith, I almost felt like petitioning Shiva—the one who had inspired such love in a princess that she willingly renounced her wealth for his ascetic lifestyle—to let loose his cosmic energy and rewrite these lives.

The ghats are shallow, tiered steps, starting high above the river in front of the city's fabled temples. Each ghat has a name and a story. I went down one set of steps until I came to the bottom. Looking to my left, I saw the smoke rising from another ghat further downriver. This had to be the Manikarnika ghat, where the dead are cremated after last rites have been performed. Despite my Hindu ancestry, I had never been to a cremation ground before. Swirls of smoke rose from the pyres, mercifully obscuring the human remains that were being processed. But there was no missing the charred logs, flower garlands, and other remainders of death rituals that floated on the water. The bells ringing in the temples behind me and the chanting of Sanskrit mantras addressed to the gods filled me not with serenity, but gloom. The sluggish Ganges looked like a river to the underworld, not heaven.

I turned my back on the river, climbed up the stairs, and went into the city. The business of death can only thrive on the shoulders of the living. I needed to find a place where there was no obsession with death, widowhood, or the rituals of privation.

The secular realm of Benaras bustles with humanity, a choking, concrete miscellany of boxy office buildings and brightly painted narrow houses, dirty alleys, and traffic-clogged crossroads. Amid the crowd and the squalor, there is a spirit that is hospitable, enterprising, and pulsing with life. Like Lucknow, Benaras had a reputation for beautiful courtesans and dancing girls who entertained their guests with utmost sophistication. Although these women have vanished along with a way of life created by wealthy landlords and princes, the narrow, winding, congested lanes of Benaras are alive with another form of live entertainment. Vendors serve and customers wolf down quick-cooked fare that is cheap, hot, and freshly made, running the gamut of flavor, texture, and temperature. Benaras's fast food is not all that different from that of other cities. I saw potato patties called aloo tikias; the phuchkas we ate in Calcutta; chaats, with their typical crunchy-soft textures; and that delightful invention, kachori, which has as many incarnations as a Hindu god. Kachoris are stuffed disks of crisply fried dough, but the outer texture and the inner filling can make them either plebeian or gourmet fare. The ones sold in the fabled Kachori Galli in Benaras are to die for, their fillings including asafetida-flavored dal paste and a spicy combo of peas and potatoes. Eating piping hot kachoris together with ghugni, a concoction of chickpeas, with dollops of tart and zesty chutneys on the side, can be more satisfying than meals in many five-star restaurants. If much of the pilgrim's day is fasting and praying and cleansing the soul, more than enough compensation for the body awaits them in these hole-in-the-wall eateries.

In one undistinguished backstreet, I came upon a preparation of cubed cooked potatoes seasoned with hot, molten clarified butter, a dollop of yogurt, chopped fresh cilantro, and a dash of syrup. The taste was eclectic and delicious. There were savories galore, including the familiar samosas stuffed with peas, cauliflower, and potatoes; fritters made with chopped spinach and chickpea batter; and crisply fried pappadams. Eager jostling crowds kept lining up all afternoon and well into the evening, and a patient eavesdropper could hear conversations in multiple Indian languages.

If the street food of Benaras conforms to the greater Indian tradition, the drinks carry the city's unique signature. Despite the intrusion of colas and sodas that have become quenchers of choice in places like Calcutta and Bombay, the residents of Benaras still retain a passion for milk-based concoctions that reminded me of the American love of shakes and frappés. Coming as a student from Calcutta, where milk was expensive and sometimes unavailable, I had been blown away by the literalness with which one could describe America as the land of milk and honey. Supermarket shelves groaned under the weight of cartons and bottles of plain and flavored milk. In my dormitory cafeteria, fellow students supplemented their platefuls of food with glasses of thick, creamy milk that they downed the way I drank water. I could not acquire their taste for the white stuff, but I never ceased to marvel at its easy, cheap availability, at the tall glasses of chocolate milkshakes that I saw children drinking.

In Benaras I saw an Indian city with an enthusiasm for and seemingly equal availability of milk. Very early one morning, I wandered onto a street that widened into a small square cul-de-sac. In front of a sweetshop, the owner was already at work with a couple of assistants. Two enormous black kadhais sat on portable stoves, one containing gently bubbling milk, the other full of oil. Fascinated, I watched as, time after time, the sweet maker skimmed off the puckered skin that formed on top of the hot milk. These creamy layers would then be pressed together, cut into squares, and floated in a sweetened milk syrup scented with saffron and garnished with pistachio, to make that utterly sinful dessert—rabri.

The confectioner's head was completely shaven, except for a tiny lock of hair at the back. From the hygiene perspective, this was an easier alternative to wearing a chef's cap, especially in a hot climate, but its purpose was likely to indicate that he was a Brahmin. In caste-bound Hindu society, the Brahmin not only had status as a priest, he was also desirable as a cook, since his touch was pure enough for the food to be eaten by everybody, including other Brahmins, and also offered to the gods. After a while, although we hadn't spoken a word, the man concluded I must be hanging around waiting for the typical street breakfast of hot milk and sweets. A slightly chipped glass full of hot milk was extended to me. At this hour and in this space, I felt I could not refuse. I took small sips, and diverted myself watching the other two men frying jilebis. But not for long, since I knew I risked being handed a plate of those, too.

The Benaras residents' passion for dairy was demonstrated in countless other places. Later that same afternoon, I found myself in another section of town where vendors sold the yogurt-based lassi that has become so popular in Indian restaurants in America. The drink was served in clay containers called kulhads. Standing away from the line of customers, I watched them down their stuff and smash the containers by throwing them on the ground, as we used to do with earthen cups of chai on the trains of my childhood. For those who did not care for yogurt, there were milky concoctions in many flavors and colors, but these were served in glasses that were definitely not to be smashed. The steam arising out of some glasses again demonstrated the preference for milk to be served hot.

"Madam wants to buy a drink?"

I spun around to find a portly, balding man behind me, dressed in a crisply starched embroidered Indian kurta and white pajamas. He was no poor pilgrim, satisfying hunger and thirst at the least possible expense, as I could tell from his pudgy fingers, each adorned with a heavy gold ring sporting a different gemstone.

As the stranger's smile widened, it revealed teeth stained not only by betel leaf and areca nut, but also the telltale tint of tobacco. I glanced around and realized, that propelled by curiosity, I had unconsciously inched forward and broken into the line of customers.

"I'm sorry, I didn't mean to get in your way," I replied. Quickly, I made my way down the lane, bumping into backs, elbows, purses, and bags, marveling at the endless business of cooking, blending, and eating that was going on. This unself-conscious yet focused voracity was what I had missed in other, bigger cities. Perhaps, I thought, when a city is celebrated as a destination for dying, its residents develop an unusual intensity for living. Even within the corsetlike confines of an odorous lane where two can barely walk abreast, nothing could distract the eaters from eating, not even the massive bulls and sprightly goats that occasionally pushed their way through. Bulls have special status in Benaras, not simply because of the Hindu reverence for the sacred cow, but also because of the belief that when Shiva needs a ride, it is the great bull, Nandi, who carries him.

Before long, I found myself being accosted again by the same person. He had finished his drink and caught up with me much sooner than I would have thought possible.

"I can see you're a tourist," he said. "I don't mean to bother you, but this is my city and I could tell you a few things that guidebooks won't. That is, if you care to tell me what particularly interests you."

"Everything," I said blandly.

"Everything?" he repeated, clearly taken aback. He must have expected me to say architecture, religion, history, or some such thing.

I nodded, hoping that would make him give up on me and go away. But he was made of tenacious stuff.

"Well, here you can experience street food in Benaras, madam," he said, with an expansive gesture of his arm. "The items are not all that different from what you get in other cities, but the people of Benaras, I think, eat everything with more enjoyment."

I was surprised to have my own perceptions echoed so well.

"However," he continued, "if you want something that's really special to Benaras, you need to drink, not eat. Have you tasted the sherbets yet? Have you had thandai?"

I shook my head, slowing down despite myself.

"Oh, madam, you must. But first, I must introduce myself."

He fished out a business card from his breast pocket and held it out. I was almost about to take it, when an irrational impulse overcame me. With hindsight, I like to think it was the worldly spirit of Benaras, whispering that even the slightest intimacy should be carefully considered.

"Please," I said, smiling to take the offense out of my words, "let's not be conventional. Since this is your city, let me think of you as the voice of Benaras. Let's talk about the city, about the people, about these drinks that seem to promise such revelation, not about ourselves."

A short, fraught silence, broken by laughter. My companion was prepared to be a good sport, for the moment. And the moment was all that mattered.

"In that case, madam, let's walk. Can you . . ." he peered downward, trying to see if my sari concealed unsuitable high heels or sensible footwear.

"I can."

There followed a serendipitous afternoon during which Benaras unfolded itself as layers of history and legend were peeled back, as time and events crisscrossed back and forth. My companion, it turned out, was a superb and knowledgeable narrator. As evening fell, we found ourselves on the top steps of a ghat I had not seen before. It was the Dhobi ghat, where men and women did piles of laundry, using not only soap and water, but also the time-honored technique of beating the clothes hard on the stone steps. Perhaps, I remarked to Mr. Benaras, this was an appropriate zone for a sinner like me; my soul could do with some scrubbing and cleaning.

"I think you've heard too much history," he replied, "and you're tired. Why don't we walk back to one of my favorite sherbet sellers? If we go through this lane here, we'll be passing through the Bangali Tola. You'll see your people wandering about, speaking in Bengali."

"No," I said firmly. I did not want to be reminded again about the hapless Bengali widows, some of whom might still be found in this neighborhood. "Take me through a different route. And tell me about the sherbets."

Merely hearing about the ingredients that are used to concoct

Benarasi sherbets (tall cold drinks, but not aerated like sodas and colas) can provide a magic carpet ride to a leisurely time when the world was small and mysterious, when new spices were still being imported from unknown lands. Crystallized rose petals, the purple juice of a fruit called phalsa, the yellow pulp of a fruit called bel, saffron from Kashmir, the fragrant essences of sandalwood and screw pine flower, and many other elements lend color, scent, and sweetness to these drinks. Even more intriguing, on a really hot day, you can have the drink as a "gola." Akin to snow cones, the Benarasi gola is a handful of ice, crushed and shaped into a ball, with the chosen flavoring of the sherbet sprinkled over it. A stick poked into the ball allows you to slowly consume it like an ice-cream bar. By the time we got to a sherbet seller, my inner eye was filled with a host of historical characters—princes, courtiers, queens, eunuchs, musicians, housewives, and laborers—savoring these subtly flavored drinks not simply because of the taste, but also because of the painstaking creativity that went into their making. How can a bottle of soda, churned out by a vast manufacturing plant, slake the thirst and spike the imagination in quite the same way?

"For the people of this city, the signature drink is the thandai," Mr. Benaras told me, "far better than the usual sherbet. It's a decoction of water, sugar, melon seeds, almonds, cashews, and fragrant spices like cardamom, anise, and saffron."

"Well, then, I must have some of that," I declared, deciding not to worry about the purity of the water.

"But to really enjoy thandai," my companion said with a sly glint in his eyes, "you have to be brave. The best thandai has a dollop of bhang in it."

Oh no. Bhang was the substance that Shiva was supposed to get high on. I should have expected someone in Benaras would try to persuade me to have some.

"In my young days," he went on, "we used to go out for bhang parties. Those were great times. The bhang was very superior in quality and taste. The leaves were crushed in big mortars, and cream, orange pulp, white pepper, and almonds were added. The paste was then blended with milk or thandai. You mustn't think we did it for intoxication, the way people get drunk," he added quickly, misinterpreting the look on my face as disapproval. "For us, it was a sophisticated pleasure."

"And you think, if I were brave, I would try it."

"But I know you won't."

"Not this time. I'd rather try the sherbet with rose petals."

He paid for two glasses and handed me one. We sipped in silence. It felt like drinking cool attar, a little overwhelming at first. But in a while, the fragrance mutated to a serene sense of well-being that ran all through my body. Was this Shiva, touching me gently, trying to dissipate the melancholy of accumulated widowhood that was oppressing me? Or was it a spirit from some Middle Eastern land to which the rose was native? Mr. Benaras was looking at me with a very kind smile, as if he knew exactly how I felt.

"You must come back to Benaras when you are brave. To know this city the way you want to, you have to taste a bit of bhang here. If Benaras has a culture, it is not that of morbidity, death and salvation, nor is it the kind of frantic capitalism that's taking over all the cities in India. The real lesson of this city is that you need very little to find a kind of contentment that's both aesthetic and spiritual. But you have to make the most of that very little. There's a saying about the typical Benarasi. If he earns ten rupees, he feels he has enough. He will give his family five rupees and feel he has done his duty. Then, after a refreshing bath in the Ganges— and this goes for Hindus and Muslims alike—he will spend the rest of his money on simple but good food, followed by a betel leaf wrapped around spices and scented tobacco. Finally, he will indulge in a drink laced with a small amount of bhang. And he will feel as rich as a king."

I laughed. It really seemed like a good recipe for happiness. But I knew I wasn't gifted enough to incorporate it into my life. Maybe some day in the future. I said good-bye to Mr. Benaras, feeling we had spent just the right amount of time together. On my way back to the hotel, I saw a sign outside a restaurant advertising pizza made with yak's milk cheese from Nepal and real espresso. The moving finger was writing fast, I thought, adding to the layers of Benaras's identity.

On my last evening, I bought some hot, fragrant kachoris and a leaf bowl full of large, saffron-colored jilebis, dripping with syrup. I made my way to one of the ghats and sat down on the lower steps. Several children played hopscotch on the broad landing above me. Across the river was a setting sun, the darkening outline of an old palace, and unoccupied stretches of land. Boats carrying sightseers, students, merchants passed before me like images in a film. The failing light obscured the sludgy, sluggish quality of the river's water. I ate my kachoris slowly, letting the heat, scent, and spiciness fill my mouth. My surroundings dissolved and were replaced by a vision of legions of city dwellers all over India, touching the strands of unreal contentment—all you need is ten rupees, he had said—radiating out of this chaotic, dirty, death-oriented city that pulsed with a life that was aggressive, brash, and savvy.

By the time I was ready to eat my jilebis, dusk had become darkness with tropical speed. Little clay lamps, set afloat on the river, their wicks burning bravely despite the breeze, came sailing down my way. I ate a jilebi, crisp and syrupy, and tasted perfection. The temple bells spoke to me not about deliverance, deprivation, or exploitation. Instead, they carried the voice of Shiva, the cool, cosmic dancer with dreadlocks, encouraging me to savor this moment before it vanished.

PART THREE

Chapter Nine

ART AND TEXTURE ON THE
GUJARATI PLATTER

Time to take another look at the map. India's western coast stretched along the Arabian Sea, peppered with magical names like Goa, Bombay, Mangalore, and Cochin. But it was the upper northern and western regions of the country that held my eye. Two states lay side by side, Gujarat and Rajasthan, each endowed with its own wealth of magic and myth. Of the two, Gujarat has more variety of terrain and resources and consequently, a richer culinary history. The enterprise of the Gujaratis has made them successful immigrants in many countries, including the United States, the United Kingdom, Kenya, Uganda, and Zambia.

Throughout India, too, the spirit of Gujarati enterprise is highly visible. The people of Rajasthan (literally, land of the kings), meanwhile, have a near-mythical reputation for bravery, heroism, and survival in harsh conditions. The great Indian Thar Desert is part of Rajasthan. One interesting difference between the two states lies in public perception. Rajasthan, with its glamorous palaces, its colorful people, and arresting landscape, is a primary tourist destination for both Indian and foreign travelers. Gujarat, by contrast, has a more low-key presence, despite its wealth of art, craft, architecture, and cuisine.

The majority of the people living in these two states are vegetarians and their cooking reflects, on the one hand, a wealth of artful creativity, and on the other, an ingenious resourcefulness that is born out of harsh conditions. Religion is another important factor behind the cuisines of Gujarat and Rajasthan. The Hindu majority are not the only ones who adopt a vegetarian diet. Gujarat is also the birthplace of Jainism, a religion older even than Buddhism. In advocating ahimsa (nonviolence), Jains have adopted an extraordinarily restrictive way of eating. Muslims, as everywhere in India, are nonvegetarians, though many of them avoid shellfish and pork. But it is another Gujarati community, Parsis, whose eating habits are at the farthest extreme from those of Jains. Except for the one element of beef, Parsis have one of the most joyfully inclusive diets in the country. The coexistence of these communities in Gujarat has created an extraordinary variety of food, cooking techniques, ritual practices, and eating habits. I knew it would take many explorations to gain a thorough knowledge of all of them. For now, I was happy to enlarge my horizon in whatever way possible. And I wanted to start with the mainstream vegetarian cuisines of the region.

The first time I became aware of Gujarati food was when I was thirteen. It was a moment fraught with family tensions. At that time, my parents and I were still living with our extended family in my grandparents' large, rambling Calcutta house. Khokon, my youngest uncle, was only eight years older than I was, and I considered him more an older sibling who did fun things with me, than an uncle. To my widowed grandmother, however, he was a headache, the fatherless, youngest child whose waywardness almost outweighed his precocious academic brilliance. Culturally, he was a rebel. He used up his pocket money to buy records of Western rock and pop music that he played loudly, to my delight—he was the one who introduced me to Elvis, whose star was already waning in America, but who was unbearably exciting to a teenager in pre-MTV Calcutta—and the outrage of the elders in our orthodox family. He argued with my grandmother bitterly and often about lots of things, but mostly, being a budding gourmet, about the boring, undistinguished meals that our cook served up every day. Eating out regularly or getting takeout food from restaurants was not an option in those days unless you had plenty of money to spare.

Late one summer afternoon, as I slid down the banister from the third to the second floor—a hoydenish trick Khokon had taught me, to the great annoyance of the other adults—I came upon a scene of silent drama. Through the door of the dining room, I saw my uncle sitting at the table, helping himself to food from a tiffin carrier, the kind of contraption in which my mother and aunt had loaded a delicious meal for my first memorable train journey from Calcutta to Puri. As my grandmother stood glaring at him, Khokon filled his plate not only with bread, rice, and vegetables, but also with some intriguing-looking foods I'd never seen before. Ever curious, I marched in and asked what the stuff was. It was a signal for the outburst my grandmother had been checking till then. From her indignant tirade I gathered that Khokon, by then a medical student, had ordered a week's home delivery of food cooked by the wife of a Gujarati patient he had met at the hospital. According to him, although these Gujaratis were vegetarians, their food was still preferable to the execrable efforts of our cook, even when he made fish and meat. Ignoring my grandmother, Khokon asked me to taste anything I wanted from the plate. Eagerly, I moved closer.

"I forbid you, absolutely forbid you to touch any of that," yelled my grandmother.

"Go on, you'll see how delicious it is," urged Khokon.

I stood, hesitating between the two—but only for a few minutes. The pull of the unknown was much too strong. Quickly, I leaned forward, scanned the unfamiliar items, and helped myself to a miniature strip of yellow material, rolled up like a mat. There were several of these on the plate, garnished with white coconut shavings, dark mustard seeds, and green flakes of cilantro. The thing melted in my mouth, leaving an indescribable aura of delicacy in texture and flavor. I looked at my uncle and grinned. I knew that he knew I was on his side in this matter of importing exotic food. That yellow roll, I learned, was called khandvi, a Gujarati farsan (snack) made from a batter of chickpea flour and buttermilk. A good khandvi requires an artist's hand, and Khokon's patient's wife had that. My uncle then offered me a piece broken from a thin, brittle sheet of a bread called khakda, which looked like a brown pappadam to me. I ate it and my mouth tingled with the sharpness of cumin seed and some other unknown spice. There were also some steamed savory cakes made, like the khandvi, with chickpea flour and covered with a tamarind sauce. These, said my uncle, were called rasya dhokla (dhoklas in sauce). More substantial than the khandvi, they were equally delicious.

Years later, I pondered the contrasting geography that provides the frame within which the artists of the Gujarati kitchen create such highly textured, colorful, and savory food. To the northwest, Gujarat expands into the peninsula of Kathiawar, which juts out into the Arabian Sea. A conglomeration of small princely states at one time, Kathiawar has a long and rich history. India's most famous leader, Mahatma Gandhi, was born in its coastal town of Porbandar. The area's dairy products serve as a reminder that in 1946, Gujarat became the birthplace of India's first national dairy cooperative.

Although noted for the famous Gir National Park and Wildlife Sanctuary—the only habitat of the Asian lion—Kathiawar is more arid than lush. North and west of Kathiawar spread the desolate salt flats of the Rann of Kutch, where Gujarat abuts Pakistan. This desertlike climate has generated an immense variety of homemade pickles (athaanas) that add extra zest to a vegetarian spread. The women of northern and western Gujarat are not merely good pickle makers; their creativity, and that of the women of Rajasthan, is magnificently displayed in the vivid colors and bold embroidery of their textiles. For many years, my vision of this enormous zone consisted of a line of rural women, their clothes flamboyant against the sand and scrub of their land, heavy silver anklets sweetly chiming with their steps, going to fetch water from the wells. Some of these, called step-wells, have intricate and often beautifully carved structures surrounding them, deep underground. Image translated to reality when I observed the brightly clad women of Kathiawar in the busy, well-populated towns of central Gujarat—the state's farm belt—where they are eagerly expected migrant laborers in the winter and spring. They go from house to house, their task being to clean, sift, sieve, winnow, grind, and organize the year's supply of spices and grains, which are stored in the lofts of houses. This system works only in a dry climate. In humid Bengal, the entire stored supply would become a bug and fungus-riddled disaster in a few months' time.

I had wanted to arrive in Ahmedabad, Gujarat's former capital and still the commercial and cultural center, on or before the fourteenth of January. The day is an auspicious one in the Hindu calendar—Makar Sankranti, when the sun transits the zodiac from Sagittarius to Capricorn. In Bengal, I had grown up with the tradition that enforces a monthlong ban on eating radishes from this day. In Gujarat, however, Makar Sankranti is celebrated with a kite festival, sweets, and a special ritual of feeding cows (if you happen to own any). Unfortunately, I couldn't get a seat on a plane until the following day. As we neared the city, its aerial view evoked the embroidered symmetry of a patchwork quilt—neat fields of varying sizes, colored by the crops that grew on them, bordered by irrigation channels. The channels indicated that agriculture in Gujarat is managed with the same efficient focus that has made the people of this state so successful in business. Had Babur, the Mongol conqueror, come to Gujarat now, he would not be able to criticize the people of India, as he did in his autobiographical *Baburnama*, for not managing their crops with irrigation. Coming lower and closer, however, I was startled by what appeared to be an enormous sandy serpent coiled around the city of Ahmedabad. It took me a while to figure out that this was the dried-up bed of the Sabarmati River, beside which

Gandhi built his ashram in 1915. Today, the only part of the river that has survived nature's aridity and man's dam-building is near the ashram. The dried riverbed circling the city hints at the power of the northern desert.

Southern Gujarat is the state's greenbelt. The heavy rainfall from the southwestern monsoon brings the reward of lush and plentiful vegetables. Here, the city of Surat is a favorite destination for food connoisseurs, who may travel in the winter from other parts of the state simply to sample the superb, seasonal produce. Winter is the season to make one of the most famous Gujarati dishes, oondhiu, a mélange of vegetables dotted with dumplings. Most Gujaratis will tell you that a good oondhiu can only be home cooked, not found in a restaurant, the same as we Bengalis say about our celebrated fish jhol. Aside from produce, the southern towns of Gujarat are also noted for their individual specialties. The residents of Surat, for instance, celebrate the autumn full moon by eating ghari, a kind of fried bread with a sweet filling. According to some estimates, two hundred tons of ghari are dispatched by avid townsfolk in one day. Surat, a bustling center of commerce from medieval times, is also famed for its diamond industry. This glittering gem has taken such a hold of the local imagination that even potato chips are sold under the brand name Diamond. They come in bright-colored packages, the flavors ranging from plain salted, to chatpati masala or spicy lime.

Another southern town, Bhavnagar, posed the most intriguing conundrum in the authenticity debate during my stay in Gujarat. I had gone to the opening of a painting exhibition in Ahmedabad, invited by the artist Haku Shah and his wife, Vilu. I had met the couple several days before in their tiny, two-storied house ornamented with exquisitely carved wooden doors and windows. Over cups of afternoon tea, we had talked about the strong artistic traditions of Gujarat, the architectural heritage of Ahmedabad, and Haku Shah's efforts to promote interreligious harmony. All the time, I had been aware of an air of unworldly contentment that seemed to wrap them around like soft, handwoven Gujarati shawls.

The opening was packed; I could hardly get close to any of the paintings. After a while, I decided to wait for the crowd to thin. A long table loaded with coffee, tea, soft drinks, and munchies promised refreshment in one corner of the gallery. When I went over, an elegantly dressed man with a white goatee politely poured me out some coffee. He, too, was a nonresident like me, a visitor from England. The next morning he was going to his hometown, Bhavnagar, for a niece's wedding. We talked about wedding rituals and feasts—Bengali and Gujarati—and to my amazement, he said that no wedding in Bhavnagar is complete without ice cream. Why, of all things, ice cream? Tradition, he answered with unshakeable firmness, like Tevye the milkman in the musical *Fiddler on the Roof*. I thought of the quirky ice-cream shops that Hyderabad is justly famous for, but nowhere in India had I heard that ice cream was an obligatory part of a traditional Indian wedding. It confirmed the notion that upending the old and the new, custom and innovation, is what India is about, and has been for centuries.

Several days after the missed kite festival, I called Rathin Das, a fellow Bengali and a reporter for one of India's leading newspapers. I had got his number through some journalist friends in Calcutta. Das has lived in Gujarat long enough to speak the language fluently. We met in his office one afternoon and, over a cup of strong office-brewed tea, he listened politely as I talked about my journeys through India's food, past and present. From the bemused look on his face I guessed that though he wanted to help, he couldn't think how. However, just as I was trying to find a way to let him off the hook without appearing too cavalier, I noticed the sudden gleam in his eye. He pulled the phone toward himself and quickly dialed a number. The conversation, being in Gujarati, was beyond my ken. At the end of it, though, I had an invitation to have lunch the next day with Digant Oza, a freelance journalist and author with a passionate interest in water management issues.

Mr. Oza greeted me warmly when I turned up at his house the next day. A white-clad, portly figure with a balding head, he has the expression of a happy cherub, and an infectious, burbling laughter you wouldn't expect from reading his fiery newspaper articles berating the sectarianism of the Hindu fundamentalist party ruling Gujarat. He is also a born raconteur. Listening to his spate of stories about life and food in Gujarat, I relished the serendipitous connection that had led me to him through meeting a fellow Bengali. I asked about the caste hierarchy in Gujarat and learned about the Nager Brahmins, a subsect of Brahmins with superelevated status and an extraordinary purity of diet. The influence of the nonviolent Jains, said Mr. Oza, can be seen even among the Gujarati Hindus, many of whom prefer to avoid tomatoes or red lentils because the color reminds them of blood. But the best story he told me was about one Gujarati's determination to defy the unfairness of the colonial rulers. At the end of a train journey, this man was suddenly informed that "regulations" required him to pay an extra surcharge to transport his box of thirty-two pounds of pedas—a rich sweet made with solidified evaporated milk—before being allowed to cross over to the other side of the station. If the railway officials were hoping to get a free load of sweets, they were disappointed. The man got off the train, sat on the platform, defiantly consumed the entire consignment of pedas, crossed over, and went on his merry way.

Digant Oza and his wife had a relative visiting them from New Jersey. The Ozas' daughter, Kajal Oza-Vaidya, a novelist and a scriptwriter for Gujarati television, had also dropped in. Kajal told me that her mother was considered a superb cook, an expert in all the traditional Gujarati dishes. When we all sat down for a vegetarian lunch—that home-cooked meal I was so longing for after weeks of travel and eating in hotels, shops, and restaurants—the first thing I noticed was the rolled-up khandvi that I had once tasted from my uncle Khokon's plate. To one used to the Bengali hierarchy of eating, the typical Gujarati meal seems to be rather haphazard. Partly this may be because there is no transition from vegetarian items to fish and meat. On the Oza's dining table, there were snack-type foods like khandvi and dhokla, along with complex vegetable preparations to be eaten with fried whole wheat breads called theplas. Frequent dips into the pickle containers were irresistible. In between, we sampled laddoos—spherical sweets, made with wheat flour, brown sugar and ghee. Portions of rice and khichdi (rice cooked together with green, not yellow, moong dal) were served with hot, melted ghee poured on top. Small, individual serving bowls contained the famous kadhi, eaten both in Gujarat and in neighboring Rajasthan—a soup made with buttermilk and chickpea flour. When at last oondhiu, that classic of the Gujarati cuisine, made its appearance, I noticed that my own excitement was matched by the anticipatory exhalations of everyone around me. And why not? It was a perfect blend of seasonal vegetables, exquisitely spiced, and dotted with tiny dumplings flavored with fenugreek greens. Mrs. Oza certainly deserved her reputation as a culinary genius. At the end of this feast, I could only manage a tiny spoonful of the almond-and-milk dessert that she brought out. The Ozas claimed the meal was nothing special. To me it demonstrated the one thing I had heard about Gujarati food—that it is all about texture. When I left my hosts, after receiving a farewell hug from Mrs. Oza and an open invitation for the future, I felt that hunger might be the best sauce, as popular wisdom has it, but spontaneous hospitality showered on a stranger came a close second.

I had often wondered why a coastal state like Gujarat should have a primarily vegetarian cuisine, and the delightful meal at the Ozas' again raised the question in my mind. All along the western coast of India south of Gujarat, people enjoy fish and meat, especially fish. Why was Gujarat so notably different? Of all the Indian states, this is the one with the highest percentage of vegetarians.

Everyone I spoke to agreed it was the predominance of Buddhism and Jainism for many centuries in Gujarat that was the biggest factor behind this preference for vegetarianism. In the third century B.C., the Hindu emperor Asoka, who started out as a ruthless conqueror, was eventually so sickened by the carnage of war that he converted to Buddhism. From that point forward, he zealously promoted nonviolence with edicts and proclamations engraved on stone pillars. One of these, still standing in Girnar, Gujarat, declares, "No living being may be slaughtered for sacrifice," directly flouting Hindu ways of worship dating back to the Vedic period.

Jainism, whose origins predate Buddhism, was even more emphatic about every creature's right to live. Jains totally reject Hinduism's caste hierarchy and the concept of obtaining merit through ritual and sacrifice. For them, it is the individual's conduct that matters. As children in Calcutta, my friends and I were familiar with stories about Jains who walk with extreme caution, lest a single ant or beetle be crushed under their footsteps, while some even wear masks lest they inhale or swallow a tiny flying insect. These, however, are the extreme observances of ascetics. The average urban Jain, trying to make a living and raise a family, gets around like the rest of us. Instead of being unworldly philosophers pondering the questions of life, death, and nonviolence, many Jains are extremely successful entrepreneurs. Even the art of cooking has been turned into an opportunity for making money; Jain pickles and packaged snacks are hugely popular in cities all over India.

With regard to food, however, most Jains still remain strict vegetarians. In Gujarat, I learned about some of their more orthodox practices. They avoid tubers and roots (potatoes, radishes, carrots, onions, garlic, ginger, or turmeric), since digging these up might harm insects that live underground. They also avoid multiseeded fruits and vegetables, such as figs and eggplant. The promise of life inherent in such produce is too important to be sacrificed to the lust of the palate, a point of view that might seem excessive even to the most ardent pro-lifers in America. Honey is forbidden food, since removing it from the comb would involve the death of bees. Even betel leaves, the pan-Indian after-dinner chaser, are out of bounds, since they are always smeared with a lime paste to which ground-up shells are often added. As for the thin silver foil that is used as a decorative coating for cardamom seeds or sweets, Jains won't touch it, since the metal has to be beaten to papery thinness between layers of soft leather or, worse, the intestines of cows. One evening in Ahmedabad, I saw a restaurant sign proclaiming the availability of "Jain pizza," that is, pizza without onions in the topping. Like so much in India, this, too, was an example of ingenious adaptation, being the other end of the spectrum from the chicken tikka masala pizza. On reflection, I felt that never being able to taste the pleasures of onion and garlic and potatoes was a loss, but there was some consolation in the fact that no observant Jain would be tempted to gorge on the great evil of the modern Western diet, "supersized" French fries.

As if living with so many dietary restrictions was not enough, Jains also have an annual eight-day fast for further mortification of body and soul, during the holy festival of Paryushan. It falls in the middle of the rainy season, and a Jain ascetic is supposed to survive only on boiled water during this period. Most people, even observant ones, find it impossible to be so rigorous. Instead, the usual human compromises are made—some will fast on the first and last day, others may choose a few days in the middle. Those who eat during Paryushan have greater-than-usual restrictions on what foods are permissible. Greens, normally relished, are forbidden at this time, in a symbolic acknowledgment that the monsoon rains bring to life a host of insects that might cling to the leaves. Jains don't even garnish their khandvis and dhoklas with fresh coriander leaves. As a result, they tend to make the most of legumes and beans, rice, wheat, milk products, and permissible fruits and vegetables. I used to think that Bengalis displayed the greatest ingenuity in the use of the banana, until I came across two items in a Paryushan menu. Gujarati Jains take ripe, unpeeled bananas, split them partially, and stuff them with chickpea flour seasoned with a chili-cumin-coriander powder, a bit of sugar, and a few green chilies, and fry the bananas over low heat. Another tasty but unexpected use of the same fruit entails taking the skins of ripe bananas, frying them with spices, and coating them in a sauce of chickpea flour.

Most Gujaratis, of course, are neither Buddhists nor Jains, but Hindus. Vaishnavs, a major sect among Gujarat's Hindus, are followers of the god Vishnu (better known as one of his incarnations, Krishna). They, too, advocate nonviolence and purity in food and tend to be vegetarians. In fifteenth-century Gujarat, vegetarianism as a general preference got a shot in the arm when a Vaishnav guru settled there and acquired large numbers of followers, from all segments of society.

In the context of dietary choices and habits, India is a rare instance of a land where nature has been an enabler in the adoption of vegetarianism for almost three millennia (the first practitioners of Jainism go back to the seventh and eighth centuries B.C.). The sheer size of the land and the variations in climate and geography have made it possible to adopt a diverse, healthful, and tasty diet made up of cereals (rice, wheat, millet, barley, corn, sorghum), vegetables, fruits, and dairy products. The process of cooking transforms the raw material with flavorful oils and ghee, zesty spices, and, in the case of desserts, sugar (from the indigenous sugarcane) and honey. As a result, eating vegetarian in India has never been a condition of deprivation or asceticism—unless you deliberately made it so—as it would be in colder, northern terrains or vast areas of desert. A fine culinary imagination has made the Gujarati vegetarian platter particularly artful and delicious.

Inevitably, the question of vegetarianism made me contrast Gujarat with my native Bengal. For several centuries, Buddhism was a major influence there, though the people who converted from Hinduism were mostly from the lower rungs of the caste and economic ladder, not the powerful opinion makers or trendsetters. The same Vaishnav tenets of nonviolence that Gujarat adopted in the fifteenth century were also enthusiastically adopted by many Bengalis around the same time, because of the charismatic Bengali preacher Chaitanya. Both Buddhism and Vaishnav beliefs have left their mark in Bengal's rich and varied vegetable dishes and Bengalis' love of many kinds of dal (pulses) as a protein substitute. Yet, the overall preference for fish has never been eradicated. Nature, which has filled the terrain with countless rivers and lakes teeming with fish, has been a bigger deciding factor than any manmade religion. In Gujarat, the tension between geography and faith is manifest in the fact that residents of the coastal areas have not let their diet be influenced by Buddhism, Jainism, or Vaishnavism. Having regular access to fish, they relish a varied oceanic harvest that includes such marine species as siya, dantiya, and kunga. The fact that many of Gujarat's fisherfolk also happen to be Muslims and tribal people adds to the complexity of the picture.

There was one question about food that I wanted answered before leaving Gujarat—was there any truth to the popular misconception that it is an overwhelmingly sweet cuisine? My personal eating experiences so far had not supported the notion. For an expert answer, I decided to talk with Abhay Mangaldas, the proprietor of Agashiye (Terrace) in Ahmedabad, a rooftop restaurant with a flamboyantly multicolored canopy that reminds the beholder of Gujarat's other claim to fame, textiles. I invited Haku and Vilu Shah to have lunch with me there, as they also happened to know Mangaldas.

We ordered the deluxe thali. In India, the well-traveled person sometimes bemoans the lack of aesthetic food presentation, compared to what is seen in other Asian countries, especially Japan. I've always felt that the aesthetics exist in India, but in a style suited to the heartier, spicier cuisines of the land and the habit of eating with one's hands. However, if there were any awards to be given for food presentation, the thali at Agashiye (the actual plates are made of kansa, an alloy of five metals traditionally considered good for memory and purifying the blood) would be a strong contender. Even peripheral items like pickles gladdened the eye. I was particularly charmed by one I had never had, pickled young turmeric, the tiny pieces set out on half a betel leaf. Its sharp yet delicate taste was nothing like the taste of the spice we use in cooking, the powder made from dried turmeric rhizomes. Haku and Vilu were amused by my ecstatic response. In Gujarat, said Vilu, the turmeric is considered auspicious, as in many other parts of India. It is welcomed at all times except in Hindu houses of mourning, where it is forbidden. Tiny cubes of ginger pickle, lying on another half of a betel leaf, provided a different kind of sharpness. Both these rhizomes are considered digestives in the Indian traditional system of medicine, Ayurveda.

As we made our way through a number of vegetable dishes, I could see that Agashiye's claim to providing the freshest produce of the day was not an empty boast. The seasoning was minimal, but the taste ambrosial. The meal began with rotis (breads), which included both plain wheat chapattis and theplas, the latter fragrant with ghee, to be eaten with four different vegetable dishes. Well-known Gujarati farsans (snacks) including khandvi and dhokla were also presented, providing the tongue with a different textural interlude. Bowls of yellow moong dal and kadhi came next, and I dipped pieces of chapatti in them, a departure from my usual habit of eating dal with rice.

Before the rice and some more vegetables were served, we were given some rabri, a liquid milky dessert, flavored with pistachio and saffron. Unlike the frozen northern Indian kulfi or the rich Bengali rabri, this was light and refreshing, almost serving as a palate cleanser, the way sorbet does in French cuisine. In the Gujarati tradition of eating freshly made sweets along with the main meal, there was a very rich halvah, made with white gourd and evaporated milk. After the rice, served with a couple of different vegetable dishes, we segued to khichdi. As I had seen in the home of the Ozas, liquid ghee was poured on top of the khichdi. Guests at Agashiye are free to ask for as much ghee as they want—an option that Haku Shah made the most of. Watching the waiter pour the tiny spoonfuls from a metal bowl, I envied the way Haku's trim figure had defied ghee's effects.

Finally, it was time for dessert, the kind that is supposed to end the meal. The waiter appeared with two kinds of ice cream. Was there no getting away from this foreign confection? The Shahs informed me that Ahmedabad restaurants take pride in making their own ice cream; they don't serve the commercially packaged brands. In which case, I thought, remembering the man from Bhavnagar, perhaps it is not such an oddity for a town to adopt ice cream as a "traditional" part of the wedding banquet. A perfect triangle of plain vanilla ice cream was placed before me in a translucent gray-green bowl—a nineteenth-century American novelty, embraced with enthusiasm and now integrated into the native food pantheon. Agashiye ends the meal with some chasers and mouth fresheners—betel leaves wrapped around sweet spices, supplemented with miniature titillations for the palate, such as cubes of candied tamarind pulp seasoned with cumin and other spices, freshly grated coconut, and tiny pieces of excellent chocolate.

After lunch, we went downstairs to take a look at the courtyard restaurant, where the ambience is that of a casual café. Already, the staff was getting ready for clients who would turn up for tea and snacks. In one corner, three people were busy making yet another sweet item, malpoa. This is not unique to Gujarat; aside from neighboring states like Rajasthan, far-away Bengal, too, makes a fetish of malpoa. When made well, it is irresistible. Large dollops of flour and evaporated milk are first deep-fried in ghee and then dipped into syrup. In Bengal, the dough is flavored with the seeds of the large black cardamom, whose fragrance is more potent than that of the green variety. At Agashiye, malpoa was flavored with saffron, a richer perfume harking back to the sultans' court.

It was in this atrium-like restaurant that I had the opportunity to spend some time talking to Abhay Mangaldas about Gujarati food and cooking. The son of a wealthy Gujarati family, Mangaldas spent several years in the United States, studying communications at Boston University. He is tall and on the slim side, with a neatly trimmed black beard. His casually sophisticated manner is more than complemented by his boundless energy and hands-on style. One of the first things he asked me was how long I was staying in Ahmedabad. When I told him, he looked disappointed.

"Pity," he said. "I would have organized a Bengali cooking class with you, but it wouldn't be possible till the end of next week."

Relieved at not having, myself, to teach anyone else to cook, I changed the subject to his restaurant's fortuitously historic location. It is part of an enormous redbrick structure owned by the Mangaldas family. Directly opposite stands the exquisite Sidi Saiyad Mosque, named for a slave in the court of the sixteenth-century Muslim ruler Ahmed Shah. That there were African slaves in India is a commonly forgotten footnote to the country's history. They were brought to India by the Arab traders as early as nine centuries ago. Some were also brought by the Portuguese in the sixteenth and seventeenth centuries, from their African colonies in Mozambique and Angola. But many Africans also came to India on the Arab merchant ships as traders, soldiers of fortune, and travelers, and eventually settled down along the country's western coastal areas. Their descendants, called Sidis, are to be found now in Indian cities, especially Bombay, but the largest concentration is in a village in Gujarat called Jambur. The Sufi Islam they practice is enriched by singing and drumming in the style of many African communities. But their food shows no link with Africa. They have wholeheartedly adopted the rice, dal, bread, and vegetables of their adopted land. The delicate stone filigree work on the Sidi Saiyad Mosque presents a nice counterpoint to the solidity of the Mangaldas edifice, which has now been declared a heritage site.

To maintain high standards, Mangaldas said he makes a point of serving only the freshest of seasonal produce in his restaurant; the menu changes almost daily, depending on what the market offers. All aspects of the business, from shopping to creating the daily menu to supervising the kitchen, pass under his eagle eye. He described the Gujarati thali as a basic template on which you can add, subtract, change, and modify a whole range of vegetables, cereals, legumes, condiments, pickles, chutneys. When I asked him about the supposed preponderance of the sweet element in the region's food, Mangaldas was quick to refute the idea.

"It's a misunderstanding," he said. "The reason is that many of the cooks in Gujarati restaurants are from the neighboring state of Rajasthan. They have migrated here in large numbers in search of better economic opportunities. The dominant note of sweetness is a characteristic of the food of many parts of Rajasthan, and these cooks have continued their own cooking style. Authentic Gujarati food is not sweet at all."

However, he pointed out, eating habits are changing in Gujarat, as everywhere else, and many Gujarati Hindus are now nonvegetarians. The concession they make is in limiting the consumption of such items to outside the home, which is still kept free of polluting animal foods. This was nothing new to me. I had met plenty of Marwaris in Calcutta who did the same.

The migration of sweet-fingered cooks from Rajasthan to Gujarat provides one of numerous fascinating examples of influence and metamorphosis within India. It is only natural that cooks from Rajasthan, a land where survival is a struggle and nature far from bountiful will make the most of nonperishable elements like sugar and ghee and buttermilk to give tone, depth, and nuance to their food. A wide variety of breads, plain and fried, as well as stuffed with spices and nuts, is a big part of the

Rajasthani diet. The region's best-known dish is possibly one called dal-baati-churma, in which five kinds of dal are cooked together and served with flaky baked bread, the baati. Leftover dough is deep-fried in ghee, crumbled into pieces, and mixed with brown sugar to be eaten as an impromptu dessert, the churma.

Since fresh vegetables are limited in Rajasthan, whatever is harvested has to be dried and preserved for long-term use. One legendary dish called ker sangri consists of wild berries and beans that flourish even under the harshest conditions. Dried and sold in the markets, they are combined with oil, spices, and powdered, dried green mango (to add tartness to the dish). So popular is it that few traditional weddings take place without having this on the menu. Vegetarian or not, food in Rajasthan has a rich undertone, since people have compensated for the scarcity of water by cooking with plenty of oil and ghee. To balance the richness, digestive spices like asafetida, ginger, and ajwain are liberally used. Royalty here, as everywhere else, made a practice of hunting, and meat was certainly a feature in the royal banquets. Lal maas (literally, red meat, though it denotes the color of the gravy, not the type of meat) is a noted presence on the nonvegetarian's plate. The arid shrub terrain actually produces the best kid goat meat in the country, according to some experts.

Aside from sending migrating cooks to neighboring Gujarat, Rajasthan is notable for its Marwari business community, whose spectacular grasp on business and the ability to create wealth could have provided ample fodder for economists from Adam Smith onward. The world's largest steel enterprise is now owned and operated by a Marwari from Calcutta, Laxmi Mittal. And Marwari enterprise is not limited to inedible steel. Haldiram, a company originating in the Rajasthani city of Bikaner, has become a byword for packaged sweets and savory snacks throughout India. Bengal owes a special debt to Haldiram for popularizing its classic confections, such as the rajbhog, rosogolla, and pantua, in other parts of the country. These are canned and shipped by Haldiram not only within India, but also for the consumption of Indians abroad.

★ ★ ★

Eating Gujarati food day after day was making my thoughts wander off in strange directions. True, the theory about this cuisine being sweetly one-dimensional had been laid to rest as a fallacy. Nevertheless, I found myself laboring under the cumulative effect of all the sweets I had been eating. Even with my Bengali sweet tooth, I felt badly in need of a saline immersion, figurative, if not literal. On the map, I looked again at Gujarat's northwestern reaches, the salt flats of the Rann of Kutch. The area had been devastated by the terrible earthquake of 2001. But its people, mostly tribals, are hardy souls. Processing salt is one way they earn a living. Strange myths emanate out of the region, like the one about a demigod named Lord Dattaray who once chopped off his hand to feed a hungry jackal. At his shrine, food is still cooked and offered not only to the god but to the local jackals as well.

Salt is earth, salt is life, and nowhere is salt sprinkled more thoroughly through the historic narrative than in Gujarat. Salt created a significant turning point in India's freedom struggle because of Gujarat's famous son, Gandhi. During colonial rule, the British government had a monopoly on the production of salt. Its sale or production by any other person or group was punishable by law. In a humid, tropical country like India, salt is even more necessary for survival than in colder temperate zones. For ordinary people, especially for those living in the low-lying coastal areas, salt was an easily available natural resource. Yet, the British forced Indians to pay for it through the salt tax, generating profit for themselves. Gandhi decided to organize a nonviolent protest. On March 12, 1930, he set out with a group of male followers on foot, for the coastal village of Dandi, where they planned to make the prohibited commodity by boiling sand in seawater. Despite violent attacks by the police, Gandhi and his followers, joined by local people, persevered. Richard Attenborough's biopic *Gandhi* includes a dramatic depiction of the incident. The effect of the Salt March—whose symbolism is as potent as that of the Boston Tea Party—was electric and felt all across India. Making salt became a way of nonviolent agitation against colonial rule. In today's mechanized world, coastal people in Gujarat still make salt by trapping seawater in dams. The salt they make is stored in highly visible piles on the beach.

I thought again of all the Gujarati pickles I had eaten and the role of salt in preserving food and adding savor to it. There could be no pickles without salt; no cooked food would last even half a day without salt in this hot zone. Gandhi, growing up in the home of traditional Gujarati parents, must have had his share of mouthwatering pickles with which the vegetarian thali is enlivened. Yet, as an adult and the leader of the nation, he expressed an attitude toward food that bordered on the ascetic. On the walls of the Gandhi Ashram by the Sabarmati River, are large framed excerpts of his thoughts on this matter. "Eating is necessary only for sustaining the body and keeping it a fit instrument for service and must never be practiced for self-indulgence. Food must therefore be taken like medicine, under proper restraint. In pursuance of this principle, one must eschew exciting foods, such as spices and condiments . . . this principle requires abstinence from the feasts or dinners which have pleasure as its object."

Of course such rules could only be imposed on the members of his ashram, his direct followers. Even so, I found it hard to accept such total repudiation of spice—a commodity that had drawn so many to India for so long—from an Indian. No wonder the mahatma breezed through long periods of fasting as frequently as he did. To the colonial rulers, for whom India had been such a long-standing source of wealth, luxury, and exotic pleasures, a man like this must have been unfathomable.

Gujarat's other extraordinary community, creators of one of India's richest cuisines, are the Parsis. Descendants of Persian Zoroastrians, they arrived in India after the Muslim conquest of Iran in the seventh century. Fleeing from oppression, carrying the sacred fire they worshipped, many of them made their way to other countries in the Middle East. Some of them later set sail for India, and the story of their arrival is one of my favorite food myths.

Shipwrecked off the coast of Gujarat, the Zoroastrians sent three of their *dasturs* (priests) to the king to ask for permission to settle in his land. But when the king saw them, he guessed their intent and tried to turn them away. Instead of a rude rebuff, however, he used a symbolic gesture, showing them a bowl filled to the brim with milk. The message was that his kingdom had no room for outsiders. The chief of the dasturs, equally adept at diplomatic communication, sprinkled some sugar into the milk and said that the milk was sweetened, but it had not overflowed. The king was impressed. He allowed them to stay and practice their religion on condition that they conform to local cultural norms. From these beginnings, rose a community whose achievements in culture, business, law, medicine, and cuisine are inversely matched by the smallness of their numbers. Although their presence is now concentrated in Bombay and other large Indian cities where business and professional opportunities took them, Parsis still speak Gujarati among themselves and have many customs in common with their fellow Gujaratis.

The story about their arrival appeals to me for two reasons. It reminds me of European communities that once came to the New World in the hopes of escaping persecution and finding religious freedom. It is also, intrinsically, a very Indian myth. The idea of blending two elements we consume, so that the lesser loses its separate identity and yet lends character and flavor to the greater, occurs in another instance centuries earlier, in the ancient Indian philosophical text, the *Upanishads*. The son of a famous sage asked his father how he would define Atman, the universal spirit. The father took a pitcher of water and sprinkled a handful of salt over it. Once the salt had dissolved, he asked his son to drink the water and describe the taste. Salty, said the son. But, replied the sage, though one can taste it, one cannot see the salt; Atman, too, is like that, invisible even as it permeates all forms of existence.

The Parsi community's wide-ranging, inclusive cuisine (its major omission being beef, in deference to the Hindu kingdom that had given shelter to the original Zoroastrian refugees) is the product of one of India's most fascinating stories of origin, merger, and transformation. During my school and college years in Calcutta, I never personally got to know any Parsis. Their numbers are small and the largest concentration is in Bombay. But it was impossible not to be aware of them. The leading English newspaper in the city, the *Statesman*, was edited and owned by a Parsi. The biggest business conglomerate in India at that time, the Tata Group, owed its origin and success to a notable Parsi family. And on some evenings, when my mother's older brother, a doctor, saw patients in his office on the first floor of our house, I would see a shiny black Mercedes pull up, from which descended a portly lady wearing her sari in the Gujarati fashion—my uncle's sole Parsi patient. When I left home for graduate studies in the United States, a friend and colleague of my mother's gave me an exquisite "tanchoi" brocade sari as a farewell present, telling me that the technique of weaving this textile had been brought to India from China in the nineteenth century by three Parsi brothers who traded in Chinese silks.

Given their high achieving history, one might expect Parsis to be intense type-A personalities, who have no time for the pleasures of the table. In reality, the Parsis have imbued their culinary tradition with joyful creativity. Their religious/ethical beliefs, focusing on "good thought, good word and good deed," do not include rigorous, self-mortifying, lengthy fasts nor do they focus on abstemiousness as a virtue. Vegetarianism is almost unheard of among Parsis. Even the fabled Gujarati oondhiu, which I ate in the house of the Ozas, undergoes an extraordinarily inventive carnivorous transmutation in the hands of the Parsi cook and becomes the oomberiu. Potatoes, eggplant, onions, garlic, and a kind of bean called papri are combined either with lamb or game birds like partridge or quail, whole eggs, oil, and spices, and layered inside an earthen pot lined with banana leaves and mango leaves. The mouth of the pot is tightly sealed with several layers of banana leaves. A hole dug in the ground is filled with twigs and straw, which are set on fire. When the flames die down a bit, a large whole potato is put in the center, the sealed pot inverted over the potato and the flames kept alive for a couple of hours, while the meat and vegetables cook gently. Once the potato is cooked, the contents of the pot are done. Like the vegetarian oondhiu, oomberiu is a winter dish. It is easy to imagine the enjoyment derived from the smoky flavors of the meat and vegetables in a clay pot, savored in the smoky dusk of an Indian winter.

Parsis' distant origins in Iran are still reflected in the rich festive pilafs they make, studded with nuts and raisins, often combined with the meat

of lamb and kid goat, and flavored with saffron. And in spite of now being dispersed in major Indian cities, they still observe customs that are
rooted in their earliest days as an agricultural community in Gujarat.
Some involve ascribing connotations, auspicious or otherwise, to food,
much as the Hindus do. Thus prawns, normally a great favorite, are never
served on important, celebratory occasions like weddings or coming-of-
age. Parsis believe that prawns, being bottom-feeders, live on the flesh of
the dead. Conversely, no celebration can be complete without liberal supplies of three items—sweet yogurt, a puddinglike confection of semolina,
and a sticky, syrupy, fragrantly spiced dish made with vermicelli.

One custom that has survived from the Parsis' rural roots has little
to do with actual cooking, but everything to do with aesthetics. Some
time before visiting Gujarat, I happened to meet Mrs. Thritty Dastoor, a
Parsi lady in Calcutta. She asked me to come over for tea one afternoon.
As I stepped out of the elevator, I noticed exquisite patterns drawn with
rice flour on the landing and in front of the apartment door. In answer
to my query, Mrs. Dastoor, an elegant woman with a brisk manner and
a friendly smile, said that each day the floor is wiped clean and new designs are painted. The ritual is a rather charming leftover of an old rural
custom of strewing powdered lime around the house as a method of repelling insects and reptiles. This same distant past is evoked in the harvest festival that the community still celebrates, although any direct
connection with the agricultural way of life has long vanished. Parsis in
modern India are mostly urban professionals: artists, scientists, writers,
lawyers, and businesspeople.

Just as the Rajasthani cooks are supposed to have left their sweet imprint on some Gujarati cooking, Parsi food has been subjected to two distinctive influences in relatively modern times. When Goan chefs began to
work in Parsi households in Bombay, they introduced two of their staple
ingredients, coconut and kokum, a sour purple fruit that is often used in
place of tamarind in the cuisines of Goa and Mangalore. Some of the
glories of modern Parsi cuisine, like patra ni macchi, fish smothered in a
coconut and green chili paste and steamed in a banana leaf, may owe its
origins to these cooks. Parsis have also been influenced by the colonial

British, with whom they socialized because of their international business enterprises. Quick to adopt the values of Western enlightenment—Parsis opened the first girls' school in India in 1849, and the country's first woman barrister (British-trained lawyer) was a Parsi named Cornelia Sorabji—they eagerly took on Western culinary concepts and made them their own. The result is evident in Parsi menus and cookbooks, which may include custer (custard), sas (sauce), estew (stew), and roasts.

It is, of course, the wedding banquet that presents the finest and most varied examples of Parsi cooking and illustrates the interplay of influences that have enriched the original Zoroastrian repertoire. Despite having left their village roots far behind, Parsis, unlike the Bengalis, still serve their traditional wedding feast, or patra no bhonu, on a banana leaf, although in deference to modern, Westernized mores, the banana leaves are spread on tablecloths and napkins and cutlery are provided.

Thritty Dastoor described the menu for one of her family weddings. It started, Gujarati style, with tangy pickles and bread, after which the guests were served patra ni macchi; chicken in a rich sauce accompanied by julienned potatoes; a vegetable stew with Parsi seasoning (notably, the unique spice mixture called dhana-jiru); a lamb bafad, in which the meat and vegetables are cooked with hot spiced vinegar; eggs on tomatoes; the traditional wedding custard, called lagan nu custer, which is thick enough to be eaten with a knife and fork instead of a mere spoon; a rich, saffron-scented lamb pilaf with thick dal; and finally, traditional Indian kulfi. The livers and gizzards of the chickens used for the banquet were not wasted either; they were made into a dry, spicy dish called aleti paleti, which is generally eaten by the family members at the end of the banquet. Parsis actually have an affinity with Muslims in their fondness for offal; they have numerous ways of cooking the trotters, brains, hearts, lungs, and kidneys of the lambs they slaughter. As if this wedding menu was not lavish enough, there were other items on the side, such as sweet yogurt (auspicious everywhere in India), sweet fruit pickles, and one tasty incongruity, potato chips, there called wafers. The final chaser of betel leaf and spices sent the guest on his way to gentle digestion.

A single festive menu like this one presents a miniature history of the evolution of Parsi cooking in the sequence of serving the items, the ingredients used in the dishes, and the method of preparation. The custard's coming in the middle of the meal echoes the practice of sweets being served in the middle of Hindu Gujarati meals. The steamed fish and the lamb in vinegar indicate the influence of the Goan cooks. The pilaf with meat and saffron is a direct descendant of the pilafs of ancient Persia. Tomatoes cooked with the eggs are the contribution of the colonial British, as are the potato chips.

As for the eggs, the Parsi fondness for this particular item is legendary. Almost anything can be combined with eggs—the phrase being *per eeda*—to become doubly desirable. Eggs are boiled, scrambled, poached, and made into omelets for breakfast, but again with the unique Parsi touch. The eggs on tomatoes served at the Dastoor wedding were not plain, as they usually are on a British or American table, but an elaborate production seasoned with a host of ingredients—onions, ginger, garlic, green chilies, turmeric, red chili powder, a little vinegar, salt, and even a touch of sugar. Even bananas—slightly unripe—are cooked with eggs. To my mind, however, the most incongruous combination is what the Parsis call "wafer per eeda." Once I learned of its existence, I couldn't rest until I had tried it out myself—sautéing onions and green chilies in a large skillet, unloading a bag of potato chips over them, making several nesting holes among the chips into which I broke the eggs, and letting the whole thing cook until the eggs were set. Eating this was an eye-popping experience, reminding me again that texture is the dominant element in any cuisine originating in Gujarat.

The most famous Parsi dish, dhansakh, is likely to have derived from the Iranian *khoreste esfannaj*: both are a combination of meat, lentils, and spinach. It is often included in family meals—a big Sunday lunch in a traditional Parsi home generally means happily loading up on dhansakh and other delicacies, the men drinking beer, and everybody collapsing into a much-needed siesta after the meal. But it is never served on auspicious or happy occasions because of its association with death and funerals. Parsis don't eat meat for three days after a death in the family; on the fourth day, the abstinence is broken by serving dhansakh to family, friends, and visitors. Non-Parsis sometimes find themselves unable to be as enthusiastic as Parsis about this specialty (literally grain and vegetables); yet, the variety of recipes (from families and professional chefs) for dhansakh could well fill a whole booklet, indicating how it has stimulated the Parsi culinary imagination. Six kinds of dal, cubed lamb, numerous vegetables, herbs, and greens, are combined and cooked with a host of seasonings, the dish being finished off with a sweet-and-sour bath of tamarind extract, lime juice, and brown sugar. The usual accompaniments are brown rice, kebabs, and a salad of onions, tomatoes, green chilies, and cilantro, with a sour tamarind dressing.

What about sweets? Could a community put down roots in Gujarat and not be subjected to its sweet temptations? Hardly. A community that displays such a wide-ranging appreciation of food would be unlikely to limit itself merely to the custer, kulfi, sweet yogurt, or semolina and vermicelli confections. The influence of British and European cookery on the Parsi kitchen is seen in the numerous soufflés, parfaits, flans, and cakes presented at dinners and parties, many of them, like mango soufflé, skillfully adding Indian ingredients to Western techniques. Sweets from all over India, whether the halvahs and jilebis of the North, the chhana-based sweets of Bengal, the rice puddings and evaporated milk sweets such as peda—all are grist for the Parsi sweet tooth. A most delightful Parsi invention is the malai na khaja, a baklava-like dessert with a filling of sweetened, rose-flavored cream. The use of rose petals, whether in this dessert, or in jams, or in the rose water liberally sprinkled over pilafs, perfumes the memory of an ancient connection stretching back to Iran.

However, as with so many rich and traditional foods of India, the culinary culture of the Parsis, too, is endangered—not merely because fewer people have the patience to learn the intricacies of these recipes, but also because of the rapidly dwindling numbers of the community itself. Good Parsi restaurants, as there are quite a few in Bombay, cannot quite fill this vacuum. A paean of praise to Parsi cuisine, therefore, hovers on the edge of an elegy.

Chapter Ten

BOMBAY: CITY BY THE SEA

When the Portuguese wrested seven small islands on the west coast of India from the sultans of Gujarat, and gave these the collective name of Bom Bahia (Good Bay), they couldn't possibly have imagined the magnitude of size, wealth, and squalor the place would embody several centuries later. The Portuguese later ceded the islands to the British as part of the dowry brought by Catherine of Braganza when she married King Charles II in 1662. Under the British East India Company, to whom Charles II leased the property in 1668, the islands of Bom Bahia (later connected artificially) became Bombay, an enormous port, teeming with mercantile enterprise.

In postcolonial independent India, the city continues to grow. It throbs with the pulse of commerce, desire, illusion, and creativity. Like New York, it is the financial capital of a huge country. Like New York, it lures people with dreams of fortune and success, boasting an extensive mythology of rags-to-riches stories. Like New York, it can be cruel beyond imagination. And unlike New York, it is the home of one especially glamorous business: India's fantasy-peddling film industry, Bollywood.

One of the first things I did on getting into Bombay was to call a remarkable Parsi couple I had met in the 1980s, the painter Jehangir Sabavala and his beautiful wife Shirin. Even after all these years, they remembered me and, with characteristic Parsi hospitality, they invited me to dinner the next evening. The Sabavalas' apartment, near Kemp's Corner, is exquisitely decorated. From my previous visit, I recognized the fine wood furniture with intricate carvings, the bookshelves, and the paintings. Most of all, I recognized the high, spacious balcony where I sat with their other guests and enjoyed the freshening touch of a salty evening breeze blowing in from the Arabian Sea.

What astonished me, however, was how remarkably unchanged both Jehangir and Shirin were. Their good looks and charm had successfully defied age; and, talking to Jehangir, I was again touched by his cultured gentleness. At eighty, he is still painting as actively as ever. Indian art is now slowly acquiring buyers in the international market, and Shirin proudly told me about her husband's works being auctioned at Sotheby's. When dinner was served, I noticed that both husband and wife anxiously supervised the arrangement of the food on the table, instead of leaving it to the servants. I did not remember much of what I had eaten in their house seventeen years ago, except that it had been delicious. On this evening, however, I had the opportunity to see the Parsi imagination—a combination of East and West—in the items on the table. There were crêpes with a vegetable and fish filling, covered with a white sauce; a large serving dish of pilaf sat next to a plate of plain chapattis. A spicy preparation of sautéed okra—left whole to display their elegant length—was good enough to make a whole meal with. But the star of the show was a glorious rawas (salmon), stuffed with spices and roasted whole. Even as he urged his guests to eat well, Jehangir, I noticed, hardly touched anything

except a salad of dressed lettuce, claiming that his digestion was too delicate to tolerate much at night. However, his pleasure in our enjoyment of
the meal was evident. Afterward, when dessert, a chocolate mousse–like
confection, was brought in, I was touched and amused to see the great
Parsi painter help himself liberally. A child was still alive inside the artist
who had lived through so much. When we hugged each other to say
good-bye, I felt almost tearful.

Extremes abound in Bombay, which has been recently renamed Mumbai
after a Hindu goddess. The necklace of lights around the city's Marine
Drive at night and the tall-towered skyline of Nariman Point during
the day are mesmerizing. Secretive mansions along the leafy inclines of
Malabar Hills hint at the presence of wealthy celebrities. A handsome,
uninhabited building in this area is the house where the architect of
Pakistan, Mohammad Ali Jinnah, once resided. Under a dipping western
sun, the imperial majesty of the Gateway of India monument, built by
the British, confronts the dark outlines of catamarans casting small,
humble shadows on the Arabian Sea.

But there are also hungry-eyed urchins fighting over a section of
watermelon around the town-size slums of Dharavi; road-choking, polluting traffic; throngs of workers disembarking at Victoria Station; and
hundreds of men and women manually washing the city's clothes at
Dhobighat, an enormous space full of concrete water tanks and scrubbing stones. They provide the counterpoint to the glittering image the
city loves to cultivate.

Sitting with a sandwich and lemonade in a roadside café, I managed
the odd interval of contemplation. The residents of Bombay paraded
before my eye, loitering, rushing, arguing, playing cards, and selling, selling, selling. Another day, at a restaurant called Badshah, established in
1905, I sampled the famous Parsi drink called falooda, a favorite of the
Mughal emperor Jahangir—whole milk, combined with ice cream, rose
syrup, and frozen cornstarch noodles in a tall glass—before strolling into
the colonial enclosure of Crawford Market. Having stopped to admire a
pyramid of fresh pineapples, I jumped back with a scream as a white

turkey nonchalantly stepped over my feet, and Bombay burst into up-
roarious laughter around me.

Like New York, Bombay is a city where local, national, and international
cuisines are forever fusing into something different. The diversity of its
neighborhoods is matched by the variety of its eateries—upscale, mid-
level, and downright casual. In this city, filet mignon is as available as bitter melon, avocados as much as Alfonso mangoes, all depending on the
consumer's wallet and preference. The city's street food, including items
like bhel puri and pao bhaji, has long become the stuff of urban legend.
One look at the crowd of happy eaters outside the ornate structure of
Victoria Terminus is enough to confirm the excellence of these mouthwatering snacks. Suketu Mehta, in his book *Maximum City*, calls Bombay
the "city of vada-pao," vada being a spiced potato and chickpea flour fritter sandwiched between two pieces of pao (bread). Office goers often
buy this en route to work, the way Americans pick up a doughnut and
coffee. Bombay chefs, like Bombay industrialists, are forever trying to
lure customers by remaking, renaming, or rediscovering their offerings.
Keenly aware of the international element in the city's transient population, they display a global perspective on food and cuisine.

Hemant Oberoi, the executive chef at Bombay's grande dame of
hotels, the century-old Taj Mahal Palace Hotel, is one of them. De-
scending from the beautiful lobby and residential suites to the chef's
domain in the belly of the hotel makes you feel like Jonah being swal-
lowed by the whale. There is, however, nothing biblical about the way
the extensive kitchens are operated. A modern, clockwork efficiency
permeates the creative, almost manic chaos that provides the food served
in the hotel's seven restaurants. The dominant presence is that of fish.
Seafood, including species with names like rawas, pomfret, surmai, and
bombil (the dried version of which has been called Bombay duck since
colonial times), is the prized item on Bombay's menu.

Sitting behind a desk cluttered with paper and memorabilia, Oberoi
described the seafood craze that has given rise to thirty to forty new
restaurants in the last few years. I looked over his head at the wall,

decorated with photographs of the chef with well-known faces—
former U.S. president Bill Clinton and India's former prime minister
Atal Behari Vajpayee, among them. Why, I asked him, don't the city's
residents and guests go for freshwater fish, the way my fellow Calcuttans
do? Apparently, they never have. But today's seafood mania, Oberoi
pointed out, is directly related to the growing popularity of two southern cuisines, those of Kerala and Karnataka, both of which have many
delectable ways of preparing seafood. I remembered the zesty, chili-
coated fillets of ladyfish on my thali, many hundred miles away in Bangalore. Interestingly, as I learned later, the economic muscle behind
the burgeoning seafood restaurants in Bombay happens to be the same
Shetty family who first made their mark on India's restaurant scene with
a chain of eateries called Udupi, serving the vegetarian food of southern
India.

Trends aside, Bombay attracted me as a city of secrets and singularities.
Take the unique phenomenon called *dabbawallahs*—an army of men
who pick up meals cooked by wives and family members in suburban
homes and packed into containers (dabbas). Operating a relay system,
they transport the lunch containers by train, scooter, and bike to office
workers in the city's commercial districts. Although the men delivering
the food are only half-literate, they have a remarkable record of accu-
racy, vital in a country where different religious beliefs and traditions
impose a variety of dietary restrictions. The meal eaten, the dabbas are
taken back to the family home. The system has been in place since the
nineteenth century and is a marvel of low-cost efficiency.

Standing outside Bombay's Churchgate train station at noon, I saw a
large group of dabbawallahs spilling out and continuing their journey
on waiting bicycles. Why did no such group of "lunch from home"
purveyors exist in the other major Indian cities? Was it simply an
instance of this city's entrepreneurial spirit—a spirit that wouldn't be
denied, that would carve out a window of profit even in the most un-
felicitous circumstances? This didn't seem to answer the question. The
Marwaris and the Punjabis, to mention only two groups, are noted for

their ruthless focus on opportunity and profit. But neither Calcutta nor Delhi, where these groups hold sway, has any dabbawallahs. Very likely, the phenomenon is rooted in economics and geography—the huge distances that Bombay's suburban workers have to travel to work and the expense of eating out. Whatever the reason for their continued existence, the dabbawallahs of Bombay present a unique example of a food-related trend, born to fill a need at a particular point in a society's evolution, and going on to be a cultural trademark, an ineradicable part of life in Bombay.

However, I was after a much less visible community in Bombay—the East Indians. Their numbers are few, but their cuisine distinctive. Their ancestors inhabited the villages surrounding the city. In the sixteenth and early seventeenth centuries—that is, before Bombay was handed over to the English as Catherine of Braganza's dowry—these villagers were converted to Catholicism by the Portuguese who had already established a stronghold in Goa. Over time, with dwindling numbers, disruption of families, intermarriage with other communities, the East Indian Catholics of Bombay have become an endangered community. Fortunately, a few gifted chefs are trying to revive and popularize their way of cooking. Like the cuisines of Goa, Mangalore, and parts of Cochin, as well as that of the Anglo-Indians of Calcutta, East Indian food is a product of the interchange of two religions and two races. Its authenticity can only be preserved if people are motivated to study the community's history and present it to the world.

There is some disagreement as to why the community is called East Indian. The obvious answer, offered by many, is that they are descended from Indian Catholics who worked for the British East India Company. Others, like Fleur D'Souza, a professor of history at Bombay's St. Xavier's College, dispute that. She believes that the East Indians of Bombay have a mixed ethnic heritage, being the product of Portuguese liaisons with local Indians. Goa, the predominant Portuguese settlement, had far greater numbers of these Luso-Indians. But as the British became the dominant colonial power in India, many Goanese of mixed parentage migrated to Bombay in search of jobs and property. Being

Christians, they anticipated that the British would give them preferential treatment over Hindu and Muslim Indians. Their knowledge of one European language, Portuguese, would also help in making the transition to English. To the Bombay Catholics, however, these Goanese Catholics were direct competitors. To counter the threat, the former tried to carve out a distinctive, unmistakable identity. According to Professor D'Souza, they called themselves East Indians after the huge British merchant ships called East Indiamen that regularly docked in Bombay harbor, not after the East India Company. As evidence, she points out that the Bombay East India Association was formed only in 1885, whereas the East India Company had been marginalized long ago by the British government and had become totally defunct by 1857.

Fascinating as these facets of the past were, what I really wanted was to discover the taste and ingredients of East Indian cuisine as it is today. My first call was to Antoine Lewis, the editor of *Savvy Cookbook* magazine, who agreed to meet with me two days later. Antoine's youthful features under a head of thick, wavy hair belie his experience and knowledge as a food writer. He described the two distinctive aspects of this cuisine—the artful variety of sweets and desserts and the use of "bottle masala." I was taken aback. Masala (as spices are collectively and individually called in India) was always bottled, wasn't it? How else would it keep its flavor? But no, that was not what he meant. East Indian bottle masala is a combination of many spices, sun-dried, roasted, powdered, and bottled. The masala makers tend to live in Bombay's Bandra area and each family has its own individual formulation. The year's supply is prepared in April, the hottest, driest time of year.

I cast a retrospective eye over three Indian cuisines, geographically close to each other—Gujarati, Goanese, and Bombay East Indian. They had many ingredients in common, yet each had its own way of applying them. In Gujarat, too, the annual grinding and bottling of spices takes place in April, but each spice is kept in its own separate container, allowing the cook to make up whatever combination is required. In Goa, spices may be ground together, but they are always ground fresh, prior to cooking, instead of being preground and preserved. And it seems the

East Indian has a third way, preferring prepackaged combinations. Whatever the spice formula, East Indian food is never stinging hot like some chili-laden dishes from Goa or the southern states; it is subtly flavorful, the spiciness mitigated by a strong European influence. Once purchased, the particular combination in the spice bottle determines the taste of widely diverse food, from fish to meat to a simple summer treat like tart, raw slices of green mango.

Antoine and I went for lunch to the Konkan Café. Konkan is the magically beautiful area through which my friend Sandip and I had once traveled by train to Goa. It lies between the mountain range of the Western Ghats and the Arabian Sea, extending from Bombay to Mangalore, the port city of Karnataka whose food I had tasted with Ajith Saldana in Bangalore. Right below is another narrow strip of land, which is the state of Kerala. The sea and the mountains have nurtured the different communities of the Konkan region, including the East Indians.

Although the Konkan Café serves several different cuisines, the chef, Ananda Solomon, specializes in East Indian food. Ignoring the printed menu, he made up a meal for us that considerably extended my gastronomic horizon. The equivalent of the American roll and butter appeared as soon as we sat down—crisp, light-as-air rice pappadams with three different chutneys. One of these consisted of bitter melon, coconut, and dark palm sugar. Sampling it, I found that the bitterness had been amazingly transformed into a taste that was neither sweet, nor overly salty, but indescribable, like the Japanese umami. Then came two appetizers: clams cooked with coconut, and chicken pieces with a fragrant spice coating, most probably the trademark bottle masala. I could make out only a few of the spices—garlic, black pepper, and cardamom—but I marveled at the coexistence of subtlety and heat. For entrées, we had Bombay's glory, rawas fish, steamed inside a banana leaf with a different set of intriguing spices, a bowl of sambhar (yellow lentil stew), and a chicken stew with coconut milk and saffron. All were served with rice. But it was a drink called solkadi which appeared toward the end of the meal at Antoine's suggestion, that was the real eye-opener. Coconut milk (yes, the ubiquitous coconut of coastal India) had been blended with the sour fruit called kokum, which grows in the rain forests of the Western Ghats. The color was mauve, the texture light yet emollient. This was the Konkan equivalent of the northern Indian lassi.

Reeling from the effects of the meal, Antoine and I strolled out into the lambent sunshine of Bombay's winter. What I really needed was to sit down over a cup of tea and slowly digest my lunch. But I also wanted to meet a friend of Antoine's, the journalist and food columnist, Vikram Doctor. When Antoine put away his cell phone to say that Vikram had agreed to meet us, I didn't bother to ask where. We got into a cab and Antoine gave some directions to the driver. A short ride later, we got out in front of an office building near Churchgate station, from which I had seen the dabbawallahs pouring out. As I followed Antoine up the shallow steps into a large, undistinguished building, my eyes fell on the sign over the entrance. I could hardly believe my eyes. It said Tea Centre.

Over the years, one of my biggest disappointments in India has been the difficulty of finding a decent cup of tea in cafés and restaurants. Even in posh hotels, tea bags rule. The glorious first- and second-flush Darjeeling teas—the pride of India—are more likely to be found in the boutique tea shops of the West or the homes of wealthy tea estate owners and their friends. The average Indian seems content with strong black tea, lacking in flavor and bouquet. Even the much-touted blends sold by big tea companies are disappointing. Lately, the increasing popularity of sophisticated blends of coffee has given birth to a host of coffee shops à la Starbucks for the young and the trendy, signaling a further decline in the republic of tea. So when I walked into the unassuming, Miss Marple–style interior of the Tea Centre, my expectations were minimal.

Opened in the 1950s by the Indian Tea Board, the Tea Centre is now privately owned. Its menu includes strange and exotic blends like Hot Buttered Apple Tea (recommended by Vikram), Thai Chai, Rose Petal Tea, Yogic Assam, and even Mango Chai (iced). But the regular varieties, such as Darjeeling, Assam, and Nilgiri, were also on offer. I ordered a pot of Darjeeling and was pleasantly surprised by the flavor and the taste.

Sipping the tea, I listened to Vikram tell me about the latest food books, about the growing sophistication of the readership in India, about restaurants run in central Bombay (where the British built their cotton mills) by upper- and lower-caste migrants to the city. The ones run by lower-caste owners specialize in serving meat, particularly offal. Chopped intestines, spleen, kidneys, testicles—all are made into spicy delectables. If the tongue or the stomach quails at the thought of such a plateful, one can try the eateries run by the migrant Brahmins. Like the Brahmins of Bengal and unlike those of northern and southern India, the Brahmins of the Konkan region (called Saraswat Brahmins) relish the fish so generously provided by the Arabian Sea. Vikram seemed much taken by one of these Brahmin establishments, where a fixed amount of food is cooked every day. Clients are served on a first-come, first-served basis, and when the food runs out, the waiters brusquely turn you away. Their indifference, bordering on rudeness, sounded similar to that of the waiters at Boston's legendary Durgin Park restaurant. But the food is so good that customers keep lining up day after day, hoping to get lucky.

Vikram has a way with words. It is not for nothing that he is one of the best food columnists in India today. But even as I listened to his vastly entertaining stories, the fragrance of the tea evoked a different story in the back of my mind, one about the same Catherine of Braganza whose dowry had brought Bombay under the British. Unlikely as it sounds today, it was she who popularized tea among the British elite. At the time of her marriage, the Portuguese court was already habituated to the custom of drinking tea, possibly because of Portugal's trade links with China. Not so with the British. When Catherine arrived in London after a long sea voyage and asked for a cup of tea to refresh herself, all she got was a glass of ale! Soon after, though, as the British East India Company began to make the most of its monopoly Catherine's husband had granted them on trade with the Indies, the British tea trade began to flourish. In England, Catherine's continued fondness for the leaf gave it the requisite cachet for the nobility and the gentry to start to adopt tea drinking as a mark of refinement. In India, the addiction to tea was a direct result of colonial rule. Once the British had discovered that several regions of India possessed the right altitude and climate for tea cultivation, they carried out a systematic advertising campaign about this new beverage, encouraging the locals with giveaway samples until tea-drinking became widespread. A Chinese leaf thus gave birth to an Indian habit, with the midwifery of an acquisitive trading company that had already been responsible for reinforcing the same custom in its native country. Which of these domains should claim tea as its authentic beverage today, especially given the waxing passion everywhere for coffee?

I said good-bye to Vikram, rather regretful that I could not go with him to any of the restaurants he had mentioned. But our lunch had been gargantuan and I needed to finish packing before catching a late night flight out of Bombay.

It had been a long day under the western sun, which sets later over the Arabian Sea than it does on the Bay of Bengal in the east. At four in the morning, I had gone over to the southernmost tip of the Colaba area to watch the fishing boats—stocky vessels painted in loud, tacky colors—coming in with their catch from the sea. The day before, I had gone there in the afternoon and suddenly found myself in the middle of a crowd celebrating a festival in honor of Ganesh (though not the big annual celebration of Ganesh Chaturthi), the elephant-headed god of success and prosperity. A statue of the god in a portable clay shrine painted gold, pink, and blue was being carried by a group of local fishermen, while a larger group of men and women danced around it, clapping and chanting to the accompaniment of drums and cymbals. Under a banyan tree, several women distributed food, probably offerings to the god, among which I saw puran-polis—fried whole wheat breads stuffed with chickpea flour, coconut, brown sugar, and small quantities of sesame, poppy seeds, and cardamom seeds. Puran-polis are a favorite throughout the state of Maharashtra.

In the morning, though, there were no signs of these frenetic festivities. It was time to buy and sell. Some hotels and restaurants have stopped buying from the Colaba fishermen because of concerns that they may be fishing in polluted waters very close to the coastline. Those establishments prefer to get their supplies from Ratnagiri, further up the coast. Even so, there were plenty of takers in Colaba, as I observed. The dawn sky was still dark as the crowd of wholesale buyers noisily jostled and competed with one another for the best consignment at the best price. Among them were the new dealers and suppliers (mostly dressed in cheap but flashy Western clothes) as well as the habitués, the inheritors of Bom Bahia, whose faces were lined with insider knowledge, cynicism, and a touch of resignation. Old and new, past and present, imbued the fishy air as the sky slowly lightened.

Late that night, as the glittering garlands of Bombay's lights spread out below my rising plane, I thought again about the East Indians of this city, particularly their vividly colorful wedding feasts and Christmas dinners as described by Michael Swamy Fernandes, a cordon bleu chef who is partly East Indian himself and is also the author of *Enduring Flavours: In Appreciation of East Indian Cuisine.* He had been out of town during most of my stay in Bombay, but we did manage to have a brief yet illuminating phone conversation.

For festive meals, he told me, particularly Christmas dinner, East Indians, like Goans, glory in their pork vindaloo and sorpotel. Other delicacies include whole roasted suckling pig; duck indad, seasoned with Kashmiri red chilies; mutton tope (lamb thickened with rice flakes); and chicken moile. Fish preparations, such as stuffed pomfret and fried mackerel, are also popular in the community. Unlike the majority of their fellow Indians, East Indians are not strong on vegetables. But like their Indian forebears, they avoid beef, even though Christianity has no injunctions against eating the sacred cow. And then there are the small delights such as fugeas, fried rolls made with dough that combines flour with coconut milk, sugar, toddy, and a bit of cottage cheese. A basketful of fugeas is an obligatory part of the East Indian Christmas table.

Fernandes was most nostalgic about the colorful weddings of his childhood, when East Indians celebrated for seven days, following the tradition of their Hindu Indian compatriots. In the villages, the women decked themselves out in traditional clothes and jewelry, and painted their houses with colored powders. The wedding rice was garnished with raisins and fried onions, exactly as it was in many Hindu and Muslim homes. And thalis full of local sweets, taken by the bride's family to the groom's house, held pride of place alongside a Western-style wedding cake. It reminded me of the tatto sent by Bengali Hindu grooms to the bride's house on the wedding day.

I asked Fernandes about the East Indians' Portuguese heritage, especially with regard to sweets, for which the Portuguese had acquired such a reputation several centuries ago. The East Indian repertoire, he said, is similar to that of Goa. There are endless types of boles (cakes), including coconut cake, a halvah made with guavas (itself a Portuguese import from the New World), honey bread, lethri (fine rice noodles sprinkled with coconut), newries, and of course the all-time favorite, marzipan, called mazapao in Goa. Newries? I asked. Fernandes described the sweet as a pastry shell containing a filling of semolina, sugar, raisins, cashew nuts, poppy seeds, and a bit of cardamom. The stuffed shell is deep-fried in oil until golden brown.

I tried to imagine the crisp, sweet, fragrant, richness of a newri, and promised myself a future visit to the city on Bom Bahia, just to taste one of these. For now, I was going to take some time out to reflect on my varied experiences and plan a journey to Cochin, the ancient spice entrepôt in the western state of Kerala.

Chapter Eleven

KERALA: RICH CUISINES
OF THE PEPPER KINGDOM

As my plane descended into Cochin, the most famous city in Kerala, I felt as if I was plunging into an ocean of green. A density of coconut, palm, and banana trees hugs the coastline of Kerala, defining the land as they have for millennia. Even the Bengal coastline does not look as intensely green from above. The greenness of this western prospect soothed my eye and reminded me of the Bengali folk belief that merely looking at something green is good for one's vision.

The coconut tree not only outlines the coast, it can also serve as a focal point for exploring life and food in Kerala. Like other coastal peoples in India, the inhabitants of this state have found an extraordinary range of applications for this nurturing product that is both a fruit and a nut. Not only is it an essential part of the diet, its fiber and flesh are also important commercial products. Many family fortunes have been made by buying and selling coir and copra. For an ingenious utilization of coconuts, one only has to look at the gleaming floor of Cochin's Dutch Palace (built by the Portuguese, taken over by the Dutch, and eventually handed over to the local rajahs). Although it resembles polished black stone, it is actually made from a unique combination of burned coconut shells, charcoal, lime, egg white, and juices extracted from various plants.

A young woman in the lobby of my hotel handed me a coconut, its top sliced off and a straw inserted into it—a traditional gesture of welcome. Unlike in Bengal, where the young coconut is always green, in Cochin, I noticed, it was a pale shade of saffron. It reminded me of the interior of the ripe palms of Bengal, the ones that come into the market in August and September, their pulp exuding a fragrance both tempting and overpowering. When I drank, the Kerala coconut's water had an undertaste of salt that you don't get in Bengal. The Arabian Sea, I sensed, was much more of a parent to it than the Bay of Bengal to the coconuts in my native soil. As I slowly sipped the sweet-salty water and gazed out at the quiet streets of Cochin, I felt that the coconut was as emblematic of this narrow strip of southwestern India as the banana leaf was of the Bengal delta. Unexpectedly, I felt the stirrings of romance, the romance of discovering a promised land, outlined by coconut trees and beckoning mariners and traders from far countries to brave the perils of unknown seas.

Once I had checked in to my room and done some minimal unpacking, I called the two people whom I had met during a previous visit—Radha and her husband, Chandran. They had been expecting my call, and Radha asked me to meet her early the next morning so that we could both go to the Krishna temple near her house. She was a devout Hindu, belonging to the Nair (warrior) caste and a daily morning visit to the temple was part of her life.

As soon as we walked in through the temple gates, I saw the coconut in an extraordinary demonstration of "rendition." Rows of coconut halves—a pleasing contrast of husky brown shell and creamy white flesh—were being used as votive lamps, the cotton wicks burning merrily in a little bit of oil poured into the shell and continuously replenished by the coconut's own supply of oil.

The pillared, flat-roofed structure of the temple with its open courtyard was very different from the Bengali temples I was used to, with their cupolas sheltering the deity in a dark center. This small Hindu temple in Cochin aroused memories of the elaborate Hathee Singh Jain temple I had visited in the Gujarati city of Ahmedabad. As we neared the shrine where the priest was chanting Sanskrit mantras and making floral offerings to the image of Krishna, Radha and her aunt, who was visiting from Bangkok, folded their hands and prayed silently. My eyes, however, were riveted by the masses of bananas laid out as offerings—the many varieties of bananas that Kerala is justly proud of.

We left after circumambulating the temple courtyard. It was a very different experience from that of Amritsar, where the huge crowd had impressed me with its discipline. In this neighborhood temple, there were only a few visitors, though their devotion was as evident as in Amritsar. Men dressed in suits and ties, obviously on their way to work, entered, took off their shoes, made offerings, and prayed. Before leaving, some of them prostrated themselves flat on the ground, quite uncaring as to what the act might do to their office garb. Before leaving, each person was handed a small leaf containing his or her share of the temple offering, mostly bananas. Sweets—the Golden Temple's rich, ghee-laden halvah, or the soft chhana sandesh found at the Kalighat temple in Calcutta, or even the spun-sugar batashas distributed in many northern Indian temples— were noticeably absent. The South, I was reminded, has less of a sweet tooth than the rest of the country; even the Southern gods don't seem to mind the absence of man-made sweets in their offerings.

For a small state, Kerala has a wealth of legends, as Radha reminded me while we strolled back from the temple. Its mythical origins are connected to Parasuram, a quasi-god supposed to be an avatar (incarnation in human form) of Vishnu, the second of the Hindu trinity. In the *Mahabharata*, he is a tormented figure, condemned to behead his mother (who was overcome with desire for another man) on his father's orders and, later, forced to avenge his father, killed by some princes of the warrior caste. His revenge consisted of ridding the world of all members of this caste. He finally desisted from slaughter, at the request of his grandfather, and undertook arduous penance to appease gods and Brahmins, after which he retired to a monastic existence in a high mountainous region. In Kerala, however, the story goes that after completing his penance, Parasuram was given a piece of land, fertile and beautiful, by the god of the ocean and the goddess of the earth. He invited Brahmins from other parts of India to bless the land, take up residence there, and see to it that future residents obeyed the rules of gods and men. That beautiful and fertile piece of land is supposed to be Kerala.

The residential area where Radha and her family live has a hushed quietness that evokes a much older time. Its houses sit behind old brick walls, their red tiled roofs peeping out from densely growing coconut trees and banana plants that provide fruit and shade. When the two of us came back to the house, Chandran and his mother were waiting to have breakfast with us. Radha bustled around in the kitchen, getting the food ready with the help of her maid. I asked Chandran about his two daughters and learned that neither lived in Cochin. Both are in the software business, one working in Bangalore, the other in Boston.

The most prominent thing that appeared on the table that morning was a large bowl of bananas. But these were more like plantains, not very sweet, their texture a bit more chewy. They had been steamed, peeled, and cut into pieces before serving. With my first bite, as with my first sip of the coconut water, I tasted a faint trace of salt—from the Arabian Sea that impregnated the coastal area. The next unusual thing was a white cylindrical item called puttu, a combination of rice flour and ground coconut steamed in a bamboo steamer. This, as I was told, was a versatile dish, as amenable to being eaten with milk and ripe bananas (like a breakfast cereal) as with a spicy fish curry or vegetable stew. There were also idlis (steamed rice cakes) that we ate with a sauce made from peanuts and spices that Radha's maid had ground up together and blended with sesame oil. It was an unfamiliar taste but, the more I ate, the more I liked it. Radha laughed at the surprise on my face and said she would take me to a store later where a packaged version was available. I could take it back to America, and blend it with sesame oil to make a dipping sauce for fried items.

"I wish you had come a little later," she said as we drank our tea. "Then you could have seen the Pooram festival when elephants, wearing rich decorations, are brought in. The images of the gods are put on their backs and paraded around town. It is beautiful."

I nodded regretfully. I knew I was also going to miss the other major event of the Kerala year, the weeklong harvest festival of Onam, which takes place in late August and early September. Every state and community with rural roots has a harvest festival. In Bengal, it is called Nabanno, literally "new rice." Unheated milk, palm sugar, pieces of sugarcane, and small bananas are combined with uncooked, newly harvested rice and offered to the gods. Afterward, the rice is cooked with milk and palm sugar to make a rich pudding that the families share with each other. In the South, the eastern state of Tamil Nadu has a notable harvest festival called Pongal, which is celebrated by eating a khichuri-like concoction of rice, moong beans, and ghee, spiced with ground black pepper, kari leaves, red chilies, and cumin seeds. There is also a sweet version of the dish called shakkarpongal, made with rice, milk, moong beans, sugar, coconut chips, raisins, and ghee.

In Kerala, the harvesting process and the celebratory foods are rooted in another ancient legend, the story of King Mahabali, who grew so powerful that even the gods and demons became concerned about his power. They all prayed to the god Vishnu and asked him to take measures to rein in Mahabali. The king was not only brave and powerful, he also prided himself on his charity. So Vishnu took the form of a midget and appeared in his court, asking for a boon. The king was magnanimous. "Name it and it shall be yours," he told the midget, who then asked for enough land to cover three of his own footsteps. The king laughed uproariously and granted this small request. Instantly, the midget was transformed into the great god Vishnu. With one step he covered the sky, with the other the earth, and the third he placed on Mahabali's head, pushing him down to the underworld. At this, the king cried out, begging forgiveness for his past arrogance. His people, too, wailed at the prospect of losing a king who, whatever his intimidating displays of prowess, had looked after them. Vishnu relented and said that, once a year, Mahabali would be allowed to return from the nether regions and stay with his people for a week. That, said Radha, is the week of Onam. I was reminded of the classical Roman myth of the harvest goddess Ceres (Demeter in Greece) whose daughter was carried off by Pluto, god of the underworld. But Ceres was more fortunate than the people of Kerala. Since her daughter Proserpina had eaten only six seeds of pomegranate during her stay in Pluto's realm, she was allowed to come back to earth for six months every year.

Cochin and its commercial center of Ernakulam extend over a widespread area consisting of mainland, peninsula, and islands, of which only Willingdon Island was artificially created by material dredged from Cochin harbor. The drive from the airport takes one over the Periyar River and provides glimpses of Kerala's legendary backwaters. Unlike the Mouths of the Ganges in Bengal, these backwater channels are not enveloped in sinister mangrove forests, nor do man-eating tigers or other dangerous carnivores lurk in the green shadows. For those interested in wildlife, the place to visit is the Lake Periyar Wildlife Sanctuary near the central Kerala town of Thekkady. Near Cochin, boating in the backwaters is a safe and unmitigated pleasure. Traveling the streets of Ernakulam, however, means exposing oneself to all the hazards of a growing Indian city. Unruly traffic, crowded shopping centers, multiplex office towers, and large signs advertising tutorial and employment opportunities in the software business add up to a very modern bustle, far removed from the quiet, semicolonial murmurs of Radha's residential area.

Exploring Ernakulam, I was struck by the frequency with which churches, temples, and mosques appeared along the way. Religiosity of all kinds seemed to flourish hand in hand with material enterprise, a trend that I had noticed in many other Indian cities. Probably in no other country does one see so many businessmen of all economic levels paying their daily dues to the divine before happily immersing themselves in activities of questionable ethics or ruthless manipulation. As the sun rose high and beat down harshly on me, I stopped at a church in front of which a large crowd was observing some kind of ritual. Coming closer, I realized a baptism ceremony was in progress in the front portico of the church. The priest and his assistants read the liturgy in a language unfamiliar to me, while the mother held the baby in a huge froth of white lace. The crowd around them probably consisted of family, friends, and the odd visitor like me. All the women were richly dressed, some in colorful silks and others in the fine white Kerala cotton saris with narrow gold borders. All wore fragrant jasmine garlands in their shining black hair. With sweat beading my forehead, hair frizzing in the humidity, and a sari crumpled with creases, I must have been a sorely anomalous figure.

Still, I stood and watched the ceremony, until my eyes were suddenly transfixed by an object I had never expected to see in a Catholic church. Behind the priests stood a tiered brass pillar with a circle of oil lamps burning in every tier, the kind that is a regular fixture of Hindu temples. I had not seen one of these in any other church I had visited, whether in Calcutta, or Bombay, or Goa, or even in the small western Bengali town of Bandel, which boasts the earliest church in Bengal. Christianity, which first came to Kerala sometime between A.D. 50 and 52, has obviously had no problems adopting ritual objects from the majority faith of Hinduism. Beyond the tiered standing lamp was a waist-high stone slab on which shone row upon row of coconut halves, flaming wicks in the center, just like the ones I had seen in Radha's temple. I watched the white-robed priest pour holy water over the infant's head and momentarily wondered if that, too, had been taken from the coconut.

Modern Kerala, like so many other states in India, was formed after independence. It was officially created in 1956 by combining the regions

of Malabar (north), Cochin (center), and Travancore (south). Nature
has blessed this long leaf-shaped piece of land with beauty and many
resources that drew merchants from ancient times. A state tourism
brochure proclaims: "With the Arabian Sea to the west, the Western
Ghats towering 500–2,700 meters to the east and networked by forty-
four rivers, Kerala enjoys unique geographical features that have made it
one of the most sought after tourism destinations in Asia. A long shoreline with serene beaches . . . lush hill stations and exotic wildlife . . .
sprawling plantations and paddy fields." Happily, these claims are well
founded, which is one reason why tourism is the most rapidly growing
industry in Kerala. Unfortunately, some of the formerly pristine beaches
are already marked by the adverse effects of intense human activity.

If religious harmony inspired tourism, then Kerala would certainly
qualify as the prime destination within India. Three major communities—
Hindus, Christians, and Muslims, not to speak of the tiny but distinctive
Jewish minority—live side by side without a history of rancor or conflict.
While the state's high level of literacy and education may be a current factor behind this amity, interreligious harmony has a long and ancient history here.

The three territories that combined to form the state roughly corre-
spond to its three main religious communities. Here, Muslims, who are
the majority in the northern Malabar area, are called Moplahs, the modern variant of *mapillai* or *maha pillai*, meaning "bridegroom." They are
the descendants of Arab merchants from ancient times who married local women (thus becoming bridegrooms) and settled down here to better carry on their business. They also increased their numbers through
conversion.

The central part of the state is the bastion of Christians, originally
converted by Saint Thomas the Apostle, the one called Doubting
Thomas, who eventually moved on to proselytize in Tamil Nadu, where
he was assassinated by a Hindu priest. His grave in Mylapore (near
Madras) is still an important pilgrimage spot. Many centuries after the
apostle's death (around A.D. 78), a fresh wave of proselytizing was spear-
headed by Thomas Cana, a Syrian Christian merchant, who persuaded a

fair number of his fellow Syrians to come and settle on the Malabar Coast so that Christianity could flourish there once again. The Scriptures they read were written in Syriac, a dialect of Aramaic. These two factors eventually led to the Kerala community being called Syrian Christians. Word about their presence got around in a garbled fashion to the courts of Europe; the Indian Christians were believed to be the subjects of the legendary king of ancient Abyssinia, Prester John. That is why Vasco da Gama, on making his historic landfall in Calicut in 1498, is supposed to have declared that he was looking for spices and Christians. In the seventeenth century, the Portuguese set out to convert the local people, especially the fisherfolk living along the coast. Their descendants have formed the community of Kerala Catholics.

The southernmost part of Kerala, which was originally the kingdom of Travancore, has a Hindu majority. Among them the Namboodiri Brahmins and the Nairs, who were originally the warrior caste, are the elite. My friends Radha and Chandran belong to the latter group.

Each of these groups has developed a distinctive style of cooking, but certain items—made with rice, coconut, milk, and palm sugar—are common to all of them. As a rice-eating Bengali, I used to be proud of the many ways we process this one cereal—steamed rice, pilaf, popped rice, puffed rice, flattened/flaked rice, thin rice flour chapattis, and steamed or griddle-baked sweets, also made of rice flour. Although I was familiar with the South Indian dosas and idlis (both made from a fermented dough of rice and dal) that are now eaten all over India, I still felt Bengal had the edge in terms of versatility. It was during my visits to Cochin, when I tasted Kerala's appams—those exquisite, gravid-looking, yeasty rice flour pancakes with crisp, slightly curled up edges—that I began to think that Bengal had a few things to learn from Kerala. Mopping up stews and curries with appams is a pleasure that borders on the celestial. There are several variants on the appam, each with a different name. One delightful item, the iddiappam, consists of thin strands of rice flour dough, formed into little nests that are steamed and served with coconut milk and sugar for breakfast, or with stews and soups at dinner. The iddiappam, which became "string hoppers" in English through a peculiar colonial permutation, is also popular in Sri Lanka, where it is often served at breakfast with a poached or fried egg in the middle—a delightful South Asian variation on English breakfast food. For those used to the enormous dosas—semicrisp crêpes folded into a cylindrical shape and stretching out over both sides of an average dinner plate—commonly served in other parts of the country, the dosas of Kerala are a surprise. They are thick, small, and soft, and can be manipulated like a chapatti to scoop up vegetables or chutneys. The coconut–green chili chutney, served with dosas, is however, the same everywhere in India.

Given the rich culinary history of Kerala, I knew that the best way to learn the most would be from a professional. I managed to track down a fellow Bengali, Nabhojit Ghosh, who is the executive chef at Cochin's quaint, colonial-style Taj Malabar Hotel on Willingdon Island. I waited for him in his quiet first-floor office, where the screen saver on the computer was a beautiful image of a cantilevered fishing net, the kind that are called Chinese fishing nets, commonly seen in the harbor area. It is one of the most familiar visual icons of Cochin, harking back to an extended past that has seen a parade of nationalities—Romans, Arabs, Phoenicians, Chinese, Portuguese, Dutch, French, British—avidly pursuing the international spice trade and other business opportunities there.

As I kept looking at the computer screen, another Kerala image, from my earlier visit, was superimposed on it—dark outlines of fishing boats rocking on the sparkling waters bordering Kovalam Beach, and further away, a lone fisherman, standing in his boat and flinging his net into the sea with a motion as richly fluid as the waves he rode. These were the images I had taken away with me as I drove to the airport in Trivandrum, the state capital, to catch a flight back to Bombay. Seven days earlier, I had driven from Cochin to Trivandrum, accompanied by Radha's husband, Chandran, and one of his cousins. The journey, along one of India's national highways, had taken four hours, and we stopped for lunch at a spacious restaurant run by the tourism department. The thali there— so different from the one in Bangalore—was strictly vegetarian, the food colors more pastel than vivid. But the most intriguing item was the rice, plump, parboiled grains with a purplish tinge, a world apart from the fluffy, light basmati or the delicate small-grained varieties like gobindab-hog that I had grown up eating in Bengal.

It was in Trivandrum that I met Indira, a friend of Radha and Chandran's. When an unexpected surgery landed me in the hospital for a few days, Indira became an angelic presence during my incarceration. Every day, she brought me lunch that she had cooked herself, since the hospital staff had warned us that the food in their cafeteria was not par-ticularly suitable for a patient. Like Radha, Indira was a vegetarian, and her cooking was both savory and light. Often she brought fruit to end the meal. That was how I learned about the bananas of Kerala—varied in shape, texture, taste, so different from the ones I had grown up eating in Bengal or the South American ones we get in the States. It's no won-der that banana chips are a common snack in Kerala. She also brought me several bags of those. One day, there were two particularly delightful surprises—a bowl full of pomegranate sections, gleaming ruby red, and a mild dessert made of rice flour, ground coconut, and dark palm sugar, all wrapped and steamed in a banana leaf. I knew her only for seven days, but when I left Trivandrum, it was as hard to say good-bye to her as to a family member.

"Sorry to keep you waiting, but things suddenly got busy in the kitchen," Nabhojit Ghosh's voice broke into my reflections.

"Not to worry. I was admiring your screen saver here."

I watched Ghosh fold his tall body into the chair facing me. Despite the chef's white toque and jacket, he looked like an energetic, youthful professor, an impression that was further confirmed as he promptly launched into a discourse on all the cuisines of Kerala. He had spent only a few years in Cochin, he confessed, but he had fallen in love with all of them. One of his favorites was a Syrian Christian dish, fish moily, which is simple, subtle, and tasty, a compulsory item at weddings and during Christmas. Cooked in a shallow clay pot called a mann chatti, the dish involves preparing a clove- and cinnamon-flavored sauce made with onions, ginger, garlic, green chilies, and coconut milk (tomatoes being optional) and gently simmering pieces of whitefish in it. The final garnish is often a pinch of ground black pepper.

In a coastal state like Kerala, it is not surprising that such ocean fish as red snapper, gray mullet, mackerel, and black pomfret (similar to the pompano of Florida) should figure prominently on the nonvegetarians' plate. And as in other coastal cuisines, like those of Mangalore or Goa, using coconut milk and ground coconut in combination with spices is a natural way of employing what is most available. But was freshwater fish totally absent from the kitchen? I asked Nabhojit Ghosh. He smiled at this obvious Bengali question. Cochin being a port city, marine species would naturally be preferred, but in places like Trichur or Kottayam, fish is caught from the rivers and made into delicious tart preparations with the kokum fruit or slices of green mango. In northern Kerala, green mussels and yellow clams are popular, made into hot, spicy concoctions.

The one notable exception to the marine roster even in Cochin, said Ghosh, was called karimeen in Malayalam (pearl spot in English), a small pomfret-size fish caught in the state's backwaters. Its delicate flavor is much prized, and it is served in one classic dish called meen pollichathu. Pepper, chilies, turmeric, ginger, and garlic are sautéed with onions and tomatoes until a paste is formed. This is applied liberally to the fish, which is then wrapped in a banana leaf coated with oil. The package is gently roasted on a shallow pan till the fish is done. Since the process is laborious and time consuming, the dish is usually reserved for special occasions. As is only to be expected, other seafood, such as crabs and prawns—white, red, tiger—are eaten with great relish, cooked in many different ways. As in Bengal, the prawns are served with their heads. But the glorious galda chingri (king prawn) that figured in my aunt's wedding feast is not available in Kerala. It is a freshwater species and limited to our eastern zone.

The Syrian Christians, the only Indian community with no food restrictions, have also created a whole slew of recipes for meat including beef, pork, duck, and chicken. Possibly the best-known dish (which also has a vegetarian version) is a stew called ishtoo, which combines pieces of meat with potatoes and a few other vegetables like carrots, beans, and green peas in a lightly seasoned broth. The cooking medium is coconut oil, which is first flavored with whole cinnamon, cardamom, and cloves. Onions, garlic, ginger, and green chilies are sautéed in the oil before the pieces of meat are tossed in and fresh coconut milk added to make the broth. Ishtoo is usually served with appams. It can be a starter at an elaborate formal meal; it can even be eaten at breakfast.

My thoughts turned again to the days I had spent in the hospital in Trivandrum, the doleful warnings I had received about the cafeteria food. Surely, it was possible for even the most basic kitchen to serve appam and ishtoo? The way Ghosh was describing the taste, I felt I could have eaten these two things every day for a week. Perhaps the hospital cooks were all vegetarian Hindus, and even a vegetable ishtoo was not an item they commonly made. Even Indira, I recalled, had never brought me these items.

Among other Syrian Christian dishes there are several mouthwatering preparations. Chicken is cooked either in a spicy sauce made with both red and green chilies, star anise, and crushed cashews, or with grated and fried coconut. Duck is gently simmered with coconut milk, and, most intriguing of all, chunks of beef are combined with large pieces of coconut, fried together with spices. This last often makes its appearance at Syrian Christian weddings. Hearing about it, I felt the usual regret of the casual traveler about not living in a place long enough to know people and be invited to participate in their family celebrations. A Syrian Christian wedding, even today, seemed to promise far better fare than the peculiar mishmash of catered food I had seen being served at the Bengali wedding in Calcutta. This community also has a love for hot, spicy pickles. Unlike the northern Indians, who bestow their pickle-making genius on fruits and vegetables, the Syrian Christians of Kerala transform and preserve both beef and fish with vinegar, sesame oil, coconut oil, and flavorings such as asafetida, chilies, garlic, ginger, fenugreek, and mustard.

At this point in Ghosh's litany, I felt I needed to hear about vegetables. These, too, are cooked in a variety of savory combinations, some of the dishes being common to all communities, Hindus, Muslims, and Christians. Avial, one of Kerala's signature dishes, was one I had eaten at

Radha's house for lunch one afternoon. Vegetables, including carrots, sweet potatoes, baby cucumbers, eggplants, snake gourd, potatoes, and drumsticks (the long, fleshy pods of the *Moringa oleifera* tree, given their English name because of their appearance) are all assembled and painstakingly cut into matchstick-size pieces. They are then boiled with onion, salt, turmeric, and chili powder until cooked. A paste of grated coconut, garlic, and cumin seeds is stirred in. The final touch is the addition of coconut oil and a garnish of fresh kari leaves. While Bengal has many mixed vegetable dishes, I had never come across one where the oil was one of the final ingredients in cooking. The taste of avial, however, is light, not rich and oily.

Stir-fried vegetable dishes, called thorans, are also very popular across the state, and usually are made with a single vegetable, or even some species of small fish. Mustard and chilies are first tossed into hot oil for flavoring before the vegetables are added, with salt, green chilies, and fresh kari leaves providing taste, fire, and garnish. My favorite banana blossom often figures in a Kerala thoran. The concept is very similar to the Bengali chachhari, but some combinations—such as a thoran made with bitter melon and grated coconut—seem bizarre to the Bengali palate.

Although I had already discovered that the South does not have the same predilection for sweets that one sees in the North, or in Bengal, I was still surprised that, except for important religious occasions like Christmas or Easter, cakes don't figure all that much on the Syrian Christian menu. Like the rest of their fellow Keralites, they seem happy to end their meals with rice puddings (payasam), confections of coconut and palm sugar, sweet fruits such as mango, jackfruit, banana, and pineapple, and a few oddities, for instance, palm syrup poured over ripe bananas and mashed with yogurt.

The quiet, relatively unvisited Malabar region of northern Kerala is the birthplace of the distinctive cuisine of the Moplahs. This includes, as one would expect from any Muslim community, many kinds of biryanis and pilafs, not simply combining rice with meat and chicken, but also with many kinds of fish—a natural development of a coastal state. However, instead of using the long-grained basmati that is the standard for biryanis and pilafs in northern India, Moplahs use "kaima" rice, a local short-grained variety.

One difference from the other Muslim cuisines of India is the infrequency with which kebabs appear on the Moplah plate. The place of kebabs is taken by very dry and very spicy meat (beef and lamb since pork is forbidden to Muslims) dishes. Wedding banquets will include biryani, meats in rich sauces, and these dry-cooked meat dishes. Among their specialties is roast chicken made on the stovetop, instead of in a conventional oven. The bird is stuffed with spices and a hard-boiled egg, and slowly fried over very low heat in a deep pot. Also, wheat and meat are combined in various ways. Wheat is coarsely ground for a porridge called aleesa. Or it is left whole, and combined with minced meat, for a dish called kiskiya.

While the liberal use of coconut milk, oil, and grated coconut is common to all three regions of Kerala, as is the frequent appearance of bananas at meals, there are some exquisite dishes that are solely the product of the Moplah imagination. One of the best known and most delicious dishes among the Moplahs is neichoru, rice fried in ghee with onions, cloves, cinnamon, and cardamom. It is a dish that is commonly served on the eve of a wedding. Rice flour is made into breads called pathiris, some thin like chapattis, some thick, some deep-fried. During the fasting month of Ramadan, the evening's dinner often consists of pathiri, and meat and chicken dishes. Perhaps the most famous Moplah dish is a dessert called mutta-mala (literally, a garland of eggs), which also features in wedding banquets. Egg yolks are cooked in syrup until they form long strands. They are then removed from the syrup and spread out on a plate. An accompanying dessert, egg snow pudding, is then made by beating the egg whites until fluffy, blending them with the leftover syrup, and then cooking the mixture in a steamer. The soft white confection is cut into diamonds and served with the yellow egg strands. Once again, I wished there was a Moplah wedding I could walk into.

The food of the Hindu Nairs and Namboodiris (the latter are strict vegetarians) in southern Kerala's Travancore region is the mildest of all the Kerala cuisines. However, as Nabhojit Ghosh pointed out and as I had already discovered from Radha's table, it has an ineffable yet unforgettable delicacy of taste. Not too many vegetables grow in Kerala; most of the ones in Cochin's markets these days are imported from neighboring Tamil Nadu. But the Hindu vegetarians have learned to make the most of whatever nature has given them. At Radha's house, I found a simple dish made with chopped arbi (a tarolike root) so delicious that I could have forgone all the other items. The dal she served, which was the sambhar made with toor dal common to all of South India, did not have the tongue-blistering heat of some Tamil versions of the dish. The curd-rice with which we ended the meal was the same I had eaten in Bangalore, but there were no pungent fried chilies to be crumbled into it.

This same savory mildness is apparent in what is called elasadya (temple food), which is served to devotees on banana leaves. People sit on the ground, and designated servers walk by, ladling the food onto the leaf. Dry or fried items are served first. Then, a heaping portion of rice—a parboiled variety with thick, reddish grains that Kerala is famed for—is placed on the center of the leaf. A bit of dal and a bit of ghee is poured over the top. Finally, the sambhar and vegetable dishes are served around the rice. The auspicious aura of this vegetarian temple menu is so strong that sometimes Hindu families will serve exactly the same dishes on special celebratory occasions.

I told Nabhojit Ghosh I knew what he was talking about, from my stay in the hospital at Trivandrum, because of Sister Sreeja, the young nurse who looked after me. My first encounter with her was mildly hilarious. Lying alone in bed, I had been thinking about my future travels, when suddenly there was a knock at the door, followed by the sound of girlish giggling.

"Who is it?" I asked.

"Sister, madam."

"Well, come in."

"Any bystanders, madam?"

For a moment, I was stumped. Bystanders? Who were they? What did she mean? Then it dawned on me that perhaps she was displaying an acute sensitivity to my privacy. If I had friends or relatives visiting me, she would come back later. The giggling, I later understood, came from several other trainee nurses who couldn't speak English and wanted to vicariously participate in an encounter with the patient from America. During the next few days, Sister Sreeja not only looked after me assiduously, she also talked to me about her parents and siblings; about the foods she loved to cook ("Malayali food very good, madam, next time you come to my house and I cook fish and prawn for you, madam"); about her longing for her husband, an electrician who was working in the Persian Gulf and whom she hadn't seen in three years. A large percentage of Kerala residents work in the Gulf; the money they remit home has significantly contributed to the state's economic health.

"But that's terrible," I said. "Why don't you go and join him? Or at least make a short visit?"

"Not possible right now, madam. But he will come back at some point. Meanwhile, I adjust, madam, I adjust."

No doubt it was to find the strength to adjust that she went whenever she could to the great Padmanavaswami Temple in Trivandrum. The day before I left, she made an afternoon visit and came back with a portion of temple food for me, wrapped in a piece of banana leaf.

"Eat this, madam. You will recover fully, you'll see."

Faithless, but moved, I ate it. It was mild and delicious, just like Sister Sreeja.

Radha was true to her word. One afternoon, she took me shopping to a well-stocked grocery store, where I bought several packets of the spice combination that had been blended with sesame oil for us to eat with the breakfast idlis. Afterward, she suggested that we drop in on P. C. Marcus, a retired professor who was a Syrian Christian and also happened to be the father of Jacob, the young man married to Radha's elder daughter, Soumya.

The living room of the Marcus house was shaded with heavy curtains, providing a welcome respite from the sun outside. The professor was sitting with a book, while his wife and one of her sisters talked to each other.

As soon as we entered, they jumped up and welcomed me effusively. A large slab of cake—rather like a Sara Lee pound cake—made its appearance along with a cool glass of lemonade. Though not very hungry, I was dutifully trying to make my way through the cake, when Mrs. Marcus said something in Malayalam, glancing inquiringly from me to her husband and to Radha. Her sister also seemed to perk up at the suggestion, and gave me a broad smile. The latter had recently visited Israel, Radha explained, and had brought back a bottle of wine produced in Canaa, the same ancient site where Jesus had once turned water into wine. Would I like to taste some? I couldn't possibly say no. The bottle was brought, and the red liquid ceremoniously poured for me. It was a bit on the sweet side but I was only too glad to have a taste of biblical history in a twenty-first-century version, offered to me by the followers of Doubting Thomas.

Professor Marcus reminded me of Digant Oza in Ahmedabad. Both had cherubic smiles, were great raconteurs, and tended to burst into laughter after each of their humorous stories. I told him about eating appam and ishtoo in one of the restaurants supervised by Nabhojit Ghosh, and he gave me the kind of tolerant smile that a teacher gives a student trying very hard.

I learned that Syrian Christians were a rich community; most were plantation owners, though their ancestors had been spice traders. It was not uncommon for a family to have a pepper vine growing in the backyard. Mrs. Marcus said she often plucked the peppercorns from the garden behind the house, to use in her cooking. I couldn't resist sharing with them my own unexpected encounter with this vine in the unlikely locale of a Bengali small town—Shantiniketan, renowned for the university founded there by Rabindranath Tagore. Among the earliest teachers was the great Bengali painter Nandalal Bose, whose grandson Supratik Bose has, like me, made his home in the Boston area. I went to Shantiniketan when Supratik also happened to be visiting and he took me to visit his older cousin, whom he called Barda. It was a small house with a large garden, filled with rosebushes and jasmine plants, with clumps of coconut and palm trees in the corners. Twined around the knobbly trunk of a coconut tree, grew a vine with heart-shaped leaves and clusters of tiny berries. "Know what this is?" asked Barda. I shook my head. "Black pepper," he said. I had not known until then that the pepper plant was a vine, not a bush.

Of all the spices that were traded in ancient and medieval times, the one that was most sought after for the longest period was undoubtedly black pepper, *Piper nigrum*. And for many centuries, Kerala was the source. A medieval traveler referred to the state as the "pepper kingdom." Although pepper is now extensively cultivated in several other countries (Vietnam being the largest producer), nothing can rival the taste and flavor of Kerala's Tellicherry peppercorns. Emperors, artists, writers, have all waxed eloquent about it. Sybille Bedford, in her book *A Visit to Don Otavio*, describes her first meal on the long train journey from New York to Mexico and mentions a pepper mill filled with the "truffle-black grains of Tellicherry." Apart from pepper, nature has also bestowed the largesse of several other fragrant spices on Kerala— cinnamon, cardamom, even vanilla. The verdant forests of the Western Ghats mountain chain that borders Kerala on the east provide ideal conditions for their cultivation.

Unveiling the long history of the spice trade is a continuous process. The remnants of a port recently uncovered by archeologists in the small town of Pattanam, north of Cochin, provides significant evidence about the spice trade between India and the Roman Empire. Historians have long speculated that the trade lasted from the first century B.C. to the first century A.D., although there are some indications that it might have continued, on an irregular basis, until even the sixth and seventh centuries. To control the pepper trade the Romans had built a port on the southwest Malabar Coast and Roman documents of the time refer to it as Muziris. Its location is described as being on a river. The locals called the Roman Muziris by the name of Vanchi, and Sanskrit texts refer to ships coming there with gold and going back with pepper and other aromatic spices. But its precise location eluded modern historians for many years—with some speculation as to whether it might have been Cranganore—until this recent discovery. Numerous shards of ancient Mediterranean pottery and glass beads testify to the onetime Roman presence.

In the historic area of Mattancherry, home to the Jewish community and Cochin's sole surviving synagogue, the yellow building of the Pepper Exchange is a reminder of the old days when a fast and furious international trade was conducted here. Computers, monitors, telephones—all the trappings of modern business have now been installed, but not too many traders operate here any longer. A comparative somnolence has overtaken the place. In the old warehouses, black pepper is still processed and graded the traditional way. Women sift and shake it in trays so that the smaller berries will fall out through the steel mesh, leaving the larger ones to be graded as top quality. Near the Pepper Exchange is a row of tiny shops where vendors display their spices in bowls and plastic bags. Each time I went inside one to take a look, the dusty scent of a host of spices entered my nostrils. I felt I was becoming part of two millennias' worth of human adventure in search of a commodity that was never necessary but always desired. In the last shop, a young boy displayed a long chain made of tiny plastic envelopes joined together. Each envelope contained a different spice, whole not ground. As an Indian, I did not find any of them exotic. Nevertheless, I bought the chain to hang up in my American kitchen as an evocation of a whole world of fragrance.

Although Vasco da Gama landed in Calicut, ninety-one miles northwest of Cochin, after his epoch-making voyage in 1498, it was the Portuguese viceroy Afonso de Albuquerque who built the first Portuguese settlement in Cochin (Fort Cochin). The Portuguese settlers who came with him also included five priests, since conversion was as much on the agenda as trading in spices. Albuquerque built St. Francis Church (the first European church in India) in 1510. Vasco da Gama returned to India in 1524. But he died that same year and was buried in this church. It was not till 1538 that his body was disinterred and shipped back to Lisbon.

The Portuguese realized early on that the importance of the Malabar Coast lay not only in the availability there of Indian spices, but also in the fact that it could serve as a holding point for ships bringing the rarer nutmeg and clove from the Indonesian Spice Islands, the Moluccas. These ships could take on the additional cargo of Kerala spices before making the westward journey to Europe. By establishing strongholds on both coasts of India as well as the East Indies, they succeeded admirably in their objective of destroying the Arab monopoly on the spice trade with Europe and Africa. For almost a century they were the undisputed lords of the Indian Ocean trade.

Standing outside the spice shop with my purchase, I had this odd fancy that with the right kind of vision, one could look all the way across peninsular India from the Malabar Coast to the Coromandel Coast, just as the Portuguese seem to have done. This is a zone that continues to beckon the wanderer. Someday, I know, I will embark on another set of journeys simply to delve into the diversity and mystery of the many cuisines of the South, which embrace both the radical and the conservative. There are myths galore, some to be explored, others to be exploded. And there are countless stories to be heard and told.

One that fascinates me is that of the Chettiyar community of Tamil Nadu. With their voracious love of meat and rich foods, the Chettiyars are the antithesis of the orthodox, vegetarian Brahmins that most of us think of when Tamils are mentioned. Traditionally moneylenders, the Chettiyars are from Sivaganga, in the heart of Tamil Nadu, about twenty-five miles inland from the Coromandel Coast. Over time, they migrated to different destinations, one of the supposed reasons being the punishing hot climate of their native region. Now large populations of Chettiyars are found in Southeast Asia (from where they have picked up a fondness for many kinds of noodles), Burma, and some countries of the West. Their business acumen brought them financial success even in foreign lands, and gradually, many of them have been returning to India and building palatial homes whose architecture evokes southern traditions of the past, with their carved wood columns and wide courtyards.

As a wealthy community, Chettiyars have always been able to indulge in meat and fish along with a variety of tropical vegetables. What is notable is the spicy and aromatic nature of their cooking. Generous amounts of peppercorn, cardamom, nutmeg, and green and red chilies are used. One local favorite is varuval, a dry preparation of chicken (or fish or even vegetables) fried with onions and spices. Another is pepper chicken. Coconut milk also comes into play in a stew called kuzambu. They cook crab with whole fenugreek, mustard, fennel, sliced onions, chili powder, turmeric, and coriander. Depth and tartness are endowed by pureed tomatoes and tamarind juice. Chickpea flour and ground coconut are used to create a thick sauce. Some of the seasonings that distinguish the fiery Chettinad cooking include kalpasi (a kind of dried flower), Marathi mugh (a tiny fruit), sukku (dried ginger), kokum (the same that is used so frequently in Goa and Kerala), and cinnamon from Sri Lanka, which is subtler in flavor than the more commonly used cassia. Star anise is also occasionally used for flavoring.

I said good-bye to Radha and Chandran late in the evening of my last day in Cochin. Earlier in the afternoon, I had had the pleasure of meeting Indira's twin daughters. The girls are enrolled in law school in Cochin, and Radha and Chandran are their de facto local guardians. Since their dormitory is only a short bus ride away from Radha's house, the girls came over after classes to meet me. Over tea, banana fritters, pappadams, and a few other homemade goodies, I reminisced with them about the wonderful meals Indira had cooked for me during my week-long incarceration in the hospital. They were shy and quiet, but when they smiled, a hint of mischief lighting up their eyes, the resemblance to their mother tugged at my heart. As darkness gathered, they went off to catch the bus again, waving cheerily to us.

"Remember what you said to me, the last time I was in Kerala?" I asked Radha.

"What did I say?"

"That I had to come back to Cochin and see you again."

"Well, so you did."

She held my hand and smiled at her husband, who nodded.

"This time *I* want to say the same thing. I have to come back. There's still so much to see, so much to learn, so much to taste. I've never felt so at home in an unknown place as I have in Kerala. And it's because of you two. So be prepared. I'll be back."

I leaned out of the window as the car pulled away from the house. In the failing light, I suddenly noticed bunches of unknown white flowers and pink bougainvilleas trailing against the walls of the houses. I remembered Radha telling me that during the harvest festival of Onam, women gather huge quantities of flowers, shred the petals, and create extensive multicolored patterns by arranging them on the ground. It is a work of art that lasts only a few hours or a day. But it seemed to me to represent the renewable soul of a beautiful, fertile land.

Chapter Twelve

THE VANISHING JEWS OF INDIA

"There are only sixteen of us left, you know," she said, and quickly walked away from me, barefoot on the hot paved street of Cochin's Jew Town. I had seen her step out of a beautiful old house embellished with blue panels of intricate wood carvings. Dressed in a gauzy white skirt and a pastel printed blouse, her curly hair framing a pale face and gray eyes, she walked rapidly, utterly oblivious of her surroundings. Something in her manner, the air of being wrapped in an alternate reality, reminded me of Wilkie Collins's *Woman in White*. But this was no dark, misty, mysterious night in cold England. It was a Saturday afternoon in Cochin, where even the January sun is hot enough for a hat or parasol to be desirable.

It was also the Jewish Sabbath. The city's synagogues were barred to all outsiders and the shops owned by Jewish people either closed for business, or left open—for browsing, not selling—under the kind supervision of non-Jewish neighbors. On this second, brief visit to Cochin, I had been plagued by delays and cancellations of flights out of Bombay and arrived almost twenty-four hours later than scheduled. Saturday was the only full day I had left. On Sunday I was to leave for Bombay again and from there, return to Calcutta for a few days, before catching a flight to Boston. It turned out to be the most frustrating Saturday of my travels. Not surprisingly, every attempt I made to meet with any member of Cochin's tiny Jewish community on such a day was in vain. Phone call after phone call ended with the same polite refusal to talk to me on the Sabbath. In the picturesque area known as Jew Town—no shades of the ghetto here, despite the oddly abrasive-sounding name, which is only a territorial identification akin to saying Chinatown—I saw people looking out of their windows, enjoying the mild breeze on their balconies. But nothing could convince them that talking to a stranger about their food or customs would not flout the spirit and observance of Sabbath. Why, I found myself thinking in despair, couldn't I find a single nonobservant Jewish person? And then I saw her, a beautiful apparition, but more European than Indian in appearance.

"She's one of them," muttered a man sitting on a stool outside an antique shop.

I went up to her and explained my mission. But she shook her head.

"No one will talk to you, not today."

"Can I call you late in the evening? Or someone else? I only want to learn about your ways, your food and cooking, and tell the world about it."

"What's the point? We are disappearing. There are only sixteen of us left, you know."

"Wait," I said, following her as she increased her pace.

She turned to look at me, an enigmatic, yet sad smile lighting those extraordinary gray eyes, and shook her head again, as if ruefully amused at the obduracy of a child. Then she vanished into a narrow lane, leaving me to retrace my steps toward the exquisite Paradesi Synagogue for one last look from outside. I remembered the descriptions of its interior I had read in guidebooks—the hand-painted blue and white Chinese tiles on the floor, each with a unique design, the ladies' gallery, the hanging lamps with beautiful Belgian glass lampshades. But all I could actually see was the white outer wall with blue doors and windows, the eighteenth-century clock tower built by a Jewish merchant named Ezekiel Rahabi, and the placard commemorating the Paradesi Synagogue as a heritage site.

The Jews of Cochin constitute one of several Jewish communities of India—the other two being the Baghdadi Jews of Calcutta and the Bene Israel of Bombay—whose numbers have indeed dwindled fast since India gained independence in 1947. Outside these cities, they are hardly a blip on the collective religious consciousness, which is primarily focused on Hindus and Muslims and secondarily on Buddhists, Christians, Parsis, and Jains. For me, however, the Jews of India have long held a peculiar fascination for two reasons. Even before I came to the United States, I had learned that they were the only people who observed anything similar to the complex, arduous, and downright baffling customs that governed the purity and pollution of food in our strict Hindu Brahmin household. Later, I was intrigued by the fact that ever since India became independent, the Jews, like the Anglo-Indians, had chosen to migrate in large numbers to Israel, Europe, and America. This, despite the fact that they had never been subjected to overt acts of discrimination as their fellow Jews had in Europe. As a rule, Indian Jews had been prosperous; economic migration could not have been the motive, either. Why then did they want to leave the land that had sheltered them for centuries?

The answer to this particular question, I eventually discovered, lay in the fairly recent past, in the relationship between India's Jews and the British. As masters of colonial manipulation, the British extended many privileges to the Jewish community, as they did to the Anglo-Indians. It was a way of building small but effective pools of loyal adherence in the enormous foreign country that they ruled. However, as in the case of the Anglo-Indians, the growth of nationalism, the independence of India, and the departure of the British made the Jews feel less secure about their role and their position in the new country. Perhaps legitimately, they felt that the mainstream Indians would resent the many preferential deals they had received from the British, and that life would become difficult. Immigration to Britain and other countries of the Commonwealth, as well as to Israel, seemed a wise option. Whether their fears were justified or not, the dissolution of the community has also meant the fading away of a unique culinary style, born of the melding of Middle Eastern and regional Indian ingredients.

In Cochin, I was hoping to meet with a Jewish person, preferably a woman and a cook, who could provide the intimate descriptions I sought of daily meals, Seders, and holiday observances, and also give me a sense of what it was like to belong to an almost invisible yet longstanding community. Having arrived from other parts of the world, Jews had undergone some degree of assimilation in their adopted homeland of India. But unlike Parsis or colonial Europeans, the Jewish people adhered rigidly to the well-established set of rules and rituals that governed the way they cooked and ate. What would authenticity in food mean for them in India?

During school and college days, my knowledge of Judaism in general was extremely scanty and derived solely from Western literature. Shylock, for instance, gave me a strong awareness about facing communal discrimination, distrust, and envy in Renaissance Europe. Isaac and his daughter Rebecca, in Sir Walter Scott's novel *Ivanhoe*, touched my heart as victims of the cruel contempt with which Christians treated Jews in medieval times. But the Holocaust, though far more recent, remained only a terrible episode, outlined starkly but without too many details in the pages of our history texts. I had no idea about the differences between the Ashkenazim and the Sephardim, nor did we read in detail about Zionism or the creation of Israel, though I was aware of the Promised Land as one enticing image from the Bible. For many in my generation, there were only a few occasional reminders of the existence of this elusive, intriguing community in our city—the grand proportions

of the beautiful Jewish synagogues, especially the Magen David synagogue in Calcutta, built by David Ezra in 1884; pictures of the Torah
scrolls in books; and most pleasurable of all, a visit to New Market to go
to the legendary Jewish bakery, Nahoum and Sons, founded in 1902.
Aside from a whole range of pastries, cakes, and patties (meat encased in
an envelope of flaky dough), Nahoum's was the source of two exotic
treats—braided challah bread, sold around the Jewish New Year (though
we were hardly aware of the event), and a plaited cheese—similar to the
one still made and eaten by Syrian Jews in America during the autumn
festival of Sukkot—which we tore off in strips to eat.

Of the three main Jewish communities of India, which are settled in
Cochin, Bombay, and Calcutta, the one in Cochin seems to be the most
observant of the articles of faith. Although the Jews of Cochin have
adopted the language, clothes, and cooking style of the people of Kerala,
they have steadfastly avoided assimilation through intermarriage with
locals. The zeal with which they have sought to preserve their identity
has therefore also reinforced the prospect of their disappearance from
the place that so many generations have known as home.

They are also noted for a dual presence, being split into two groups:
Black, or Malabar, Jews; and White Jews. The woman I saw must have
belonged to the latter group, who built the Paradesi (literally, from a foreign country) Synagogue in 1568 on land given to them by the Hindu
king, next to his own palace. They came to India as traders and refugees
in the sixteenth century, escaping oppression from Muslim regimes in
several Middle Eastern countries as well as Christian persecution in
Spain. Since many of them were noticeably fair-skinned, the sobriquet
"White Jews" was a natural development.

The Black Jews, however, claim to be the original Jews of Kerala.
One theory is that they are part of the original Babylonian diaspora and
arrived on the western coast of India as early as the sixth century B.C.
The other is that they came after the fall of the Second Temple, to
escape persecution by the Romans. They settled in the town of
Cranganore, sixteen miles north of Cochin, and were well accepted by

the local Indians, particularly after the fourth-century monarch, Ravi Varma, guaranteed them a safe and undisturbed existence. The community prospered by engaging in trade and other activities. In the sixteenth century, however, the arrival of the Portuguese, filled with proselytizing zeal and steeped in the anti-Semitic prejudices of the Inquisition, bent on exterminating the Jews even here, disrupted the security of the Black Jews of Kerala. Uprooting themselves from Cranganore, where the Portuguese were at war with the local king, they fled to Cochin, hoping for a quieter life. But the harassment continued. The Portuguese even destroyed the Paradesi Synagogue of the White Jews. It could be rebuilt only in 1664, when the Dutch ousted the Portuguese and took control of Cochin. Since the Dutch did not pursue an overt agenda of anti-Semitism, both Black and White Jews again prospered and Cochin became a well-known center of Judaic presence in India. At one point, there were several active synagogues in town, and all the Jewish festivals were celebrated with much pomp and observance. In the 1950s, however, almost the entire group of Black Jews moved to Israel. The White Jews lingered—the Paradesi Synagogue is the only operational temple now—but over time, they, too, have been emigrating. As a result, the vivid multicultural fabric of this spice emporium of a city is being diminished in color and richness.

While all Judaic communities in India have strictly followed the rules of keeping kosher, the Jews of Cochin are—as I had guessed—nearly as obsessive about their food rituals and kitchen practices as orthodox Hindus. I grew up in a house where a whole slew of arcane rules governed who or what could touch food, utensils, cooking pots, and eating areas at different times and on different occasions. As a rebellious teenager, I tried to flout as many of these "irrational" restrictions as I could, precipitating loud arguments with my mother and grandmother. What, after all, could be the justification for washing my hands simply because they had fleetingly touched a bowl containing mashed potatoes seasoned with chopped onions? Apparently because onions were as impure as meat in the hierarchy of foods. But the onion was part of the vegetable kingdom, I objected. Perhaps, but since it was used mostly to cook meat, the combination somehow tainted them. What was probably left unsaid was the strong popular association of onions, garlic, and meat with the "other" community of Muslims, who were considered un-touchable and impure for devout Hindus even a few decades ago. Then there was the conundrum that touching a tin of uncooked rice, or even plunging my hands into it, did not affect the cleanliness of my hands, whereas the merest contact (aside from the act of eating) with a pot of *cooked* rice required immediate ablution before one touched anything else in the home. Questioning this stricture, I was told, was particularly heinous. It has the weight of antiquity to support it, with Sanskrit texts containing references to the transformation of the purity of food when it is cooked. Collectively, these rules of cleanliness and pollution, called bichar-achar in Bengal, have built up over centuries—part ancient scrip-tural injunctions, part folklore—and, ultimately, the blanket response to all my protests was that rules were rules; they had to be followed simply because they had been there forever. Power being in the hand of the adults, a rebellious teenager could only fume in silence and begrudg-ingly comply with soap and water.

After my failed encounter with the young woman in Jew Town, I consoled myself with a stroll through the streets of the quarter. The af-ternoon had lengthened by then and people were waking up from their siestas and coming out of their houses. Suddenly, a sign caught my eye—Incy Bella: The Book Shop. Intrigued, I went into the tiny shop and was rewarded not only with several fascinating books, but also a wo-ven jute shopping bag emblazoned with the name of the bookstore and its address, Synagogue Lane, Jew Town, Cochin. How will it sound, I wondered, when Synagogue Lane loses the living dimension of hav-ing devotees attending a synagogue? Later, scanning the pages of a book on Indian Jewish identity edited by Nathan Katz, I found further con-firmation of my theories. The extraordinarily obsessive watchfulness about food among the Jews of Cochin, as described by Katz, seemed to imply that the rules of kosher had been further influenced by Hindu orthodoxy.

During Passover, for instance, the Jewish women of Cochin are so determined to ensure the purity of the wheat with which their matzo (called massa in Cochin) is made that they spend hours sorting the wheat to remove any grains that show the slightest sign of being cracked or damaged, since polluting elements can enter through these cracks. Once the process is completed and the wheat kept in a container, it is absolutely forbidden for any non-Jewish person to touch the container or even the surface on which it rests. On the appointed day, the wheat is taken to a flour mill where the equipment, having already been cleaned by the owner, is given a second thorough cleaning by a Jewish woman before the wheat is processed into flour. During the week of Passover, the Jews—who normally have friendly, social relations with their Hindu, Muslim, Christian, and Jain neighbors—take great care not to eat anything from those households, because there is no way to ensure that the food has not come into contact with unsanctioned items.

Aside from sacred and ritual occasions, however, the cooking and diet of a Cochin Jewish household is not all that different from those of people belonging to other faiths. As Sarah Cohen, the matriarch of the community, said to me on the phone—when I did finally reach her after sundown—cooking meat is a rarity because there is no one qualified to do ritual slaughtering. But perhaps this is not such a terrible loss. After hundreds of years in Kerala, and living in a hot, humid climate, the Jewish palate has evolved from its Middle Eastern roots and may well find little burden in being limited to fish, vegetables, eggs, and the occasional chicken. In terms of culinary techniques, the Cochin Jews have enthusiastically adopted the special offerings of their land, just as they have made Malayalam their mother tongue. In Kerala, land of spices, they liberally season their meals with hot chilies, fenugreek, kari leaves, mustard seeds, ginger, and coriander. Fish fillets, fried dark and crisp, are coated with chilies and enlivened with coconut-vinegar and cardamom. Or fish is marinated in a paste of crushed herbs and cooked with small onions. Like southern Indians all over, they love to eat yogurt in different forms, including the curd-rice combination, tempered with dried chilies and fresh kari leaves. The Middle East or Spain, where their ancestors once lived, has receded far from their kitchens.

The most mysterious Jewish community of India, the Bene Israel of the state of Maharashtra (of which Bombay is the capital) were, for many centuries, at the opposite end of the spectrum, in terms of detailed observance of ritual and orthodoxy. Some have theorized that they are one of the lost tribes of Israel—the tribe of Reuben—and not much was generally known about them until the eighteenth century, although they are supposed to have lived in India almost from the beginning of the last millennium. Their story, like that of the Parsis, is one of flight, arrival, and asylum; the western coast of India seems particularly likely to give rise to such legends of origin. The Bene Israel themselves believe that their ancestors were from Galilee. Fleeing the oppression of the Greek overlord, Antiochus Epiphanes, around 175 B.C., they were shipwrecked in the Indian Ocean. Seven men and seven women are supposed to have survived—a human Noah's ark with reproductive capabilities—and found shelter in the port of Navagaon, on the Konkan coast.

Though they managed to cling to some of their religious customs and dietary laws, by and large the Bene Israel adopted the language and customs of their new land. As time went by and collective memory faded, they continued to observe only the Sabbath and a few important Jewish holidays. Unlike the entrepreneurial Jews of Cochin and Calcutta, also, the Bene Israel remained a rural people for centuries. Most of them worked as oil pressers, a clear identity that fit in well with the Hindu caste hierarchy. It was only when Bombay became a thriving mercantile center under the British, and Jewish merchants from Cochin and Calcutta gravitated to that area in the eighteenth century, that the Bene Israel were discovered, re-educated in the detailed observance of the Jewish faith, and thus brought back into the larger fold of the Indian Jewish community. They moved out of their villages, settled in Bombay, and established several synagogues. However, after the independence of India in 1947, they, like their fellow Indian Jews, felt the pull of migration. Israel and the West promised greater security for their Jewish identity. Their numbers dwindled from 24,000 in 1947, to 13,000 in 1969, to less than a thousand at present.

The history of their long cohabitation with the villagers of Maharashtra meant that the daily meals in Bene Israel homes were almost identical with those in Hindu households. The Bene Israel have learned to relish the ingredients of the land—coconut milk, garam masala, turmeric, ginger, and cumin. During important occasions like Passover, they clean their houses, prepare matzo (though rice is not forbidden to them) and observe all the typical Jewish traditions, but without the obsessive attention of the White Jews of Cochin.

Calcutta has been home to India's youngest Jewish community, which consists of people from Syria, Iran, Yemen, and Iraq. The Iraqis are the largest group, which has led to their being referred to as Baghdadi Jews. The founding patriarch, Shalom Obadiah Ha-Cohen, was an enterprising merchant from Aleppo, Syria, who came to Calcutta on hearing of the enormous business opportunities being provided by the British trading houses. After a brief stint on India's west coast, in the city of Surat in Gujarat, Ha-Cohen settled down for good in Calcutta in 1798 and began trading in diamonds, indigo, and textiles. As he prospered, family members and friends followed him to India in search of wealth—and a community was born. In the roughly 150 years before India's independence, the Baghdadi Jews became a fixture in the city. For much of that time, they maintained their Middle Eastern heritage, especially in dress and language. However, as business ties with the British grew closer— many Baghdadi Jewish fortunes were made from the same opium trade that left Bengal with an enormous largesse of poppy seeds—the community began to socialize with them and adopted western dress and social customs. There was never much of an attempt to integrate socially with the local people, Hindus or Muslims.

After returning to Calcutta from Cochin, I went to visit Ian Zachariah, a Baghdadi Jew and well-known music critic and jazz enthusiast. His living room exhibited the pleasant clutter of a single man's home. Books, papers, magazines, and old vinyl records competed for space, and the late morning sun gleamed off an enormous fluted brass speaker of an old phonograph. When afternoon tea was served, British style, with dainty sandwiches and pastries, a visitor could sense the lingering aura of a leisurely, cultured past. That morning in his apartment, Zachariah and I shared a pot of steaming hot tea as he talked about his childhood, when the Jewish presence was far more vivid, when the synagogues were well attended and the festivals celebrated with large family meals. From the kitchen, where a maid was preparing his lunch, came the nose-tingling, sneeze-making aroma of cumin, chili, and coriander. I wondered whether she was making a typical Baghdadi Jewish dish, but could not ask. And if I had, the answer would probably have been in the negative. The maid was a local Bengali and was likely cooking in her own style.

When Zachariah was growing up, the daily meals at home were fairly simple and not overly spicy. Along with rice and vegetables, the midday meal consisted of a stew called marag (possibly derived from the Hebrew *marak*, soup), made either with chicken or fish. Although it contained onion, garlic, ginger, and other Indian spices, the seasoning was done with a light hand. Mashed potatoes were often added to the chicken stew. Dinner was somewhat more substantial and often included kebabs as well as Western or Anglo-Indian items like chops and roasts. The Baghdadi Jewish cuisine strongly reflected its Middle Eastern roots as well as Jewish dietary laws. Even in a Westernized family like Zachariah's, it was only cucumber sandwiches that were served with afternoon tea; sandwiches that contained meat were not permissible as tea was always taken with milk. If something more substantial was required, the family produced mahmoosa, which consists of eggs scrambled with potatoes and tomatoes.

As any immigrant community does, the Baghdadi Jews initially held on to many of their traditional foods as they settled down and made their fortunes in Calcutta. But the strong flavors of India could not be kept at bay. Stuffed tomatoes, eggplant, and cabbage leaves were accompanied by a vegetable stew called khatta (the Hindi word for "sour"), which combined items like okra and potatoes in a sauce flavored with lemon and sugar. This inclination for a sweet-and-sour taste, which also characterized many dishes of the imperial Mughal kitchen, can be observed throughout the Middle East. But in Indian Jewish homes, the taste was enhanced with the addition of such spices as turmeric, ginger, chili, or coriander.

Zachariah's eyes lit up when he described tiny meat-filled dumplings called kooba that were added to soups and stews, including khatta.

A variant of the Middle Eastern kibbe, the dumplings were labor inten-sive. Ground rice and meat were blended together and formed into tiny balls. These were then hollowed out and spiced meat added as a filling before the dumplings were deep-fried.

But did the mistress of a prosperous Jewish home really spend the time laboriously making large quantities of dumplings? Ian Zachariah gave me a mischievous smile as he shook his head. In the oblique light of the shifting sun, I could almost trace his Middle Eastern ancestry in his features.

"Haven't you heard of Jewish cooks? Those legendary masters of the kitchen whose disappearance is still being lamented by those of us who are left in Calcutta?"

I confessed that I had not. It appears the Jewish cooks of Calcutta are one of India's many conundrums. The current political tensions in the Middle East, as well as the prevailing view in the West, underline distance and hostility between Muslims and Jews. In India, however, it has always been the tensions between Hindus and Muslims that have torn the social fabric apart. The minorities have dealt well with each other. In the pros-perous Calcutta homes of the Baghdadi Jews, the "Jewish cooks" were ac-tually Muslims from an area in southern Bengal called Midnapore. Their nimble fingers made heaps of tiny dumplings, and garnished the soups and stews with them. With their ancestral knowledge, they also produced lavish pilafs and biryanis—including those in which fish, not meat, was layered with potatoes and rice—for celebratory meals. To cater to the An-glicized tastes of their employers and British or European guests, these cooks also learned to make Western-style roasts and puddings. Most mem-orably, they followed the instructions of the Jewish ladies of the house, and went on to create inimitable dishes like chitarnee and, of course, that leg-endary item of Baghdadi Jewish cuisine, aloo makalla.

A simple translation of *aloo makalla* would be "fried potatoes." Yet, what a world of difference there is between the average French fry and aloo makalla. The latter is now an endangered pleasure, as so few are left who know how to make it. The only hope for its survival lies with the Baghdadi Jewish diaspora in the West and in Israel who might still be making it to celebrate Sabbath, as their ancestors in Calcutta used to do. According to Ian Zachariah, the potatoes for aloo makalla were usually grown in northern India's Dehra Dun region, as renowned for its spuds as is Idaho in the United States. Culinary aesthetics required that the potatoes be of the same size, and the cooks often pared the larger ones down to match the smaller. The peeled potatoes were first dropped into a large pot of boiling salted water and cooked for five minutes. After being drained and cooled, they were pierced all over with a fork, placed in a pot and covered with oil (to produce a pareve dish—neither meat nor dairy—the Baghdadi Jews favored peanut or sesame oil as their cooking medium instead of the clarified butter that Indians generally love). The potatoes were then cooked, immersed in oil, over medium-low heat for a couple of hours. By then, the exterior would take on a pale golden tone. Just before serving, the heat was turned up, and the potatoes fried until the crust turned a crisp golden brown. Simple as it seems, only the expert cook, with a fine calibration of timing and temperature, could produce the ideal aloo makalla—crispy brown on the outside, soft and tenderly white on the inside. In fact, so crusty was the exterior, that an intital attempt to pierce it with a dinner fork often failed, making the potatoes jump. That is why they were often jokingly referred to as "jumping potatoes." Served usually with roasted, stuffed chicken called hashwa, these potatoes always made the festive or Sabbath meal something to anticipate with relish.

Zachariah's other favorite, chitarnee, is a chicken dish that embodies the union of the Middle East and India. Its sweet-and-sour taste is achieved through the combination of tamarind and sugar. Onions are lavishly used to form the base of the sauce and supplemented with typical Indian spices such as ginger, turmeric, cumin, coriander, garlic, and cardamom. Tomatoes and chili powder add piquancy and color. Chicken was also made into a stew called hamin (common in the Middle East, but usually made with beef and flavored with allspice, cinnamon, and saffron) and gazar meetha, in which the sauce was enhanced with grated carrots.

As delicious as these dishes sound, the predominance of chicken and fish (in stews and dumplings, as well as unusual pilafs) in the diet of the

Baghdadi Jews is a poignant indication of a group whose choice of food
was affected both by a slow attrition of their numbers and the require-
ments of their faith. Beef or lamb was replaced by chicken in many in-
stances, including that of kooba dumplings, which required minced meat
because, for many years, there was no butcher who was qualified to ritually slaughter the larger animals. It was the same problem that Sarah
Cohen had mentioned in Cochin. Several decades ago, the wealthiest
families would fly in a butcher from Bombay to do the slaughtering for
important festive meals, but now even that has become a rarity. The
Jewish table in Calcutta and elsewhere has been shaped by many such
small adjustments. The Muslims known as "Jewish cooks" were trained
to keep kosher and make necessary innovations. Aside from not using
any butter or ghee in cooking meat, they also avoided marinating it in
yogurt or cream. Instead, coconut milk was added to increase flavor and
tenderness. In shopping for fish from the plentiful markets of Calcutta,
they had to make sure not to buy any fish without scales as well as the
prawns and shrimp that the Bengalis around them enjoyed with gusto.

As my conversation with Zachariah lengthened from morning to
early afternoon and the sunlight receded to the other side of the building, I was touched with the unspoken melancholy of all groups that are
forced to confront the prospect of their own extinction. Under his
cheerful equanimity, someone like Zachariah had to be living with a
constant and growing sense of loss. How much harder it must be, I
thought, for the elderly members of Calcutta's Jewish community—now
numbering only thirty—who had lived long enough to remember the
vibrancy of the past, and contrast it with the inevitability of future demise. How did it feel to be part of a group that had almost vanished, to
be surrounded by people who hardly knew anything about your traditions or your heritage, to count on your fingers those who still did,
to chalk up each obituary as a further erasure of communal identity?
Surely, each Jewish person still left in the city must wonder who would
outlast the others, which year would see the final celebration of Passover
and the last Seder laid out on a Calcutta table.

Chapter Thirteen

THE INDIGENOUS POT

Pondering the fate of lost tribes and less visible communities inevitably makes me think of India's own native tribes. Like indigenous people in many countries, they tend to hover distantly on the edges of mainstream consciousness unless economic need or conflict of interest brings them face-to-face with the "outsiders" who have infiltrated the land and created industrial or agricultural societies. Even as tribal people have sought work in the tea estates of Bengal and Assam or the coal mines of Bihar and Bengal, they have striven to maintain their separate ethnic identities and unique cultures. This does not mean there is perpetual hostility between the mainstream and the tribes. Historically, there have been occasions when the tribal people cooperated with their neighbors in a time of need. The royal families of Rajasthan, for instance, are known to have asked the local Bhil tribesmen for help during their battles against the encroaching Muslim conquerors.

Numerous indigenous groups are scattered throughout the country. According to the 2001 census, tribal people make up 8 percent of the nation's population. The greatest concentration is probably in the state of Madhya Pradesh, home of the Bastar tribe. The area known as Chota Nagpur spills over from Madhya Pradesh into the state of Bihar and is populated by such tribes as the Oraons, Mundas, and Santhals. On the eastern side of Bihar, my home state of West Bengal has the eponymous zone of Santhal Pargana, where there are significant concentrations of Santhal tribes. East and north of Bengal stretch the seven states collectively referred to as the Northeast—the domain of a different set of tribes whose ways of life and food have been influenced by Bengal, Southeast Asia, and Tibet. Language, social organization, religious affiliation, and self-identification are the usual criteria for identifying tribes in India.

Many food terms in modern Indian languages can trace their ancestry back to the dialects of the tribal people, who might have adopted them from ancient travelers from other parts of the globe. A particularly interesting example is the word for coconut—*narikela*, or *nariyal*—which, experts believe, entered the ancient tribal dialects from Southeast Asia and then passed into Sanskrit and later, modern Indian languages like Bengali and Hindi. This idea ties in with the theory espoused by many botanists that the coconut originated in the Melanesian area of the Pacific, from where it was taken, in prehistoric times, to Asia. The term *niu, ngai,* or *niyor,* writes the eminent food historian K. T. Achaya, signifying essence or oil, was combined with the term *kolai* (nut), to describe this "oily nut."

Even more fascinating is the way indigenous people were named by the Aryans who migrated into India during the late third and second millennium B.C. The Indo-Aryan dialects they spoke later developed into Sanskrit. The initial encounters between these pastoral and nomadic people and the indigenous hunting communities were probably

fraught with suspicion and fear on both sides. Among the many names
the Aryans used for indigenous people, one is Nishada. According to
some historians, the term is rooted in the Sanskrit term *nisha*, which can
mean both "night" and the spice "turmeric." A Nishada, according to
this theory, could be a person who eats turmeric. Subsects among the
Nishadas were called Chandalas (dog-eaters), Svanin (dog-keepers), and
Punjistha (those who hunt and trap birds). Not only do these terms imply that the indigenous people had considerable knowledge of edible
roots and rhizomes, or that dogs and fowl had been domesticated in India before the arrival of the Aryans (the domestic chicken is descended
from a native Indian bird), it also indicates how a growing sense of superiority and separateness on the part of Aryans might have led to the
categorization of dogs and chickens as impure animals, fit to be associated with only tribal people. In modern times, urban Indians often jokingly refer to a supposed delicacy of the Naga tribes—dog meat.

In the final section of the *Mahabharata*, there is an unforgettable
story of how the virtuous Pandava prince, Yudhisthira, is tested on his
way to heaven. Having renounced earthly life, he sets out for the Himalayas (where the gods of the Hindu universe resided) with his four
brothers and their common wife, Draupadi. A stray dog begins to follow
them, but Yudhisthira won't allow him to be shooed away, even though
his companions shudder at the proximity of this impure animal. Along
the way, all four of Yudhisthira's brothers and Draupadi drop dead; each
is guilty of a particular sin and therefore unfit to enter heaven. Finally,
when Yudhisthira reaches the gates of heaven, Indra, king of the gods,
welcomes him at the gate, but says he can't come in with a dirty animal
like the dog. Yudhisthira immediately turns his back on heaven, for he
cannot possibly abandon a creature that has sought his protection. At
this point, the dog is transformed into Dharma, the god of virtue, who
says that he was only testing whether Yudhisthira's great reputation for
virtue was deserved or not. Even in the Aryan canon, protecting the asylum seeker transcended the value of being immaculately pure.

India's oldest epic, the *Ramayana*, depicts two encounters between
Rama, a prince who was exiled to the forest due to the machinations of

his stepmother, and members of forest tribes. The stories are meant to indicate Rama's exceptional greatness of heart, underlining the distance that normally prevailed between the two communities. On seeing Guhak, the king of the Nishadas, Rama embraces him and greets him as a dear friend. The two had met previously when Rama, like royalty everywhere, had gone hunting in the forest. He also accepts fruit and milk from the hands of a woman named Shabari who belongs to the Chandal sect, normally considered untouchable, thus flouting—or rising above—the prevailing Hindu beliefs in the purity and pollution of food as well as its acceptability. I read these stories as a schoolgirl; even as they conveyed to me a sense of power and discrimination, they also made me burn with the desire to discover what these forest dwellers ate, what secrets of herbs and vegetation they had managed to unearth, what kind of game they hunted, how they cooked it—an extensive lore that would always be beyond my ken.

Madhya Pradesh, like Kerala, or Karnataka, is a postindependence creation, assembled out of discrete areas once controlled by princely rulers—the Peshawas and Holkars of Maharashtra, the Scindias of Gwalior, and the ruling families of Ujjain (in modern Uttar Pradesh). Geographically, however, it seems to declare an affinity for the Deccan plateau. An enormous expanse of dark, unyielding rock and sparse forests harks back to a remote, even prehistoric past, when this was part of the hypothetical geological entity of Gondwanaland. Rocks, stones, caves fill the landscape instead of emerald fields of rice or orchards loaded with fruit. To a visitor here, the lush greenness of Bengal or Kerala seems to belong to another planet. As one gets out of the cities, lingering traces of Hindu kingdoms and Muslim palaces and mosques are overshadowed by an even older history. The presence of the tribal people in this and other states remind the visitor of an era when our ancestors fed themselves by hunting and gathering, when food was precious because of its uncertain availability, when its enjoyment was primal and visceral.

I had a vivid sense of that spirit in Bhimbetka, a short distance from the tragic yet beautiful city of Bhopal, the capital of Madhya Pradesh. It is an enormous outcropping of rocks, caves, and stone formations. Inside the caves are extraordinary Stone Age paintings similar to those of Lascaux in France. Hunters, armed with spears, arrows, and shields, are shown targeting such animals as deer, bison, peacock, and rhinoceros, as well as creatures that no longer exist in India, the giraffe and the ostrich. They are also depicted spearing fish or trapping them in nets. Side by side with these martial images are more domestic ones of women gathering fruit, processing food (kneading dough?) with primitive utensils, and doing other domestic chores. Although hunting large animals for food is no longer common, the images underline the physical and geographical reality of places where humans have had to make the most of nature's erratic blessings. The hunter's booty, seared over a primitive fire, is the first and most authentic human cuisine. Despite the immeasurable distance prevailing between that food and the offerings of the modern table, Bhimbetka reminds us of our origins, when all of us lived off the land, when authenticity was never an issue.

Before returning to Bhopal from Bhimbetka, I made a detour to see the twelfth-century Bhojeshwar Temple, dedicated to Shiva. The structure was never completed, but an enormous stone linga (phallus) representing the god, still stands, filling the viewer with awe. It is nothing like the "cool" image of Shiva my mother had embroidered on canvas, that serene face with the third eye and the dreadlocks. Hewn out of obdurate rock that reflects the local geology, the Bhojeshwar Temple phallus is nearly eight feet in height and eighteen feet in girth, and projects an irresistible sense of power. I found it hard to imagine that prayer and worship, however fervent, would call forth any response from this emblem of divinity. To the local people, however, the stone is alive and speaking; more important, it demands daily nourishment. Using an ingenious system of ropes and pulleys, the temple devotees "feed" the phallus by pouring fresh milk, the purest of offerings, over the top.

Worshipping Shiva in his phallic form is common throughout India. In Madhya Pradesh, the River Narmada, which has now become the symbol of a major conflict between environmentalists, villagers, and the government, speaks to that connection between man and earth. Innumerable phallic stones (shaped by nature or by prehistoric man) have been discovered along its banks and established in temples and shrines, big and small. The city of Ujjain is particularly famous for its Shiva temples.

In an interesting example of symbiosis through thousands of years of living side by side, worshipping the phallus is common among both Hindus and the indigenous people. There is much debate as to who did it first, just as there is a lot of controversy over whether tribals should be considered Hindus or not. However, it is reasonable to suppose that the animistic beliefs of the tribal people lends itself more naturally to worshipping a phallic stone or a tree as a symbol of divine power, and that these ideas later gradually infiltrated the Vedic Hinduism practiced by the Aryans. In the earliest Veda, the Rig Veda, for instance, the tribals are called, among other things, worshippers of the phallic god. The reverse process has also taken place, and tribal people are often seen to pray at Hindu shrines and make offerings to Hindu gods. Those living near urban areas, and receiving some degree of education, sometimes identify themselves as Hindus in the hopes of greater social and economic advancement in Indian society.

In Madhya Pradesh, the geological phallic propensity and the depth of devotion for Shiva that is prevalent among both Hindus and tribals have given birth to a culture of temple food similar to that in the Jagannath Temple in Puri. Daily offerings to Shiva, consisting of khichuri (rice and dal cooked together) and a mixed vegetable concoction are prepared in numerous temple kitchens and distributed among the devotees. The simplicity of preparation, which belies the delicious taste, might well have evolved from a simpler, tribal way of life. The cooks prepare for their tasks in the morning, after being bathed and cleansed and wearing freshly laundered clothes, so that no touch of impurity can defile the offerings. The vegetables are often kept whole and can be anything that is in season—small eggplants, potatoes, flat beans, gourds. They are combined with oil and spices, and put on wood fires in tightly sealed pots. No stirring, mixing, frying, or uncovering of the lid during the cooking process is permitted. This allows the vegetables to release their moisture, blend their flavors, and mingle into an explosively flavorful dish. The khichuri, too, is cooked in the same slow-pressurized way, without any stirring, mixing, or seasoning after it has been put on the fire. Five or six thousand years ago, a tribal woman, like the ones I saw depicted in the Bhimbetka caves, could have prepared a pot of vegetables the same way for her family, even if rice and dal had not yet become part of the daily diet.

Unlike the members of the lowest rungs of the Hindu caste ladder, tribal people in India are not technically considered "untouchables," though there are always small pockets of exception, as with the Chandal sect mentioned in the *Ramayana*, who are still confined to the outskirts of villages, condemned to do the kind of work others will not. But whether they are untouchable or not, most of them have not climbed very high on the social ladder even after half a century of independence and the assistance available to them under affirmative action programs. Their visibility depends on perceived need—for their labor, for votes in a political campaign, for anthropological representation in books and films. The commonest exchanges between tribal people and the dominant communities take place when the former come to work as servants and laborers in homes, fields, mines and plantations. Rarely are they approached as sources of native wisdom or for their age-old insights about their land.

Gandhi, that maverick voice of India who campaigned ardently against untouchability in the Hindu caste system, was also a champion of indigenous people, to whom he gave the name Girijan (people of the forest). In Ahmedabad, in his native state of Gujarat, he founded an institution called Gujarat Vidyapeeth, which houses the extraordinary Tribal Museum depicting life, food, and religion among the twenty-five tribal communities in the state. Models of huts and villages, people and animals, all made by tribal artists, fill the exhibition area and indicate that over time, they have become farmers and sharecroppers by default. Their daily activities now include milking cows, feeding calves, grinding maize (corn) on a stone, cooking meals, and cleaning the house. One of the most intriguing tribal artifacts on display is an enormous food storage container made of clay and rice husks. Shaped like a fat-bellied jar with a square lid, this indigenous refrigerator has three separate clay chambers in which different types of cooked food can be preserved for several days even in the heat of the Gujarati summer, when the mercury frequently tops a hundred degrees. A similar ingenuity and adaptation to the climate are displayed in the design of tribal huts. The Gonds, for instance, construct delightful round structures with tiny barred windows and conical thatched roofs, whose interiors are surprisingly cool even when fiery desert storms are raging outside.

A peep into a different part of the exhibit space reveals that despite being tamed into an agricultural way of life, the tribes of Gujarat still hold on to many ancient beliefs. In their pantheon, trees and forest creatures hold superhuman power and are worshipped and placated with offerings. I was not surprised to see numerous images of snakes, adorned with vermilion paint, as part of this collection. In front of a wall of deities, a large collection of terra-cotta horses represented an ancient custom of sacrificing a horse when someone dies. To the Gujarati tribes, the horse symbolizes power, energy, and stamina—all values that must have been cherished in prehistoric and ancient times. Since they cannot possibly kill a real horse after each death today, the terra-cotta images are offered as substitutes.

A rich mélange of religious beliefs and customs prevails among the varied tribes residing in India's Northeast, which comprises the states of Arunachal Pradesh, Assam, Manipur, Mizoram, Meghalaya, Nagaland, and Tripura. Hinduism, Buddhism, Christianity, and even Islam have sent out tendrils of influence here and intertwined with the original animistic beliefs. The migration of people from neighboring states has also diluted tribal identity to a certain extent.

The landscape is significantly different from that of Madhya Pradesh or even Gujarat. Verdant mountains and green terraces allow the liberal growth of herbs and vegetables that can adapt to the high altitude. Bamboo groves are plentiful in the area, and the bamboo shoot is both a staple and a delicacy. The enormous stretch of the Northeast includes several microclimate zones that produce a wide array of fruits and vegetables, as well as an exotic abundance of orchids. Among the unique products are a basil-like herb called lengmaser and a fruit called patkia.

The one notable element in the cuisines of all the tribes, however, is the relative absence of fats and oils. Ginger, garlic, chilies, fresh turmeric, all are used to impart flavor and heat to food—often added just before the pot is taken off the stove—but the taste of lipids, especially the clarified butter that is so beloved throughout northern India, is markedly absent. An instinct for health or perhaps lack of access to these fats seems to have prevailed among these people, keeping them agile and fit for a life of hunting and gathering in a mountainous terrain.

The closest I came to tasting anything remotely resembling the cuisine of this area was in the eastern Bangladeshi province of Sylhet, which is contiguous with two Northeastern states, Tripura and Assam. In pre-Partition days, when modern West Bengal, Bangladesh, and the seven Northeastern states were all part of the Indian entity, provincial borders existed more in the mind than on the map, allowing for a continuous interchange of ideas and influence. In Sylhet, I discovered that even mainstream people are very fond of a fermented fish product they call hindol, which is made from a freshwater fish called sarpunti (sardinelike creatures harvested from lakes). These are cleaned, salted, and laid in clay pots under a layer of mustard oil. The pot is buried for three or four weeks, until the product reaches the right degree of fermentation and pungency. Hindol is definitely an acquired taste, and not for the meek of palate. But it imparts a flavor all its own to numerous vegetable dishes and fish stews. In Tripura, I found, exactly the same product is used, by both mainstream and tribal people, under the name of shidal. Like Bengalis, the people of Tripura are avid rice lovers, and they will sometimes just cook their shidal with onions and chilies, and make a meal of it with rice. Fermented fish is a common theme in the Northeastern zone, and certain variants reflect the influence of Southeast Asia. The Bodos of Assam, for instance, make extensive use of a fermented fish sauce called napham, which is clearly a cousin of the Thai *nam pla* and the Vietnamese *nuoc mam*. Fish, however, is not the only fermented item in the Northeast. The people of Meghalaya, for instance, relish fermented soybeans, with which they cook their meat.

Over the years, Bengalis have migrated and settled in Tripura and Assam, sometimes precipitating land-related conflicts but mostly keeping their distance. One of the culinary influences of this process has been the incorporation of dal into the Northeastern diet, which was originally based on rice, fish, and vegetables. For their part, the Bengalis have learned to eat some of the offerings that belong to this area, one of which is a delicate fern called dheki shak. It is mentioned as *dhekiya* in an Assamese text dating back to the seventh century. As with the hindol of Sylhet, I learned about this edible fern from a Bangladeshi friend. Later, when my mother and I discovered it being sold in a Calcutta market, we bought it to make the delicate yet mouthwatering dish that had been described to us—dheki shak with ground mustard, shredded coconut, green chilies, and tiny shrimp. It was good enough to make a whole meal of this with rice.

The Bodos, the indigenous tribe of Assam, love meat, especially pork, which is skewered, salted, and smoked for preservation. Portions of this preserved meat are added to other dishes—as fermented fish sauce is used elsewhere—to impart flavor. One of their classic preparations combines chicken with unmilled urad dal. It is a festive item, served during the April celebration called Rongali, which begins the new agricultural season. In a curious parallel to a Bengali wedding ritual, newly wed Bodo brides have to make this chicken dish for their in-laws to display their culinary skills. Pork is also cooked and enjoyed the same way. Along with other Assam tribes such as the Karbi, Mishing, and Rabha, the Bodos often drink alcohol on celebratory occasions. The commonest drink is zou, a kind of rice beer.

Among other uniquely Northeastern ingredients is tangal. According to cookbook writer Hoihnu Hauzel, the Hmar tribe of Manipur and the Garo tribe of Meghalaya are particularly fond of this alkaline extract made by burning the trunks of dead banana trees and mixing the ashes with water. The liquid that percolates out of the mixture is called soda by outsiders. Leafy greens cooked with this liquid are relished by these tribes.

The Northeastern tribes that have converted to Christianity and Buddhism primarily favor nonvegetarian food. Christianity imposes no restrictions on the diet, and tribal Christians are therefore free to enjoy beef and pork (and raise pigs and water buffalo themselves), as well as chicken, goat, and fish, along with rice and vegetables. Momos, steamed dumplings filled with minced beef, pork or chicken, are a common delicacy in the northern states of the Northeast. The Hindus, depending on which area they come from, will either limit themselves to fish or eat both fish and goat.

The Shan tribes from Burma, who conquered the Bodo territory and ruled as a dominant race for six hundred years, are responsible for popularizing the use of the wok and for introducing cooking techniques like steaming as well as preservation methods like drying and smoking. The preference for items like bamboo shoots, fermented soybeans, and sticky rice must also have resulted from the interaction with the interlopers from Burma and Thailand.

But all of this and much else remain far from the daily consciousness of most Indians. The indigenous people and their kitchens are not visible to the mainstream. Nevertheless, it is easy to see that the migration of people from neighboring states, the arrival of Christian missionaries and British tea planters, as well as the Thai and Burmese incursions, have all had a significant effect on the life, faith, and food of the tribes.

The tribal people Bengalis are most familiar with are the Santhals, who live in the large area called Santhal Pargana that lies along the western border of Bengal and extends to neighboring Bihar. Living side by side with the Bengalis, the Santhals have found regular employment in Bengali households and farms. The region's writers and artists, such as Rabindranath Tagore and Jamini Roy, have been fascinated by their physical energy, beauty, and simplicity, and by the ancient customs to which they still adhere. As with the other tribal groups, alcohol is a regular part of Santhal life, especially on festive occasions, accompanied by music and dance. They make a powerful drink from the flowers of the mahua tree, just as the Northeastern tribes make beer from rice and millet. The alcohol is not merely for human consumption; it is also offered to the tribal gods.

In modern times, having become farmers, the Santhals and their fellow tribes in this area treat rice as a sacred crop, much as the Hindu majority does. One of their important festivals, the spring rite of sarhul (also called baha), a celebration of the shaal tree which comes into bloom at that time, demonstrates this. Tribal priests and shamans take handfuls of rice and bless them. The rice is then stored for the following sowing season. Hunting and fishing, however, have not been totally supplanted by agricultural activities; they remain the fallback options for obtaining food when other supplies run low due to droughts or floods or financial problems. The festival in honor of the shaal tree therefore also includes special prayers to the forest gods for the welfare of animals and birds that live in the forest. Chickens—the birds that were first domesticated by the ancient forebears of modern tribes—are sacrificed to ensure the favor of these deities. This is a custom that sets the tribal people apart from both Hindus and Muslims. The latter offer up cows and goats on the occasion of Id-ul-Azha, commemorating Abraham's willingness to sacrifice his son to the Lord. The Hindu sects that do practice animal sacrifice, in honor of the goddess Kali, will usually slaughter goats. The Aryan prejudice against the domestic chicken as an impure creature, unfit for the gods, has survived through the ages among the Hindus, in spite of its being generally acceptable as part of the regular diet. In the nineteenth century, for instance, the chicken was considered a heathen bird by Hindus, not because of any association with indigenous people, but because it was eaten by Muslims and Christians. The birds of choice for the Hindu kitchen were the duck and a few other game birds.

Growing up in a city like Calcutta, I had no interaction with any people from the tribal communities. My only knowledge was through the occasional mention I came across in books and the rare depiction in films. In *Days and Nights in the Forest*, a film by the great Indian director Satyajit

Ray (based on a novel by the eminent Bengali writer Sunil Gangopad-hyay), a group of young Bengali urbanites have a soul-stirring encounter with some Santhal people in a forest. That such a thing could happen was an attractive notion. Yet I fear that for many viewers, the lingering image from that film is the tribal woman (played by Simi Garewal), her eyes, features, and body relaxed under the influence of the alcoholic mahua she has consumed, holding the men spellbound with her exotic appeal.

My father went to school in the Birbhum area of Bengal, where many of the Santhal villages are located. A few years ago, when I happened to visit that area, I remembered some of the stories he used to tell me, especially about attempts to persuade tribal villagers to give the schoolboys a taste of their alcoholic drinks—attempts that never met with success. Having heard that there was a Santhal village next to the Hindu village I was visiting, I wandered over to take a look. The first thing that struck me was the exquisite neatness of the place. The second thing I noticed was the intricate, colorful patterns that had been painted on the walls of the cottages. The patterns were unrelated to any festival or celebration, I discovered; they were merely the expression of a spontaneous, native artistry.

The village lay in the middle of the vast Bengali poppy-growing zone where the British had once held Bengali farmers hostage to the cultivation of this one particular crop. Indian opium continues to be some of the best in the world, and the poppy is cultivated in different states under government supervision. I remembered the old stories about the British smuggling contraband opium into China, the two wars that were fought over this narcotic, and the curious culinary by-product that became part of the Bengali platter—the poppy seed, called posto. Had the Santhal tribes also acquired a taste for posto? Walking through the village with a friend who had a smattering of the Santhali language, I came across an old man sitting in front of his cottage and mending the holes in a woven mat while keeping an eye on his grandson, who was playing with a baby goat under a tree.

Questioned about posto, the old man nodded vigorously. The Santhals loved it, just as the Bengalis did. They added ground posto when cooking vegetables, made a tart chutney with posto and tamarind, and ate uncooked ground posto flavored with mustard oil and green chilies, as a starter with rice. But, he added, shaking his head, it was becoming very expensive. I commiserated but suggested that delicious though it was, posto was in the end nothing more than a seasoning, a condiment, not really an important or essential part of the diet. The old man gave me a scornful look. What do these city slickers know, he seemed to be thinking. Posto, he told us, was indeed important; it cleansed the blood and kept you healthy, even in old age.

I was not sure how credible this was, but I found the concept intriguing. It echoed many other theories regarding the purification of the blood that exist in the ancient Ayurvedic system of medicine. Posto is considered an element that promotes strength and good looks; but there is no mention of its blood-cleansing properties. More than a year later, however, when I was doing some research for an article on posto, I came across some data on the chemical content of poppy-seed oil. I learned that it is particularly rich in unsaturated fats such as linoleic acid, which is scientifically proven to enhance cardiac health. With a sudden rush of recall, I saw the old Santhal man's face again, the look of scorn in his eyes. In this one matter, at least, he had been right, without benefit of literacy or science. Had it been possible, I would have run straight back to his village and asked him several more questions. Sadly, distance, time, and lack of opportunity have kept us incommunicado, and a veil lies between us.

Chapter Fourteen

SAFFRON DESIRES

Back home in America, I spread out and peruse the large detailed map of India that I had acquired long before I began my travels. It vividly resurrects the aromas, tastes, colors, and revelations that India has brought to me. Every time I see her familiar outline, broad at the top, narrow and triangular at the bottom, I think of a song inspired by the delirious nationalism that permeated the country in the early twentieth century. It describes India rising from the blue depths of an ocean, or rather, from the conflux of the three watery entities that surround her— the Bay of Bengal, the Indian Ocean, and the Arabian Sea. The song happens to be the product of a Bengali imagination. But it evokes for me a very Western image—Sandro Botticelli's painting of the birth of

Venus, of beauty and mystery rising from the sea. For millennia, India's beauty and mystery have captured the imagination of people from distant shores and lured them to her coasts. Although much of the old mystique may have dissipated in this age of accessible travel and overflowing information, the lure is there, perpetually reincarnating itself. And food remains a great part of it.

For a traveler like me, who was born and raised in India before migrating and settling elsewhere, the map possesses many levels of meaning and mystery, much like the sumptuous Goanese cake bebinca, baked in multiple overtopping layers and turned upside down to be cooled before serving. I look east, at the region I know best, Bengal. Surrounded by a diversity of cultures and languages and cuisines, it glows for me like a fine gem in a setting of precious metals. Focusing on the gem in my mind, I magnify each of its many facets—the shared meals, the rituals I have performed or watched being performed, the festivities that marked the year, the significant events of my life, the relationships that bound me to them. The distant past, personal, cultural, and physical, manifests itself in the observed map, as does the more recent remembrance of my travels. Together, they speak to me about a country that has an incomparable genius for assimilation and regeneration, an ideal immigrant nation, just like the country I have now adopted as my own. I had set out on a search for authenticity in food, but I have ended up as a witness to endless synthesis.

From my beginnings in Calcutta, I trace the downward curve of the eastern coast of Bengal. My finger pauses over the fjordlike rivulets called the Mouths of the Ganges. Around these waters spread the great mangrove forests of the Sunderbans, tempting men with a bounty of honey and fish, but delivering the unwary into the terrifying jaws of the tiger. The coconut, the palm, the banana—I imagine a wealth of leaves, fronds, and edible fruits covering this land as I move my finger downward to the neighboring state of Orissa. This is an overwhelmingly green coastline.

En route from Bengal to Orissa, the coast forms a gentle swell, like the belly of a pregnant woman—pregnant with secrets, with the stirrings of history, the blending and cooking of flavors. Where the belly again merges into the body stands the legendary Sun Temple of Konark. I pause each time my finger touches this point, for it reminds me of the felicitous connection that was once forged between settlers from a small European country, Portugal, and the people of Bengal, allowing the latter to discover the pleasures of sweets made with cottage cheese. In the sixteenth and seventeenth centuries, when the Portuguese sailed around India's southern tip and moved up the eastern coast, one of the landmarks that helped them get their bearings was this temple, which they called the Black Pagoda because of the dark color of the edifice's stone roof. You cannot see the same landmark anymore, even if you make the same sea voyage. Years of encroachment by the sandy beach have shifted the temple three miles inland, and not much of the original structure has escaped the depredations of climate and conquest. But when it was built by King Narasimhadeva in 1278 (possibly to celebrate a victory over a Muslim ruler), it stood right on the coast, a massive structure in the shape of a chariot drawn by horses, the black granite of the roof in marked contrast with the paler stone of the body of the chariot.

The Bengali poet Tagore once wrote that, at Konark, the language of stone has surpassed that of man. Despite the ravages of time, what remains standing on the shifting sands today is indeed breathtaking. I can still remember being awestruck when I first saw Konark as a child of eight. I wasn't old enough to be fascinated by the extraordinary erotic sculpture gracing the wind- and sand-washed stone, nor did I appreciate the finer points of architectural design. What I saw with my child's eye was an image of arrested energy that has stayed with me. The artists who created the temple sculpted seven horses of the sun, representing the seven days of the week, eternally poised to gallop across time. The twelve wheels of the chariot they pulled were meant to mimic the rotation of the year. But more than horses (or lions and elephants in the temple courtyard), it was the three statues of Surya, the sun god himself, that enthralled me. Standing tall and still, each image conveys an extraordinary sense of serenity. Unlike any other god in India, however, the sun god, I saw, was wearing knee-high boots. The same distinctive footwear, I learned years later, can be seen in the Surya images in other Indian sun temples. It is an incongruity worth pondering.

Some historians speculate that Surya was derived from the Persian god of light, Mithra or Mithras, and was therefore dressed in the Persian/West Asian style. It is an intriguing theory. After all, the connection between Persia and India does go back to ancient times, the Aryan settlers having spread out over an extensive domain from West Asia to India. A common adoration of the sun, giver of life and food, could well have prevailed throughout this region. In India, the ancient Hindus who composed the Vedas expressed their reverence for the sun in the great Gayatri Mantra, a prayer beseeching the sun to enlighten man through his exuberant, joyful power. Later, when a newer faith, Islam, had taken over the domains of both Mithra and Surya, a new political and economic connection was forged between Persia and India, thus paving the way for the sumptuous, saffron-tinted, fruit-studded pilafs and biryanis of the Persian culinary tradition to become part of India's courtly Islamic cuisine. That an Indian sun god should be wearing boots in the style of a Persian deity is not so incongruous after all; it is merely another instance of the integration of ideas from diverse sources, the same kind of integration that has repeatedly shaped India's food.

The Portuguese mariners who looked for the landmark of the Black Pagoda came to explore a secondary realm of gold on the eastern side of India, after having established themselves in Goa on the west coast. Loaded with a cornucopia of fruits and vegetables from their colonies in the New World and Africa, eager to reach the Spice Islands of Indonesia that liberally produced what India did not—nutmeg, mace, and clove—they put up with the rigors and dangers of this extended voyage, as the vision of prosperity beckoned them onward. The ones who settled around the Bay of Bengal could not possibly have foreseen a future in which assimilation with Bengalis would erase their separateness to nothing. Were it possible to revive their ghosts and tell them about the transformation worked on Bengal's confectionary by their unique cheese- and sweets-making techniques, they would probably find it as incredible as the bacterial theory of disease.

On the map, the coast starts curving both downward and inward. The peninsular south is taking its characteristic triangular form. But the green remains steadfast as the monsoon currents flow across the ocean and the warmth of the equator reaches out from below. The border of Andhra Pradesh and Tamil Nadu merge and flow downward to form yet another fabled entity—the Coromandel Coast. Halfway down this coast is the former French enclave of Pondicherry, where a curious amalgam of East and West blossomed but remained confined within a small boundary. The French bequeathed the baguette and the croissant to the Tamil Indians, as well as recipes for pork, sausages, and beef ragout. They also took advantage of the coastal bounty of fish to create poisson capitaine, in which steamed fish is combined with garlic and mayonnaise. It reminds me of chicken country captain, so popular among the Anglo-Indians of Calcutta, though the identity of the captain in both dishes remains equally mysterious.

Shrinking inward, jutting and retreating, the Coromandel Coast finally dips down to the southernmost point of India, Kanniyakumari or, as the British called it, Cape Comorin. If I could stand at this point and look up across the immensity of space and geography—with that imagined, penetrating, all-seeing vision I have so desired, the third eye of the gods—I would focus on one of the most beautiful spots in India. Of all the places I have never managed to visit, whose food I have never managed to sample at the source, this is the one that most occupies my dreams. Its culinary tradition, at once royal and common, can boast a sophistication comparable to that of the haute cuisines of Delhi, Lucknow, and Hyderabad. It has been shaped by hundreds of years of human history, by the coexistence of several communities, Buddhist, Muslim, and Hindu, and by the unique ingredients with which nature has endowed the region. It is a place about which a Mughal emperor reportedly said, "If there is a heaven on earth, it is here, it is here, it is here." The beauty and fruitfulness of this region elicited eloquent praise from Chinese and European travelers in ancient and medieval times. In my day, however, it has become a tragic symbol of human inadequacy. An earthly paradise, whose beauty once conquered her conquerors, is now ravaged by war, terrorism, and natural disasters. Kashmir, land of the Indian saffron, possibly the finest saffron in the world, is a potent reminder of what we cannot have, despite the intensity of desire. Ever since India became independent after Partition in 1947, the fate of Kashmir (where a Hindu king once ruled over a Muslim people) has been fraught with conflict and controversy, and peace has become the most elusive commodity.

The valley of Kashmir lies between the massive peaks of the Himalayas. Legend has it that originally the place was an enormous lake, haunted by an evil demon. A holy man named Kashyap went through a rigorous period of meditation and asceticism in order to please the gods and asked them for the power to destroy this demon. The gods agreed, and Kashyap blasted some mountains away with his yogic power, drained the lake, and killed the demon. The land that lay beneath the lake became the beautiful valley that we now see in so many picture postcards. One of the best-known pictorial images of Kashmir is that of houseboats floating on lakes, the Dal Lake being the most famous of these. The lakes serve as floating vegetable gardens, the plants rooted in fertile beds of reed and mud under water. And the houseboats are a leftover from the days of the British who were originally forbidden by the king to sell their goods in Kashmir's markets. Showing the same kind of ingenuity that enabled them to transition from a commercial entity to an imperial power ruling all of India, the British merchants began selling their products from boats in the lakes. Now the British are gone, but the people of Kashmir have adopted the custom.

I still remember a postcard sent to me by a school friend when she visited Kashmir with her family many years ago. It is a picture of a beautiful girl dressed in a red outfit, her transparent red scarf thrown carelessly over her hair, highlighting the blush on her cheeks. Sitting on the front deck of her houseboat, she holds a small basket of apples on her lap, but her eyes are not directed toward the camera. Instead, they are trained on an invisible object or landscape in the distance. The look in her eyes is one of intense longing. It is a longing that has found an echo in my heart.

Once, when my uncle Khokon—the same person who had introduced me to the Gujarati khandvi and dhokla—came home from America for a visit, he took our family out for dinner at one of the well-known restaurants in Calcutta. Eating out, except for sampling the occasional street food or prohibited beef kebabs with my friends, was a major event in those days, partly because it seemed like a waste of money. In a home that boasted a cook like my mother, tasteful and varied meals were the rule rather than the exception. A staunchly middle-class Bengali family like ours would rather spend money on books, household items, or even a vacation trip. Meals, even special or festive meals, consisted of food cooked at home.

My uncle said he had chosen the restaurant on hearing that the chef was from Kashmir. In the cab that took us there, he told us about the better-known dishes of Kashmiri cuisine, the unique ingredients used in it, including lotus root (the rhizome of the plant, found underwater), and, most of all, the famous wazwans (wedding banquets), which can consist of up to thirty different dishes cooked by wazas, or master chefs, whose ancestors supposedly came from Samarkand. Rista (meatballs in gravy), gushtaba (giant meatballs in yogurt sauce), tabak maz (crisply fried spiced ribs), kebabs—the more names he mentioned, the more we felt we were about to enter a fairy-tale kingdom.

For me, the mere idea of the lotus, the flower of the gods, and considered sacred by both Hindus and Buddhists, being used as a food source for human beings was amazing. After all, the lotus grows in Bengal, too. But though we eat the stems of the water lily, lotus roots had never figured on our plates. Kashmiris, perhaps by virtue of their location near the Himalayas, the abode of the gods, are not intimidated by this beautiful flower. They make crisp fritters out of lotus roots coated in rice batter, or combine it with meat or fish or other vegetables to add a succulent texture to the dish. They also use the large round leaves of the lotus as plates, my uncle said, the way Bengalis traditionally use banana leaves. I found the notion entrancing. The beauty of the lotus leaf almost surpasses that of the banana leaf. Its surface is matte instead of shiny, but its wavy circular form is closer to the shape of a man-made dinner plate. Like the banana leaf, it is also waterproof and heatproof, ideal for holding the varied textures and consistencies of the items

served in an Indian meal. The natural water-repellent quality of the surface has inspired the oft-used Indian simile about the pains and pleasures
of life being as short-lived as droplets of water on a lotus leaf, and the
flower, rising tall and exquisite from the bed of clay under a pond, is a
frequent metaphor for beauty and purity unaffected by squalor and filth.

The restaurant we went to did not offer any formal thirty-course
banquet. But it did serve the most famous export from Kashmiri
cuisine—roghan josh (literally, red meat, the color originally achieved
with the addition of dried cockscombs—flowers of the *Celosia cristata*—
but made now with Kashmiri chilies that are strong in tint but low in
heat), a lamb preparation whose very name rolls off richly from the
tongue. We ordered it with great anticipation, along with rice pilaf and
other items such as chicken and duck. Everything was unlike anything I
had known till then. Even the duck, a preparation called shikar, cooked
with vinegar, garlic, and chilies, marched on my taste buds with a
rhythm that was foreign. But when we started on the roghan josh, the
silence that descended on our table lasted a long time. It was our first
experience with meat that had not been cooked with the inevitable
onion and garlic, and yet had a richness of taste and texture. An unfamiliar, yet luscious combination of ginger, asafetida, fennel, fenugreek,
red chilies, yogurt, and ghee in the sauce opened a door to pleasures that
were later magnified with each recall. Kashmir, which until then had
been a symbol of unattainable beauty, based on what I had read and
heard, took on the added dimension of a paradise of sensory delights.
The old pictures I had seen came back, the undulating valleys and hills,
the placid lakes full of lotuses and lilies, their petals unfurling under the
sun, the beautiful girl with her basket of apples. Alexander had been
there when he was pursuing his dreams of conquering India. I wondered whether it was the effect of Kashmir's beauty on the ruthless
Macedonian that led to the adage: Alexander came and saw, but India
conquered.

A little more familiarity with the food of this distant region brought
some surprising discoveries. Despite its northern location, and a traditional array of excellent breads, the staple food of Kashmir is rice, as it is

in Bengal. However, it is not the long-grained basmati that they prefer, even for their famous pilafs, but the slightly sticky rice that grows in the valley. Another unexpected commonality I discovered between Bengal and Kashmir was a preference for mustard oil as a cooking medium. Fields of yellow-flowering mustard are a common sight in the valley. Perhaps the most striking revelation was that Kashmir's Hindu Brahmins had no objection to enjoying fish and meat, just like Bengali Brahmins. In Bengal, we have grown used to being considered "lesser" observers of Hindu orthodoxy, primarily because Bengali Brahmins have not been able to give up the pleasures of nonvegetarian food, unlike their "purer" brethren in northern and southern India. In a rather desperate attempt at establishing their credentials, Bengali Brahmin scholars even made up a rule of exclusion for themselves—fish without scales was prohibited. Needless to say, it didn't do much to restore status in the eyes of those who never touched fish. The Kashmiri Brahmins had their own rule of exclusion. They cooked their fish, lamb, chicken, and duck without the use of onion and garlic, since these two items figure largely in the cooking of Muslims. The dual tradition of cooking that developed has only enriched the overall tapestry of Kashmiri food. Hindus focus on asafetida, ginger, fenugreek, and fennel, while Muslims combine onion (the extraordinarily flavorful Kashmiri shallot, called praan), garlic, ginger, and the fragrant spices of garam masala.

The natural beauty of Kashmir is reflected in its exquisite crafts as well as in the features of its people. In childhood, when I locked horns with my mother, refusing to eat the "healthy" slices of apple she set before me, my grandmother would try to resolve the matter with diplomacy, declaring that eating apples would make me as pretty as a Kashmiri girl. Somehow, I didn't quite believe in this miraculous power of the fruit, in spite of the pictures I had seen, of handsome men and pretty, pink-cheeked women. But for the British, as well as the Mughal rulers, Kashmir's bounty of temperate-zone fruits—apples, apricots, plums, peaches, pears, and most notably, grapes—magnified the desirability of its location. Before they created their royal orchards around Delhi and Agra, the Mughals regularly imported these fruits from Kashmir. As for grapes, Kashmiris produced a delightful fragrant wine that was enjoyed not only by the people and nobility of the region (it was often drunk to celebrate the year's first snowfall) but also the imperial Muslim rulers of Delhi, who saw no contradiction between their faith and the bottle.

It is, however, a tiny flower, not a fruit, that most evokes Kashmir's magical aura of heaven on earth. Kashmir is the only place in India where saffron is cultivated. Although the saffron crocus, called nargis in India, is native to Greece, it entered India through Persia and was cultivated in Kashmir as far back as the sixth century. Under the Mughals, obsessed with high living and fine cuisine, labor-intensive saffron cultivation flourished. According to spice experts, Kashmiri saffron is the best in the world; its deep reddish-orange color and intense fragrance transform any dish in which it is used. Even two or three strands can permeate a large pot of pilaf with flavor. Unfortunately, the world doesn't often get to enjoy the pleasures of Kashmiri saffron. Conflict and violence have made sustained cultivation and export difficult, and the international market focuses mostly on saffron from Iran and Spain. For me, this reclusive flavor, culled from the beautiful purple flowers that carpet the valleys of Rampur and Paraspur, symbolizes a negative aspect of eating India—our failure to make the most of what we have, by transforming the beauty of food into the ugliness of conflict. Each time I use my private stock of Kashmiri saffron, in an American kitchen far from the soil where it was grown, I make a silent undertaking to reach Kashmir some day, no matter what, and eat a meal on a lotus leaf. I know, if I get there, that hospitality will not be wanting. As Sandip Kachroo, a Kashmiri chef I met during my travels in South India, told me proudly, "To us, the guest is god."

Until then, Kashmir's beauty, the stuff of legends and real stories, lives in my mind, in the books I have read, in the beautiful objects made by her craftsmen, in the exquisitely embroidered woolen shawls that warm my shoulders with such comfort even in a frigid northern climate. These inimitable shawls were the only renewable direct contact we Bengalis had with Kashmir. Every winter, itinerant salesmen left their home and made their way to distant Bengal to tempt people into buying their wares. It was a centuries-old practice. Over time, the more successful among these merchants settled in Bengali cities, opened shawl shops, and hired a new group of salesmen to do the hard work of door-to-door vending.

I look at the map and visualize the Calcutta neighborhoods through which the itinerant shawl sellers moved. Throughout the short tropical winter, they went from house to house, undid the enormous cloth bundles they toted on their back or on their head, and spread out their shawls before the Bengali housewives. And what a sight it was, one jewel tone after another, inscribed with the finest of stitches to form subtle patterns.

My finger stays on Calcutta. One shawl seller made a regular stop at a house in southern Calcutta where my husband's widowed great-grandmother lived with her son Prafulla—British-trained barrister turned freedom activist—and her three grandchildren. The house has now been demolished to make way for an apartment complex, but I can imagine it, a comfortable, spacious structure, though marked by signs of neglect. Prafulla's eldest daughter is the shadowy figure in this episode of the family history. She had inherited her dead mother's beauty, and the eye of the shawl merchant—dare I think he was handsome, was he nourished with Kashmiri apples in boyhood?—fell on her. He was a Kashmiri Brahmin, his speech and manners evoking an elegant courtly tradition. And they worked their charm on a susceptible girl who had led a sheltered life. Finally, undeterred by considerations of family or social disapproval, she left home to marry him. Not much was known of the outcome of the marriage; it was unlikely that the distant Kashmiri family welcomed an unconventional Bengali bride with a formal banquet of thirty dishes, the traditional wazwan. The only information that trickled down to her family not long after was that she had died of tuberculosis, bereft of the company of her immediate relatives, hundreds of miles from home. Had she been abandoned by her beautiful Kashmiri lover? There were whispers, but no one seemed to know for sure. All that is left is a terse note made by her brother, my late father-in-law, in

the family journal: "Didi [elder sister] died on the 16th of July, 1937."
She was twenty-three.

I fold up the map and put it away. It rustles with stories, joyful, incredible, fragrant, clamorous, absurd, poignant, and downright tragic. My stories, the world's stories. The one thing I have learned from exploring the realm of India's food is that this is a civilization with an insatiable, almost childlike curiosity. India welcomes new trends and new foods with equal zeal; she consumes the old and the new with eager voracity. She has taught me that authenticity is a myth, that fusion is not a mere restaurant fad, that tradition lives because it is constantly being retouched. Even the weight of several millennia's history cannot imprison the spirit of this land into staleness for long; dark and dismal eras do come, but eventually the powerful Indian sun fights them off, with light and energy.

Once again I go back to the mythical past, when India's greatest epic, the *Mahabharata* was written. There is a story of exile here, too, as in the *Ramayana*. The five Pandava princes and their beautiful wife Draupadi are doomed to spend thirteen years in the forest before they can inherit their kingdom. Draupadi, in the role of woman and wife, is responsible for providing food, and not only to her five husbands but also to any guests (wanderers, royal hunters, forest-dwelling ascetics) who might stop by. How, she wonders, can she know how much food to prepare on any given day? The sun god, booted or not, comes to her rescue. He gives her a copper pot that has the magical power to eternally renew whatever was cooked in it, until Draupadi herself eats from it and washes the pot.

India is the sun's cooking pot. In our time, the process of renewal involves modernizing certain foods, rediscovering lost cuisines and creating a public demand for them, and also acquiring a taste for dishes from the global platter, ranging from sophisticated French or Italian concoctions to the mouth-tingling delights of Southeast Asia and China, to, let's face it, the fast-food menu of the West, which transcends language and culture.

A genius for adaptation and inventiveness is best seen in the last category. Restaurants advertise pizza with a topping of the ubiquitous
chicken tikka masala on the one hand, and on the other, a version so
strictly devoid of onion, garlic, or anything that grows under the ground
that even observant Jains can eat it, provided they are sure it does not
bear the contamination of eggs. The world's greatest fast-food chain,
McDonald's, marches in and opens outlets in India's cities, but soon
learns that it is not enough to transform the Big Mac into a chicken
burger (even lamb could be mistaken for some forbidden meat and cause
controversy). Better enticement is needed in a country full of vegetarians. Thus we see the birth of a completely new product, a new brand,
the McAloo Tikki burger, a spicy potato patty instead of a meat burger,
encased in the usual bun. Meanwhile, in parks and street corners and inside shops tucked away in narrow lanes, the "indigenous" fast foods—
the kebab rolls and tangy chats, the samosas and pakoras, the golegappas
and dahi-vadas, the jilebis and imratis—continue to be made and
mopped up with unabated relish.

So I live with the realization that Indian food is even more of a mis-
nomer than I had ever imagined. Yet there is no other satisfactory term,
since regional identities are in a permanent state of flux, all traditions
subject to being reworked, while borrowing and adapting of technique
and ingredients continue according to the perpetual migration of people within the country. Food in India has always been and still is fusion,
and a fusion that remains unfinished.

Outside my window, it is the New England autumn, the vivid fall colors reminding me of the intensely colorful celebrations of Bengal's biggest
Hindu festival, Durga Puja, which is followed three weeks later by Diwali,
festival of lights, celebrated on the night of the new moon. I make some
of the festive ritual foods that were served in my parental home to mark
the occasions—luchis, puffy fried bread made with a dough of refined
flour; chholar dal, or yellow split peas seasoned with ginger and garam
masala; aloor dam, or slow-cooked potatoes with tamarind and asafetida; a
chilled pudding of thick evaporated milk infused with shredded sections
of tangerine. Remembering the Portuguese sweets connection, I also

make some chhana and stir it with sugar over a low flame until it reaches the consistency of the Bengalis' favorite sweet, sandesh. Before taking it off the stove, I flavor it with several strands of Kashmiri saffron from my carefully stored supply.

I know that even my best efforts will produce only an approximation of what I grew up eating; things don't taste the same in India and America. Nevertheless, there is pleasure in striving to recreate remembered dishes. The joy of eating, especially for an immigrant in her adopted country, is a complex one—part nostalgia, part discovery, and part creation. In adding my personal touches to some of these ceremonial dishes, I am only doing what my mother and grandmother did when they added their signatures to the recipes they had inherited.

Hindus believe in the theory of rebirth and reincarnation. Were it possible to be reborn with the memory and vision of past lives and past journeys intact—a capacity that is indeed granted to some fortunate "seers," according to both Hindu and Buddhist legends—I, too, would be a believer. For after this odyssey, I know that one lifetime, one memory, is not enough to eat, know, and absorb India.

ACKNOWLEDGMENTS

This book would not have been possible without the generous help given to me by many people. Those listed below include old friends and new acquaintances who directly contributed to my project by sharing with me their time and knowledge, and putting me in touch with important resources.

Shermeen Ahmed, Dubai and Hyderabad
Radha Chandran and Chandran Ullatil, Cochin
Gouri Chatterjee, Calcutta
Shobha and Supratik Chatterjee, Hyderabad
Ananya Das and Debdatta Ganguly, Hyderabad
Biren Das, K. C. Das Private Ltd., Bangalore
Rathin Das, *The Hindustan Times*, Ahmedabad
Subhadra De, Calcutta
Maria D'Souza, Xavier Centre of Historical Research, Goa
Fleur D'Souza, St. Xavier's College, Bombay
Mrs. Thritty Dastoor, Calcutta
Vikram G. Doctor, *The Economic Times*, Bombay
Nabhojit Ghosh, Taj Malabar, Cochin
Samit and Elaine Ghosh, Bangalore
Rajarshi Guriya, Fortune Katriya Hotel, Hyderabad
Linda Harrar, Wayland, Massachusetts
Diya Kar Hazra, Penguin Books, New Delhi
Gourav Jaswal, Synapse, Goa
Sandip Kachroo, Taj West End, Bangalore

Anjum Katyal, Calcutta

Pradeep Khosla, Taj Krishna, Hyderabad

C. V. and Indira Krishnakumar, Trivandrum

Antoine Lewis, *The Savvy Cookbook*, Bombay

Sandip and Mou Maiti, Bombay

Abhay Mangaldas, Agashiye, Ahmedabad

Professor P. C. Marcus, Cochin

Ken and Verjik Martin, Bolton, Massachusetts

Manoj Mishra, Taj Bengal, Calcutta

Sujan Mukherjee, Taj Bengal, Calcutta

Hemant Oberoi, Taj Mahal Palace Hotel, Bombay

Mr. and Mrs. Digant Oza and Kajal Oza-Vaidya, Ahmedabad

Mr. and Mrs. D. N. Purkayastha, Calcutta

Basant Rawat, Ahmedabad

Maria de Lourdes Bravo da Costa Rodrigues, Goa

Ajith Saldana, Bangalore

Anuradha Sengupta, *DNA*, Bombay

Haku and Vilu Shah, Ahmedabad

Parthiv Shah, New Delhi

Nagendra Singh, Taj Residency, Lucknow

Rahul Verma, New Delhi

Ian Zachariah, Calcutta

I am particularly appreciative of all the efforts made by Biswaranjan Sarkar to ensure the working-out of my complex itineraries and to quickly resolve unexpected problems. Without his help, this journey would have been fraught with difficulty.

I am also immeasurably indebted to Dr. Sasikumar, Dr. Gopal S. Pillai, Dr. Sreeni, Mr. Kesava Rajendran, Sister Sreeja, and the staff and administrators of the Chaithanya Eye Hospital in Cochin and in Trivandrum, for looking after me so well during a very dark time.

To Karen Rinaldi and Amanda Katz at Bloomsbury, I owe a special debt of gratitude for gracefully accommodating unforeseen delays and providing consistent encouragement. Anne Edelstein, my agent, lavished patience, attention, and invaluable advice on me during the years of planning, traveling, and writing. Most of all, I am thankful for the unvarying support, nurturing, and motivation provided by my family. I could not have got here without them.

A NOTE ON THE AUTHOR

Chitrita Banerji grew up in Calcutta and came to the United States as a graduate student; she received her master's degree in English from Harvard University. She has since become an internationally recognized writer on Bengali food, and is the author of *Life and Food in Bengal*, *Bengali Cooking*, *Feeding the Gods*, and *Land of Milk and Honey*. A two-time winner of Sophie Coe awards in Food and History, she has written about food for *Gourmet*, *Gastronomica*, *Granta*, the *Boston Globe*, and the *American Prospect*. She lives in Cambridge, Massachusetts.